Creative Dramatics

THE BLUE BIRD.

Creative Dramatics

For the Upper Grades and Junior High School

by

Winifred Ward

Supervisor of Dramatics in the Public Schools of Evanston, Illinois;
Instructor in Dramatic Production, School of Speech,
Northwestern University

D. Appleton and Company
New York   London

TO
HAROLD A. EHRENSPERGER

Preface

This book has grown out of the creative dramatic work in the public schools of Evanston, Illinois. During the six years in which the School of Speech of Northwestern University has been supervising the dramatics of the grade schools, my dramatic teachers and I have been doing much experimental work. It was necessary to experiment, for there were no precedents to follow, no available plan for educational dramatic courses in the grades. Many junior high schools had some form of dramatic work, but most of it was scattering or unorganized. We planned tentative courses, therefore, tested them out, and revised them whenever we saw better ways of presenting our subject. It has been fascinating, this pioneer work, and it will continue to be an absorbing study, for our courses will go on developing as long as we teach them.

Certain conclusions we have reached, needless to say, because we have found by thorough tests what methods and materials were especially successful. These conclusions I have written into this book, not at all with the idea of standardizing dramatics for upper-grade children, but with the hope that they may serve as a starting point for other teachers who are given the opportunity of developing dramatic courses in the upper grades and junior high schools.

My book has been written chiefly for directors of children's dramatics. Many regular teachers, however, who wish to make their teaching more effective by using the dramatic method in studying literature, will, I trust, find the book helpful.

Others, who have been successful in directing school plays, and are, therefore, called upon whenever the school presents a dramatic program, will gain confidence, perhaps, by a study of the last half of the book.

Auditorium teachers have an opportunity of using both formal and informal dramatic work in the programs which they present. It is here suggested that a large proportion of such informal work as is described in the chapters on *Dramatization* and *Assembly Programs* be used instead of formal plays, having greater value for the players, and, as a rule, more interest for the audience.

Children's theaters are being organized all over the country, and there are few people trained to direct them. The results of five years' experience in the Children's Theatre of Evanston may be of service to those who wish to organize and direct such theaters in other cities.

Numberless opportunities present themselves, too, in community dramatics for children, but there are few trained leaders. The book may be of use, therefore, to the directors of adult dramatics who find their biggest opportunity in children's work, with the result that they must learn, either by experience or training, a new approach to the subject, a different technique, a body of fresh material.

More than all else, I hope that my book may prove something of an inspiration to my students who are about to enter the field of children's dramatics. If, with their youthful vitality and enthusiasm, they may gain also a vision that sees far beyond the day's lesson; if, when they teach, they feel the thrill which comes from setting free the creative imagination of their children, they will be truly successful. And in the measure in which my book has helped them to gain that vision and to know the joy of guiding children in a creative activity, it will be justified and I shall be happy.

My greatest debt is to Harold A. Ehrensperger, without whose help and encouragement this book would not have been written. Having urged me to write it, he was good enough to act as my critic, reading my manuscript and advising me in every problem that arose. My deepest thanks to him!

My teachers in the public-school dramatic department have been of immense service in making experiments with materials and methods, and giving me the results of their work. Belle Kennedy, Marjorie Porterfield, Helen Bittler, Evelyn Brown, and Evelyn Wiseman McKay have made an especially distinctive contribution to the cause of creative dramatics. Their original ideas, their perfect coöperation and their excellent teaching have made our six years' experiment in the Evanston schools productive of most gratifying results, and I take this opportunity to express to them publicly my pride and appreciation of their work.

The chapter concerning the school stage and its equipment is full of the ideas of Dean Farnsworth, who was my invaluable production manager for three years. For every school stage in Evanston which was built or remodeled during this time, his advice was sought, for he is a genius in stagecraft. To him I am indebted, also, for the illustrations in the chapter on The School Stage, as well as for the photographs of the Children's Theatre plays.

To Hazel Easton, my colleague and friend, I am sincerely grateful for valuable help during the writing and proof-reading of my book.

Ethel Kopp and Betty Phelps have made the tailpieces for the chapters; Ethel Kopp the costume designs.

And lastly, I wish to express my sincere appreciation to these people who have given me such hearty support and coöperation in my work with creative dramatics and with the Children's Theatre: Ralph Dennis, Dean of the School of Speech; J. Roy Skiles, Superintendent of District 75 of the Evanston Public Schools; F. W. Nichols, Superintendent, and David E. Walker, Assistant Superintendent, of District 7; and Helen Sanford, Principal of Haven Intermediate School. They have given me every opportunity possible to make my work a success and I am deeply grateful.

W. W.

Contents

CONTENTS

Creative Dramatics

Creative Dramatics

CHAPTER I

INTRODUCTION

THE new education has set its stamp of approval on creative dramatics, thus opening the doors of the schools to another of the arts. Optimistic protagonists have long seen it coming—so long, indeed, that a generation of children has had time to grow up and go off to college while it was still only dimly in sight! In 1914 G. Stanley Hall wrote in his preface to Elnora Curtis's book on *The Dramatic Instinct in Education,* "the present seems to be the psychological moment for its appreciation and also for its utilization in education." That moment passed, and many more moments, until even now it is only just arriving.

Two things have been happening, however, which are bringing about a most significant change in the old attitude toward dramatics for children. In the first place, the aims in education have so shifted as to give recognition to the heretofore unrealized possibilities of dramatic study. The old education had no place for dramatics. It was a frill, grudgingly allowed to deck holiday attire, but of no possible use for everyday wear! Mental discipline was the one important aim in the school of the last century. Facts must be stored in intellectual cupboards, rules must be learned, lessons must be memorized and recited.

Along came such leaders as John Dewey, Francis Parker and William H. Kilpatrick, who declared that an education which recognized the mind alone, or even the mind and hands, was not true education. The whole child must be developed if he was to reach his maximum growth. By means of actual, first-hand experience along the lines of his natural interests, they said, his capacity for creative self-expression should be developed; and at the same time he should grow in tolerant understanding of self and society.

This new idea of education, eagerly adopted by the experimental schools all over the country, is slowly permeating the public school system. The sacred school curriculum is being scanned minutely, and subjects which have long held an established place are compelled to justify themselves or make room for others. And because dramatics is based upon a very strong natural interest, and because it has unusual possibilities for creative self-expression, its chance has come.

Coincident with this shifting of emphasis in education has come a change in the manner of teaching dramatics. Here, too, the emphasis has shifted and this change is as important as the other in accounting for the new attitude toward the subject. In place of stressing the finished production, modern teachers of children's dramatics stress the process of developing the production. If the play built by the children around Robin Hood and his band is good, so much the better. That, however, is not so important as is the growth which comes out of the experience of creating the play. This change in emphasis from the exhibitional to the educational has made of dramatics a new subject—one that has a valuable contribution to give to education.

CREATIVE DRAMATICS

The term *creative dramatics* has grown up to distinguish this original dramatic work from the old formal study of ready-made plays. *Educational dramatics* is a more general term for what is usually the same type of work. It is dramatic expression which comes from within, rather than the imitative expression which so often characterizes the rehearsing of plays for public exhibition. Instead of memorizing set speeches and acting parts in the way the teacher directs, the children develop plays out of their own thoughts and imaginations and emotions.

The enthusiasm of the pupils in creative dramatic classes is an interesting commentary on this free type of work. Asked by a graduate student who was preparing a thesis on the subject, why they liked dramatics, sixty children from three different classes wrote answers which varied widely in the way in which they were expressed but agreed entirely as to content. "I like dramatics because it gives us a chance to use our own ideas and imaginations. We can make up our own scenes and dialogue instead of learning the speeches in the book." Such an answer was typical, as was also this: "One has a chance to put in one's own originality, and say or do as he pleases. I do not mean that dramatics is slipshod. Oh, no! But it is usually more interesting to do or watch because it is original. I have never been bored one minute in dramatics." Such an admission from a sophisticated youth in the eighth grade is indeed a tribute to creative dramatics!

THE MATERIAL

The heart of creative dramatics is dramatization. Original plays developed from activities or stories form the basis of the actual work of the courses. The material for this creative activity is to be chosen with greatest care, for the interest of the children is centered always on content, and this material must, therefore, suit their needs and their tastes if it is to bring satisfaction and growth. What, then, shall be the starting point? Shall the children create from the very beginning the stories to be dramatized? Shall they base their dramatizations on historical or geographical facts? Or shall they develop plays from literature?

The dramatizations of little children grow out of many and varied activities. They develop from rhythms, their galloping horses and strutting turkeys leading suddenly into a Humpty Dumpty play or a Thanksgiving dinner party. They grow out of playing house, when the neighbor knocks at an imaginary door and says, "Good morning. I came over to see how your little girl is to-day." Dramatic material is everywhere and the children are ever on the alert to use it. Projects such as the study of the Indian, the life of a community, Greek civilization, chivalry, may offer opportunity for the building of plays by children who are a little older.

No material offers so many possibilities for artistic growth, however, as literature. Dramatization may vitalize and crystallize the study in history, geography, civics, but its best material is undoubtedly literature. Contrast the opportunity offered by such a story as *Old Pipes and the Dryad* with the possibilities in, say, the life of Columbus or the study of chivalry. True, the latter type of project requires more ingenuity from the children in the matter of plot and character. Much is given them in the Stockton story. Which experience offers the greater chance for growth?

Stimulated sufficiently by an imaginative teacher, the children might originate a creditable play based on the life of Columbus or on the study of chivalry. The experience could well prove a valuable one, illuminating what might otherwise be an uninspired study. Nine-tenths of such plays, however, turn out to be stiff and formal, lacking any trace of imaginative charm, and cheapening the art of creative dramatics. Even with material highly stimulating to the imagination, the process of developing a play is not an easy one, so that if a class with an unskilled leader attempts to dramatize unsuitable material, the results are likely to be completely empty of real satisfaction. The pity of it is that there is a surface satisfaction which both class and teacher believe is real. Not knowing how rich the experience of dramatizing might be, they accept their own meager accomplishment as a standard. When they present for parents or schoolmates their dramatization of the industrial activities of a community, with costumes, properties, and perhaps even lighting effects, the applause and approving comments which always follow such a performance lead them to believe that their play has been a success. For the good of the art, it might have been better if the presentation of their work had resulted in failure. But no one could be hard enough to wish disaster to result from any really sincere effort.

The dramatization of an imaginative story from literature, on the other hand, is both fascinating and productive of growth. Analysis of such characters as Old Pipes, the villagers, the Echo-dwarf, and the Dryad is an absorbing study to children. Their understanding of people grows when they analyze and interpret such characters. The situations appeal to their imaginations, and they build whole scenes on incidents which are merely suggested. The truths of the story are vitalized by dramatizing them, and they help to remake experience. Indeed, literature is the perfect fabric for creative dramatics, for it is closest to drama and to life itself.

THE STORY OF SCHOOL DRAMATICS:
IN WHICH A BIT OF ALLEGORY IS INTRODUCED

Dramatics has been viewed askance by educators for so many years that she almost came to think of herself as a questionable character. Waiting outside the doors of the school, she watched her sister arts, Music and Drawing, taken into the family and given honored seats at the table. Later, even the Dance was admitted, though by the side door and in disguise! Finally, some one in a burst of generosity led her into the kindergarten. She was, and always is, welcome there. Then the upper grades found use for her. Since she was attractive to the children, they thought, perhaps she could teach them facts without their knowing it! So, by means of health plays and better English plays and safety-first plays and geography, history and science plays, she was made the slave of every other school subject. Then, indeed, was her reputation ruined! She was not recognizable as art; she was less and less welcome as a substitute for science. Only the little children saw her as a Bringer of Joy!

Through all the years, there have been those who have had faith in Dramatics as a power in education. At last their voices were heard. A few schools opened their doors to her, to find that a most surprising change had come over her. She had freshness, youth, and so great an understanding of children that she was a powerful influence in their development. The activity she offered was one they loved. What they learned through her, therefore, would the more thoroughly remake their experience. If her contributions had enough intrinsic worth, education could not afford to do without her. Consequently, more and more schools welcomed her. Where she was once frowned upon she is now embraced, and though she has far to go before she is given the place of dignity by the side of her sister arts where she belongs, Education has at last opened its doors to her, and she is to be given a chance to prove her worth.

WHAT CREATIVE DRAMATICS CAN CONTRIBUTE TO EDUCATION

Education, having devoted itself to the intellect for a great number of years, became conscious a few decades ago that children's hands, too, should be educated. Vocational training was the talk of teachers' institutes. The manual arts were introduced into the curriculum. Surely now Education was really educating!

Not for long was this state of self-satisfaction to last— if it is fair to accuse Education of self-satisfaction! "What about the emotions?" a few leaders began to say. "Isn't the way people feel about things quite as important as the way they think about them? Would it not be well to build right attitudes and appreciations in our children so that they would be better fitted to make the decisions of life? Will they not be more useful citizens if the school leads them to a tolerant understanding of the people with whom they must live?"

Others said, "Education should give the child the opportunity for fullest self-realization. This can only be done if the creative imagination of each individual child is given free play. We should include in our school curriculum, therefore, such activities as will call forth and guide this unique and precious power."

As educators in general accept the new idea of individual instead of mass education, they realize the importance of the arts. Not every child is an artist; but they are coming to see that almost every child can, if given even a little encouragement and help, express himself well enough in some art to make his life richer and happier. The public school is not trying to develop Raphaels and Bernhardts and Carusos. Its object is not to train children for artistic careers. But as educators accept the ideas of Dewey, Parker, and the other leaders, they are opening the way for many kinds of creative activities, recognizing that the creative is the richest life, both for the individual and for society. And as the drama is an integration of all the arts, it offers, probably, the greatest possible opportunity for creative self-expression.

Bound up in these great aims are all the lesser ones. The oral English training which is involved, with its development of vocabulary, voice and diction, is a tremendous help to every child in learning to express himself. Freedom in bodily expression, with the poise which results from ease of movement, fits him to appear well with his fellows. The independence, resourcefulness, and ingenuity always evident among children in a creative dramatics class develop personality and leadership.

VALUE FOR UPPER GRADES AND JUNIOR HIGH SCHOOL

At no other period in school life is creative dramatic training so needed as in the sixth, seventh, eighth, and ninth grades. If only four grades out of twelve could have creative dramatics, it should be these four. Valuable as it is in all the grades, it can be of really significant service in solving the problems of this most difficult time in a child's life. Adolescence is a highly emotional period —a period when the child can scarcely repress his feelings, yet is ashamed to give vent to them. Introspective and oversensitive, he often becomes morbid from living with his own unhealthy thoughts. Creative dramatics gives him a wholesome outlet for his emotions. According to the theory of Aristotle, it serves as a sort of *Katharsis*, or purging of emotion. Without fear of ridicule he can express his feelings in one vivid experience after another. They are vicarious experiences, it is true, but they are real enough to afford him much genuine satisfaction.

An eighth grade girl told one day of what fun she had experienced in working off her high spirits in playing Katharine. "I *love* to play Katharine," she said, beaming with joy at the recollection of her last dramatic class. "The class thinks I am too shrewish, but I just forget everything when I am on the stage, and put my whole self into the part."

Emotion is not only given an outlet in creative dramatics but it is refined and guided into legitimate channels. A boy learns control as well as expression, for his work must have balance and a certain amount of restraint, and these things can be gained only by learning to direct and curb them at will. The overbearing boy gratifies his desire for importance by playing King Robert, in *Robert of Sicily,* and as the dramatization progresses, comes to realize the beauty of humility in the man of high degree.

Self-consciousness often makes life miserable for the thirteen-year-old boy. Because he is growing rapidly he feels awkward and blundering. He wishes to appear well before people but he is so frightfully sensitive that he usually makes a very poor impression. This is a strong argument for introducing dramatic study before that trying period is reached. Sixth grade children are at a wonderfully free and natural stage. They respond joyously and whole-heartedly to creative dramatics, and if the study is continued through the eighth grade, many of them are carried through with scarcely a trace of self-consciousness. Watch eighth grade boys dramatizing a vigorous old ballad like *Robin Hood and the Widow's Three Sons* and see how utterly free and un-self-conscious they are, even with strangers watching their work. When dramatics is not begun until the eighth grade, the pupils seldom achieve the charming freedom and spontaneity which is so characteristic of their work if it has been started in the sixth or seventh grade. For most children of the seventh grade have not yet arrived at self-consciousness and can still be spared much of the unhappiness which attends that difficult period.

Psychology and experience tell us that the adolescent is a highly idealistic period. At no other time, probably, is there so great an opportunity for the school to build fine attitudes and appreciations, to inspire children with a love for high standards and ideals. Now, the material and methods used in creative dramatics, dealing as they do with actions and their effects, are such as to afford a unique opportunity for character building, and a teacher of personality and ideals will find that there is scarcely a limit to the possibilities the subject offers for the education of the junior high school pupil. Without a suggestion of preaching, without so much as a reference to ethics, the dramatic lesson vitalizes the gentleness and chivalry of Arthur, the self-reliance of Ulysses, the loyalty and good sportsmanship of Robin Hood, and the courage of the lass who traveled east of the sun and west of the moon.

PLACE IN THE CURRICULUM

An overcrowded program keeps many a school from incorporating dramatics into its curriculum. In reality, the reason lies in the failure to recognize the worth of dramatics as an educating and socializing force. There is room in the curriculum for whatever is of greatest value in education, and dramatics should not take the place of any other subject unless it can make a greater contribution. That its worth has as yet been tested by comparatively few schools is due, first, to the slow process of changing the public school curriculum, and second, to the lack of teachers educated for this particular type of work. As interest grows, both obstacles are being overcome, however, and the next ten years will see a great number of junior high schools, if not lower schools, revising their programs to include dramatics.

PLACE IN THE SCHOOLS OF EVANSTON

When, in 1924, the schools of Evanston, Illinois, were reorganized to make of the seventh and eighth grades an intermediate school, a system of electives was incorporated. By this plan, each pupil is required to take certain subjects, being allowed to exercise his personal choice in two additional courses. Along with French, special art, orchestra and a half dozen other subjects, dramatics is listed as an elective, and four progressive semester courses are offered. One forty-five minute period a day is saved by every pupil for electives, some of which are given on Monday, Wednesday and Friday, others on Tuesday and Thursday. Most of these electives are concentrated in the two noon periods, so that while half the school is at lunch, the other half is in elective classes. Thus, each pupil selects one elective which meets three times a week, and another which meets twice. Since there are several sections each of Dramatics I, II, III, and IV, some are necessarily offered twice a week and others three times. Pupils who go home for lunch take their electives at half past two, but most of the children have their lunch at school in the cafeteria.

This plan has worked out with the greatest success, and is now operating at Haven and Nichols, the two large new intermediate schools of Evanston. Such a system incorporated in all junior high schools would not only solve the problem of finding a place for dramatics, but it would render the immensely important service of giving individuals a chance for self-expression by allowing them some choice in their education.

Dramatic study in the public schools of Evanston is constantly expanding to include more grades and more schools. Starting only in seventh and eighth grades, it is now included in the program of the sixth grade, in some of the fifth grade classes, and beginning this year, in the kindergarten, first and second grades. With these tiny children, dramatic play grows out of rhythms, no effort being made to develop dramatizations until the imaginations of the children create them quite naturally from the situations which arise. Eventually, it is planned to offer some form of speech or dramatic work in all grades. Below the seventh grade, subjects are not elected, so that if dramatics is offered, every child is in the class.

Six dramatic teachers, assisted by a number of practice teachers from the School of Speech of Northwestern University, have charge of the classes, all work being under the direction of the dramatic supervisor. So many children elect the courses that not enough classes can be provided to care for them all. Twenty is the ideal number for a creative dramatics class, though this is often stretched to twenty-five when by so doing no children will have to be disappointed.

HIGH SCHOOL ENGLISH CLASSES

Many teachers have asked whether it was possible to use creative dramatics in senior high school English classes. Indeed, it is not only possible but highly advisable. Let the English teacher who has some dramatic training to her credit experiment a bit and she will find that her literature courses will take on an amazing new interest, and that her pupils will work harder and more willingly than ever before. Certain it is that they are far more keenly alive to the heart and soul of literature than to its form, and a teacher who gives them the opportunity to dramatize when the material lends itself to dramatization, helps to vitalize what to them might always have been lifeless clay.

CHAPTER II

ATTITUDE

THE measure of effectiveness in any school subject is the attitude of the students toward it by the time they finish the course. If the class in general feels like tossing up its collective hat and shouting, "Thank goodness, I never have to think of *that* again!" there is little hope that its future life will be richer for having had the course. A child who has heartily disliked poetry as taught in his school will not be likely ever to find joy in reading poems. A student who is not interested in his course in civics will not be a better citizen for having studied the subject. In order to be educative, in order really to get over into his life, a subject must not only be respected but genuinely liked by the student.

A new course introduced into a school has a better chance of succeeding if teachers and pupils have a preconceived idea that it will be a welcome addition to the curriculum. When dramatics is introduced, it is often greeted with joy by the pupils but with distrust by the teachers. This distrust is justified in schools where unwise dramatic "coaching" has been done. When outside dramatic teachers have come in and upset the school program by taking the children out of their classes to rehearse for a public play, or when the regular teachers have labored with crowds of children in school pageants, the subject of dramatics is likely to be a distasteful one.

The new dramatic department in such cases has to live down the disrepute into which the subject has fallen, and prove to the school that dramatics is worthy if rightly taught.

The attitude of the pupils, though distinctly favorable to dramatics, is based in nearly every case on an entirely wrong idea. They remember the play they took part in last year and the fun they had wearing the suits of imitation armor. They recall with self-satisfaction the applause and the congratulations of the relatives and friends who crowded the school auditorium. And they think that in the dramatic class they will begin at once to rehearse some play for just such a public performance.

Such a mistaken idea of the subject leads to an undesirable attitude on the part of the class unless the pupils have been told what to expect before the course opens. For the production of a play has appealed to most of them as more or less of a lark. They have felt that rehearsals meant relaxation from the formal discipline of the classroom and an unwonted freedom from restraint. In educational dramatics they will find, it is true, greater freedom and informality than in the ordinary classroom, for creative dramatic work requires spontaneity of expression. But along with this freedom must come understanding and respect for the work they are doing, as well as a strong sense of responsibility for the quality of the results accomplished.

At the very start, then, the pupils should be told just what the course is to be. They should understand that instead of memorizing lines they are to build their own plays, and that these plays are not to be given for the public. They should know that in the arts of play-making and acting a foundation is necessary, and that in the beginning course they will learn to use the tools of dramatic work. Fortunately, the course is to be interesting enough to the pupils so that once they understand what to expect they are entirely happy in the original pantomime and dramatization which take the place of the cut-and-dried rehearsing which they had anticipated.

When a teacher succeeds in building the right kind of an attitude toward dramatic work during the first year, she will have no difficulty thereafter. A tradition is established, and the right attitude will be handed down from one generation of students to the next. This tradition is the more easily built in schools where the lower classes are invited to the demonstrations of dramatic work given by the upper classes at the close of each semester. This custom is highly desirable, for it not only shows the pupils what to expect, but it serves as an inspiration for their own work.

There is no doubt as to the fact that the responsibility for the attitude of a school toward dramatics rests upon the person who teaches the subject. Other factors, as the stage, the equipment, the preconceived notions of parents and teachers, all influence this attitude. But if the dramatic teacher has character, personality, ability, and training, she can overcome any number of negative influences. She may have a bare platform for her stage, she may have no equipment and no costumes. The other teachers may be skeptical as to the value of dramatics. The parents may think a dramatic department a foolish waste of money. But, given a chance to work with children of average imagination and intelligence, she can in one year prove to parents, teachers, and pupils, that dramatic study is worth having in the curriculum.

The kinds of attitudes a teacher builds in her pupils have been determined long before she starts to teach. What she is and what her background has been count more in deciding her success or failure than any possible combination of teaching conditions, favorable or unfavorable.

To win the respect of her pupils she must, first of all, be master of her subject. She must know far more of it than she teaches. The greater her natural ability, the richer her knowledge of life and of literature, and the keener her understanding of the way to teach children, the deeper will be the impression she will make on those who take her courses.

A generous amount of natural dramatic ability in a teacher of dramatics is highly desirable but not indispensable. Appreciation is more important—appreciation plus a discriminating taste. Creative imagination is necessary for the greatest achievement, but a reproductive imagination may go far if combined with the power of intelligent observation.

Ability without fine traits of character and personality, however, will fail signally in dramatic work with young people. For the biggest opportunity in creative dramatics is character development, and unless a teacher has a fine sense of values herself, she will have no power to build it in her pupils.

Finally, she must have abounding faith in what she is teaching if it is to be done well. Enthusiasm is hard to summon without faith; and enthusiasm is indispensable in a dramatic class. Few subjects require more vitality on the part of the teacher. Few subjects take so much out of her. But if she has plenty of vitality to start with, she will find that as she gives it to the children their fresh enthusiasm creates ever a new supply for her.

THE ATTITUDE TOWARD DRAMATICS

All the time that a pupil is studying dramatics, he is building a certain attitude toward the subject. And what that attitude is, is largely determined by first impressions. He comes to the class with an unfortunate lack of respect for dramatics if it is new in the curriculum. He has never taken seriously the kind of training he thinks he is going to receive here. The first care of the teacher, therefore, must be to win respect for dramatics. To do this she must plan with especial care for her first introduction of her subject.

One has only to watch a group of children as they come into a classroom to know their attitude toward their teacher and toward the subject they are to study during the next hour. Perhaps they respect the instructor's authority but do not like her nor the subject she teaches. They will file in quietly, take their seats with an air of facing a disagreeable but inescapable duty. Or they may have a substitute teacher whom they like but whose authority they delight in testing. They will come in noisily and give but scant attention to what she teaches, unless she makes it so interesting that they cannot resist. But watch children when they like and respect both teacher and subject, and note the eagerness with which they come in, the feeling that something interesting and worth while is to happen here. In such a class there need be little thought of discipline. Except for an occasional child who does not "belong," the pupils center all their thought and ingenuity on the work in hand, and the atmosphere is that of joy in achievement.

THE BEGINNING

The bell rings for the classes to pass, and the children who have elected dramatics at this hour come through the halls and file into the room. And at once they begin to receive the impressions which are to determine their attitude toward dramatics. The teacher's appearance—is it pleasing? Her manner—is it friendly or forbidding? Does she look as if she would "stand for any rough-housing"? And they act according to their first impression.

When the pupils are in their seats, the teacher, if she is wise, takes her place, ready to begin as soon as all is quiet. She has the manner always of expecting courtesy in the same measure in which she shows courtesy to the class. She treats her pupils, from first to last, with the friendly regard she would give to a group of honored colleagues.

Certain preliminaries must needs be dispensed with at this first meeting. The roll must be called to see that there are no errors, and this may be made an occasion of getting acquainted. After a few meetings, however, a secretary from the class will check the roll without taking the time to call it. Then without delay comes the introduction of the subject, a thing which should be carefully planned. Among the many possible ways of gaining the interest of junior high school pupils in doing dramatic work of high quality is the following one, which has been tried with success.

"What is the difference between a professional and an amateur?" The boys, remembering certain football heroes who graduated from one into the other, will say: "A professional does a certain thing as his life work, while an amateur does it just for fun." The discussion which follows develops the idea that a professional engages in an activity with an earnest purpose, while an amateur more often does it merely to amuse himself and does it less well.

Avoiding the mistake of placing a stigma on the term "amateur," the teacher guides the class to see that a professional attitude is highly desirable. For an amateur to have a professional attitude is possible and not at all unusual—as in the case of the school football team, for instance, the orchestra and the glee club, all of whom have been doing work of which the school is proud.

On the other hand, not even an amateur likes to be called "amateurish," for the term signifies the manner of a beginner, one who does not know how to do a thing well. If one says a person taking part in a play is amateurish, he means that he is inexperienced and ignorant of the technique of acting.

Does a professional attitude make us enjoy a thing less? Which is more fun, to throw a basket ball around the gymnasium without observing the rules of the game, or to play real basket ball, trying to make every play count? And the class is prompt to say that a game is always more fun if played according to rule.

The discussion then centers on dramatics, and the

teacher may emphasize the fact that the more thought one puts into it, the more he enjoys it. And she makes her pupils see some of the difficulties in the way of imagining just how certain characters think and talk and act—characters who are entirely different from themselves. Even if they can imagine the characters, she shows them that it is not easy to impersonate until they have acquired skill in doing so. If, by chance, she herself can characterize extremely well, an illustration will point what she says better than any words of her own. If she does a characterization, it should be interesting enough to provoke a brief analysis of the character by the class.

The pupils should then be given an idea of what the course is to be. If they are beginning dramatics the teacher will make them realize the need of learning the tools of dramatic work: the correct use of voice, diction, pantomime and dramatization. She will tell them that their work is to be original. Instead of memorizing ready-made plays they will build plays of their own. They will base them on stories, as a rule, but they will originate their own dialogue, and, in many instances, create the characters themselves.

In this preliminary talk she will let the pupils feel how definitely this is their class. The plays will be their own. She herself will be a fellow worker, and because of her experience, she may be able to help them to build better than they could alone. But she will give them the delightful feeling that this is a project of their own, and that they can work out the plays themselves.

And, lastly, she will create a feeling for their theater. If the class is held in an auditorium, with a stage, the

THE THREE SPINNERS.

pupils should be led to feel a pride in it, to consider it their workshop—a place to be treated with the utmost respect. Their professional attitude will lead them to take care of the stage equipment, to conduct themselves in a becoming manner behind scenes, to put their best effort into their dramatizations.

At this time, or at the next meeting, she may explain the simplest of stage terms to them, as: wings, flies, borders, apron, cyclorama, and right and left stage, up, down, and the rest. And she will from time to time during the first meetings give them lively drills on the meaning of the words, in order that in her directions and their class criticisms they may understand and use the proper terms. Emerson Taylor's *Practical Stage Directing for Amateurs* gives a very useful list of such terms.

CRITICISM

Class attitude on the matter of criticism needs careful guidance and cultivation. In a course in creative dramatics constant criticism by the pupils is one of the most valuable aspects of the work. Only by having a critical attitude toward the plays they build can students get worthy results in their own work and acquire a discriminating taste for drama in general.

Criticism is a dangerous thing, however, in the hands of children. Without continual care on the part of the teacher it becomes destructive, with the result that the more sensitive of the pupils become self-conscious and inhibited.

Before the occasion for criticism arises, the teacher should talk to the class very clearly and impressively on the value of constructive and the danger of destructive criticism, emphasizing the former and illustrating it by examples which will be common in their experience. "Suppose," she may say, "a boy plays the part of a character who, according to the story, is a gruff, hard master. Suppose his characterization makes the man seem very mild in comparison to the other characters, whom he is supposed to bully. In our criticism shall we say, 'His characterization is all wrong; he makes the man seem weak'? Or shall we first comment on what is good about the characterization, and then tell how he could make it better? Perhaps the boy's pantomime was really good. It was quite what you would imagine the man would do. Suppose we comment on that, and then suggest that the man would be likely to have a gruffer tone of voice, and be more bullying in what he said. And let us be specific in suggesting ways of improvement. He might find fault with the farm lad for being slow in bringing the horse from the pasture, and frighten a neighbor's child who came to borrow some meal."

The teacher's principal motive in the whole talk is to build a friendly feeling in the class; to prepare the way for an impersonal type of criticism, in which the characters' names are used rather than those of the pupils; to lead the children to see the other person's point of view; and at the same time to stimulate keen, constructive criticism with real thought behind it.

THE TEACHER'S ATTITUDE

Visitors to a well-taught class in creative dramatics are likely to comment with surprise on the amount of responsibility taken by the pupils. True, the teacher fills the important place of manager and guide. But the character analysis, playing, and criticizing is done chiefly by the pupils, with the teacher acting merely as coworker. One is far more likely to find her at the back rather than the front of the room. And she is last in giving a criticism of a scene, often, indeed, leaving it entirely to the students. She knows that when a class has criticized a scene intelligently, the pupils will gain much in confidence and in discrimination if they see it improved by criticism which is their own.

What shall be the attitude of the teacher toward criticism which is well meant but poor? If she is wise, she will receive it with consideration and do one of three things with it: dispose of it quickly, but without seeming to rebuff the child who made it; put it up for discussion if it is at all worthy; or try out the suggestion contained in it, to prove that it is not practicable. The teacher's attitude influences that of the whole class, and if she treats all her pupils as if their criticisms were worthy of consideration, they will stretch up to respond to her opinion of them.

In every class there are a few pupils who are outstanding. These are the children who volunteer most eagerly for every activity of the course. Usually, though not always, they are the most talented of the pupils and, if the teacher is not careful, they will usurp the time and attention of the class. These are not the children who most need the work. It is the timid and the mediocre child who needs encouragement and care. No pupil should be urged to take part in the activities of the class, but all of them should be led to feel that it is a privilege

to do so. And a good teacher knows that she is justified in giving a generous amount of praise to those who
are lacking in self-confidence, when they make an effort
which is even mildly successful.

Theoretically, a teacher should give an equal chance to
all pupils. If John played Nick Bottom last week, he
should step aside and let Harry play him to-day, and
Frank have his turn to-morrow. And every girl should
have her turn at playing Portia. Theoretically, yes;
practically, no. Every child should be given a chance
to do what he can manage with a reasonable degree of
success, and no more. Unless some degree of satisfaction
results from the playing of a part, the child has gained
nothing from the experience. And if, by attempting
something entirely beyond him, he has made the scene a
failure, the others in the class lose interest, and unusual measures must be taken to revive its charm. A
scene must be made to "go" if it is to be of any value
educationally. One successful teacher of dramatics says
that she always chooses carefully the cast which is to
dramatize a scene for the first time so that they may set
a high standard for the others. After the first playing
she is willing to get a cast from those who volunteer.
One sees in her classes an unusually high quality of
work, with several of the most able pupils heading each
cast, and the less talented children doing surprisingly
creditable work in rôles which are not beyond their
ability to do well. And all of the children are happy in
that they are really achieving results in the characterizations they are chosen to do.

Perhaps the greatest joy which comes to the teacher
of creative dramatics is caused by the unfolding and

flowering of the timid child. So often as to be a common occurrence in the dramatic classes is there a child who sits back, afraid to express himself either in the planning or the playing of a dramatization. Then comes a day when the teacher sees a light in his eyes, an impulse to express himself. She encourages him to tell what he imagines. Whether or not his contribution is valuable she regards it as such and gives it special consideration. The next time he is a bit freer, and before long he is volunteering timidly to be one of a group of villagers or dwarfs or hunters. If the teacher is an understanding sort of person she will always notice when he volunteers and always give him the encouragement he needs. Again and again do such children become the most interested and eager pupils in the class, and because of confidence gained there, grow in self-respect and in the esteem of their classmates.

THE STANDARD OF WORK

Many teachers are too easily satisfied by the standard of work done in their classes. Encouragement is desirable and even necessary, but it should be a stimulus to further achievement. "Your pantomime made me see the old man as he walked wearily up to the door. But did you keep him old when he became angry and ran after the thief?" Or, "The dialogue of the dwarfs was excellent. Now the next time let us see if we can show better their amazement when the man asks for their mill." Only by keeping before the class the many possibilities in the story does the teacher retain their keenest interest in a dramatization.

BUILDING GENERAL ATTITUDES

Vastly more important than the attitude toward
dramatics is the great number of other attitudes which
are constantly in process of building: attitudes toward
standards of right and wrong, toward existing institu-
tions, toward qualities of character and personality.
It is in relation to the building of such attitudes as these
that the teacher of dramatics may find her widest opportunity.

A large part of the work of the class in creative
dramatics consists in analyses of character and plot. Discussions concerning the motives of the characters, concerning the ethics of certain actions, concerning cause
and effect are constantly going on, with the result that
old, childish attitudes are being laid aside, and new and
better attitudes built up in the minds of the pupils. And
these new attitudes grow not from the precepts of the
teacher but from the perspective gained through living
the story and analyzing the character and the situation.

A group of children dramatize a *Robin Hood* story and
feel a new admiration for good sportsmanship. They do
a *King Arthur* story which gives them a feeling for chivalry and honor. When they dramatize the story of *The
Knights of the Silver Shield* they awaken to the fact that
perhaps, after all, moral courage is higher than physical
courage. And as they work on the old folk tales they
become imbued with the spirit of true democracy.

Characters influence them. Honesty, cowardice, trick-
ery, gentleness, unselfishness—these and many other virtues and vices are exemplified so vividly by characters in

stories that the children cannot help judging them according to their true worth.

Without writing an entire book on the subject it would be impossible to discuss the many opportunities for building right attitudes in a dramatic class—attitudes toward one another, toward school, home, community, toward good literature and good drama. Attitudes of some sort are being constantly formed by the pupils whether the teacher realizes it or not. It is her privilege to help them to build, and if she is a person with a broad vision, her influence may be incalculable.

CHAPTER III

DRAMATIZATION

Adventurous childhood is always eager to express itself in action. A group of boys seize upon the story of *Treasure Island*, transform themselves into Long John Silver, Ben Gunn, Jim Hawkins, Dr. Livesay, and Squire Trelawney, and having been whisked by the power of imagination far off to an island in the middle of the Pacific, enact with striking realism the events of Stevenson's fascinating tale.

This is dramatization, the very heart of creative dramatics. Upon this native interest is built the whole structure of educational dramatic work. To put a story into dramatic form, whether it be played informally, or written, memorized, and acted formally, is the generally accepted meaning of the term. Every course in creative dramatics for children finds its biggest opportunity in this original type of activity.

WHY DRAMATIZE?

Dramatization, at its best, is a remarkable aid in vitalizing the study of literature. What is acted becomes far more vivid and full of meaning than what is merely read or analyzed. Incidents and phrases which would always have remained hazy in the minds of the class come to light in a dramatization and demand clearing up before the story can be acted. The building of the play demands keen thought and imagination, for it must be orderly, reasonable, convincing, permitting of no slipshod thinking and imagining.

When a class dramatizes such a tale as *Aladdin,* the children must think the story through, plan a series of scenes which are possible to act, discarding the elaborate and unnecessary details which are only confusing to an audience, and keep in mind all the while that the main story must be shown and the connection between the scenes must be made perfectly clear. The amount of thought and imagination necessary to work out such a dramatization successfully is not inconsiderable. A class will think, argue, reason, with liveliest interest all the time, before they will agree on the best version for their play. Some children will think that the point at which *Aladdin* should open is the street scene where the magician first appears to the boy. Others will contend that this starts too far back; that the play should open, rather, in the cottage of Aladdin's mother, when the magician proposes to set Aladdin up in business. All previous action could be explained easily, and the play would arrive sooner at the more fascinating scenes. "But," says the other side, "the meeting in the street is what starts everything going!" And after proving that it is important to show this scene even though a later one may have to be sacrificed in order to keep the play from being too elaborate, the scene is accepted. And so, through the process of dramatization, the children think, imagine, and test results, and by building a play of their own, learn more about structure than if they had acted a dozen ready-made plays.

In language training, too, the possibilities afforded by dramatization are worthy of consideration. Not only must vocabularies be enlarged to meet the demands of many characters in various situations, but the children must learn to think quickly, inventing their share of the conversation, answering the unexpected questions of the other characters, and all the time remembering to keep their dialogue in tone with the general style used in the story.

There will, of course, always be a wide difference in the extent to which children can develop this ability in language. In a certain dramatic class which was studying folklore, some children were at work on the dramatization of the Norwegian tale, *East of the Sun and West of the Moon*. Harriet, a highly imaginative little girl, was playing the part of the mother, and Lewis, a chubby, phlegmatic boy of twelve, was the father. From the first, Lewis found it difficult to make his rôle of father live up to Harriet's portrayal of the mother. In fact, he was entirely satisfied to sit back and let his wife do most of the talking. But after Harriet had persuaded her daughter to go away with the White Bear in order that they might be "as rich as they were now poor," the father and mother were left alone on the scene, and Lewis's position was no such easy one as it had been. For no sooner had the mother bundled her daughter off than she was apparently filled with remorse for what she had done, and she began to bewail her loss. Finally, becoming conscious that the father was not joining in her lament, she said, "Husband, is it not dreadful that our daughter has gone with the Bear? Who knows but that he may take her to his den and devour her?" Here she paused dramatically, and Lewis knew that his time had come. "Why didn't you think of that before?" he said after long hesitation. Nothing daunted by this delicate reproach, Harriet continued mourning the loss of the daughter, Lewis maintaining a discreet silence as she talked of how useless the riches would be now that her lovely child was gone. When she had worked up to a climax of eloquence without so much as a single expression of sympathy from her stoical husband, the exasperated mother bore down upon him, and said in the most scathing manner she could summon, "A fine husband *you* are!" This was too much for Lewis. Swallow such an insult? Never. So, flaming with indignation, he blurted out angrily, "The same to you!" The gift of language he had not, but when driven to the wall, he could express himself as forcefully as could his voluble wife!

That practice in dramatization stimulates initiative, resourcefulness, ingenuity in a child is a self-evident fact, to be observed in every creative dramatic class. The independence and responsibility developed by children who think out, plan, and play one story after another, guided by but not dictated to by the teacher, is a constant surprise to those who observe educational dramatic classes. Not only in the use of language do they develop resourcefulness, but in the interpretation of character, in the enriching of the details of a scene, in the use of properties. Some children playing the fable of the fox and the stork wanted to show the stork drinking from the pitcher. No pitcher being available, they substituted a vase from the teacher's desk, and then in order that the stork might seem to drink from it, the little girl playing the part promptly secured a ruler and, holding it firmly between her teeth, was able to drink with ease from the pitcher!

But in no way, probably, do children derive so much value from dramatization as from the analysis of character which it involves. The people must be understood before they can be impersonated, and the discussions which precede the actual playing of the story clear up questions of motives, conduct, and the results of good and evil acts. According to our standards, they decide, Robin Hood cannot be justified in robbing the rich to help the poor, but he may be excused to a great extent by the fact that the laws were so cruel and unjust that honest men rebelled. Long John Silver had led a wicked life and may have deserved to be left on the island with the other pirates, but his last good deed, that of saving Jim from death, justified the doctor in rewarding him.

This training in power to understand points of view widely different from one's own is perhaps the finest thing which can come from dramatizing stories. Motives and justification for acts can be seen, of course, merely by reading a story, and with more force, perhaps, when the reading is followed by analysis of character. But how much more vivid is the impression on a child's mind, when, after reading and analyzing, he actually lives the story! The opportunity here afforded the teacher for helping the children to gain a true perspective on life, to judge moral values, and to grow in tolerant understanding of society is greater, perhaps, than in any other school activity.

CHOICE OF MATERIAL

Not every piece of literature is suited to the dramatic method. Far from it! From the course of study of any grade only those classics should be chosen for dramatization which will be vitalized by being studied in this way. Such classics will depend for their effectiveness more upon action than upon beauty of language. And this action must be of the sort which can be worked out. *Robinson Crusoe* has too little dramatic action. Many of the *Arthur* stories center around tournaments, which are difficult to suggest satisfactorily in a dramatization. The *Odyssey*, while full of action, has much that cannot be used.

Stories which are very beautiful in idea should be used with caution, for there is danger of cheapening their loveliness. Children can appreciate literature which they have not the skill to portray in action, and it is wiser to choose for dramatization those classics which are within their power to do well. Such stories as *The Holy Grail, The Nightingale, The Happy Prince*, are better read than dramatized.

Literature which contains little dialogue is difficult, for the children need a model for their conversation, something to guide them in their creation of the scenes. Tales from Shakespeare must be supplemented by enough reading of the plays themselves for the children to get the tone of the dialogue. Stories from Pyle's *Robin Hood* should be read by classes dramatizing Robin Hood ballads.

Poetry seldom can be used in upper grade dramatization unless it is narrative verse. Ballads are exceptionally good, for they not only have moving stories, but they are also full of adventure and romance. Most verse, however, is of far greater value read than acted.

And lastly, the material must not be difficult until the

children have had considerable experience in dramatizing. They must feel thoroughly at home with the story or all spontaneity will be lost. And while they are learning the tools of dramatization, they must work with comparatively easy material. After they are able to express themselves freely in this medium, however, they take the keenest pleasure in dramatizing such difficult stories as *Ivanhoe, Siegfried, Don Quixote,* and the Shakespeare stories.

THE PROCESS OF DRAMATIZING

Suppose a class has chosen to make an informal dramatization of the old ballad, *King John and the Abbot of Canterbury,* which is a great favorite with seventh grade pupils. The subject of balladry has been introduced, and a background such as is suggested in Chapter VI has been given. Every dramatization, from the simplest nursery rhyme to the most complex story, should have a real background; and this background is the most important contribution of the teacher to the play which is to be built. Out of her wider knowledge and experience she can so introduce the material that the children will be able to understand and imagine the story far better than they could possibly have done with only their own limited knowledge. This introductory discussion may be only a few words which will invite the right mood. It may concern a single character, such as a miser, as in the *King Midas* story; it may deal with an institution, such as chivalry, as in the *Arthur* stories; it may have to do, as in balladry, with a description of the life and customs of a people. Whatever may be its character, its effect should be so to stimulate interest and enthusiasm that the children approach with eagerness the actual building of the play.

The teacher, then, has told the class interesting stories of medieval castles and wandering minstrels; she has read several old ballads to them, and they have chosen the one they liked best to dramatize; and they have read it aloud until they have all become very familiar with it.

Out of the reading grows a study of the characters. What kind of a man is King John? Yes, evidently a tyrant, jealous because the Abbot is reputed to be richer than he, ready to seize the Abbot's possessions and declare them forfeit to the crown. Has he any redeeming qualities? Yes, he is good sport enough to acknowledge the cleverness of the shepherd in answering his supposedly unanswerable questions; and he even wishes to reward him. He has a sense of humor, for he laughs at the man's ingenious retorts, and when he himself is valued by the shepherd at not more than twenty-nine pieces of silver, he exclaims, "By Saint Bittle, I did not think I was worth so little!" So there is something human about him after all.

How does King John look? How old do you think he is? How does he carry himself? Who will show how he would walk in and seat himself on his throne?

At this point the pantomime begins. Elements of the dramatization are best worked out before the whole story is attempted, and pantomime, always an important part of dramatic work, is here used to best advantage. Various members of the class will be eager to try to characterize King John, and several situations will grow out of their interpretations. One boy will walk in haughtily, seat himself on his throne, and wave away his attendant. The class may suggest that he would seem more dignified if he were very deliberate in his movements. Another boy will try, and he may not only be dignified enough to suit the most critical, but he may also add something to the scene by appearing to hear some music which does not please him and instantly ordering an attendant to silence the musician. After he has pantomimed this, the teacher may suggest that he add words. This gives an added opportunity, and the characterization will grow more complete as one pupil after another contributes to the understanding of the character.

The Abbot will be considered in somewhat the same way, and then the shepherd will be studied. The class will decide what other characters there shall be. They will come to an agreement as to the number of courtiers, the type of jester, the size of the Abbot's train.

Next they will decide on the scenes—an easy matter in this story, for it falls naturally into three parts: the scene at the castle, where King John learns of the Abbot's wealth, sends for him, and propounds the three questions; the road where the Abbot meets the shepherd, tells him his trouble, and receives the offer of assistance; and the final scene at the castle, when the shepherd, dressed as the Abbot, answers the questions and wins the King's pardon for the Abbot and himself.

Now comes the important question: at what point shall our play open? The subject of the Abbot's wealth must be introduced and the King must grow angry and send for the Abbot. How shall this be worked out? Some one suggests that it would be interesting to have a group of the court ladies gossiping about the Abbot, and the

King overhear the conversation and ask them about whom they are talking. But how can the Abbot be sent for and arrive in the same scene? Surely he doesn't live near by. Why not have one of the ladies sitting at the window—one of those high, castle-like windows with a step to reach the seat in front of it—and in the midst of a conversation about last night's ball, for instance, have the lady at the window exclaim about the Abbot and his attendants who are approaching on the road below. The children also decide that the splendor and the size of the Abbot's train will attract the other ladies to the window. This will be a good way, they decide, to introduce the subject of the Abbot's wealth. In the midst of their comments, the harsh voice of the King, who has entered the room, startles and silences them. Who is this that arouses such admiration in the ladies of his court? Timidly they begin to tell him of the Abbot. Each adds some detail (and these details grow more interesting and elaborate with each playing!): "My liege, it is said that the Abbot has riches greater than your own." "They say that his chests are fairly running over with silver." "That he has more servants than your majesty." And they go on, making the King more furious with every word, until he puts an end to their chatter and sends for the Abbot. Now what shall be done? In the first playing there will be a silence until the servant returns with the Abbot, but the class decides that this will not do. Shall the King tell the courtiers his plan? No, he probably hasn't thought of it yet, and if he had he would not tell them. Anyhow, the class is very sure that the questions must not be heard until he asks them of the Abbot. Finally they decide that he shall question, fume, and threaten until the time when the Abbot enters—a short interval, for, as luck will have it, the Abbot is just passing the castle! From this point the scene is easy, for practically all of the dialogue is given in the ballad, and such dialogue as is given is ordinarily used.

In the same manner the other two scenes are worked through, the first playing being crudely done, and the scenes enriched with more and more detail at each repetition. Every time that a group plays a scene it is done without a break, one of the rules of the game being that once started, the characterization must be sustained until the scene is played through to the end.

WORK WITH SMALL UNITS

The most common fault of inexperienced teachers of creative dramatics is their attempt to dramatize too large a unit of the story at one time. If a class were to undertake to play the entire first scene of *King John*, for instance, without first playing it in several small parts, the pupils would scatter their efforts over too much ground and become quite lost. In such a case the playing usually comes to a standstill in the midst of a scene, the children not knowing what to do next because of the failure of some player to give a necessary cue. In order to make the scene progress, the teacher must now step in and give instructions, or else stop it for additional discussion. The illusion is broken in either case, and the pupils lose interest in the story. When children thoroughly understand before the playing begins just what is to be done, they will invariably play through a short scene without a break, finding far greater satisfaction in the experience than if the teacher had given them directions in the midst of it. Even if they succeed in finding their way out of a long scene without assistance, there is so much to criticize that the reconstruction seems a discouraging task. By playing the *King John* story first only to the entrance of the King, and then progressing through the other two short parts of the first scene, each unit can be dramatized with the utmost satisfaction. This rule of working first with short units applies to the most advanced pupils as well as to beginners, and every teacher will follow it if her classes are to be successful.

CRITICISM

At the end of each playing of a scene there are constructive criticisms from the rest of the class, from the group that played the scene, and lastly from the teacher, who acts throughout as guide and coworker rather than as director.

Sometimes, after the first attempt, the players are asked if they wish to criticize themselves first. The boy who has played the King may admit that he overplayed the part; that after all, King John would have more dignity than to shout at the court ladies. The class, when asked for suggestions, may commend the court ladies for the naturalness of their dialogue, but criticize them for running to the window like children. They may suggest that the ladies would show more respect for the King, even though they did not admire him; that the Abbot would seem more troubled by the questions; that the scene, instead of closing with the King telling the Abbot that he must come back in a fortnight, would end better if the Abbot went sadly out and the courtiers commented on the impossibility of his finding answers for the questions.

The teacher may ask the class if they are satisfied with their arrangement of the stage. Is the King's throne in the best place? Are the windows and doors correctly placed? This will bring up a discussion of the best stage arrangement for effective playing—a discussion which would be out of place in a beginning class, but very appropriate for pupils who have finished the elementary course.

Some of the pupils will say that the throne should be center back because it will have the most importance there. Others will question the advisability of locating it there because it will cause the Abbot to turn his back to the audience all the time that he is on the stage. The first group will say that this makes no difference; that it is more important that we hear and see the King when he asks the questions. "But will not the last scene be played here, too?" some one asks. "And isn't that the shepherd's scene?" This puts a different light on the matter, for all agree that the shepherd must be important. And so a compromise is effected. The throne is placed on the side, so that the faces of the Abbot and the shepherd can be seen, but it is elevated to give the King the advantage naturally due his rank.

Such discussions are of enormous value in a dramatic class. They arouse thought, they guide the imagination, they cause careful observation, and they make the class more discriminating in judgment. A wise teacher will see to it that stimulating questions arise, for only by working out the answers to them will the pupils grow.

Whatever the dramatization, care always should be taken to keep criticism on vital points. Instead of commenting on minor details such as turning one's back on the audience, forgetting to open an imaginary door before entering, or kneeling on the wrong knee, the class should be taught to look for really important things.

A proper sense of values will lead the teacher to concentrate first on characterization. Is the Princess (in *Aladdin*) afraid of the Wicked Magician? Yes, but she is too proud to show it. How would she act? She would be very haughty while talking to him, but have a hard time to keep him from seeing her terror. What would she be likely to do when he had gone? She might not be able to keep back her sobs any longer. Such is a suggestion of the kind of questions which pupils may need if they are prone to talk about nonessentials.

Plot, too, needs emphasis. Is the story made clear by our dramatization? Have we shown (in *Old Pipes and the Dryad*) why the Echo-dwarf is so angry when Pipes becomes twenty years younger? Do we need another incident to make clear what is happening to Jim (in *Treasure Island*) when the men are in the stockade? For the time being, the children must put themselves outside the story and consider whether the story would be clear to them from this dramatization if they had never heard it before.

The enriching of a scene by more dialogue and action should be one of the chief points for comment. The first playing of *King John and the Abbot of Canterbury*, for instance, will usually start with painfully halting and stilted dialogue, so general as to be entirely lacking in interest. The discussion which follows, if it is to be helpful, will be rich in suggestion of specific material for conversation. The ladies may be in the midst of a lively argument as to whether it was the blue satin gown which Lady Agatha wore last evening which made her appear more beautiful than Lady Mary, or whether she was really lovelier. Or they may be laughing at the efforts of one of the group who is learning to embroider. Perhaps their conversation touches upon the injustice of the King in dealing with his subjects, though, of course, they take care to speak very discreetly when mentioning the King.

Suggestions may be made concerning specific action for the scene, though children are not likely to make their plays "talky." As the dialogue is perfected, however, more and more business will be possible. Grumio, in talking to the other servants (in *The Taming of the Shrew*) can find much opportunity for interesting action when he looks them over to see if boots are clean, hair is combed, and clothes are neat for the homecoming of their master and his bride. Some of the artisans (in *A Midsummer Night's Dream*) have with them the tools of their trade, in the imaginary scene given in the next chapter, and with these tools are able to accomplish much in the way of comic business.

Teamwork, so difficult for little children to understand, becomes increasingly simple as they grow older. Teamwork, however, must always be cultivated, and the teacher of dramatics finds it necessary to call attention often to the reaction of one character to another. What do the courtiers think when the King asks the shepherd what he (the King) is thinking about? They think that even though he has answered the other questions with such wit, he can never answer this one. How do they feel when he does answer it? Yes, surely, they would be highly surprised and amused. Would they say anything? They would look at the King, probably, to see how he took it, and when they saw that he laughed, they would look at one another and comment in low tones on the cleverness of the answer. This ensemble work, so necessary to a good scene, will have to be stressed again and again by the teacher before the pupils will comment upon it independently. A dramatization will never be natural until the characters do react to one another, however, and every class should be taught to be observing in the matter.

Tempo, though not referred to by name in the class, is an important item in the effectiveness of a scene, and it should be watched carefully by teacher and pupils. The tendency is to play a scene too slowly, with dialogue which is full of gaps, or pointless and long drawn out. The pupils are always critical when a scene drags, but they do not always know how to make it move more rapidly. They should be led to analyze the situation in order to find out just where the difficulty is and how to overcome it. Concrete suggestions from the class as to probable topics of conversation will do more than anything else to speed up a scene. Imaginations need to be stimulated, but, once awakened, ideas will be so plentiful that the slowest child will have something to talk about.

The action, too, often needs to be accelerated. The crowd must leave the stage more quickly, the old woman should be nearer the cupboard so that she can get there in a moment, the eating of the meal must be condensed into a minute or two. The characters should never be made to feel hurried, but the stage setting and the required action should be planned so as to make it possible for them to play the scene in the tempo most suited to the story.

Lastly, voice and diction are important. Just how thoroughly the teacher can go into this part of the work in story dramatization is still a question. Certain it is that nothing short of steady drills can correct faults of voice and diction. To tell a child that he should relax his throat is about as efficacious as to tell him to stand up straight. A few minutes' drill at the beginning of every dramatic period, with an occasional reminder to carry over into his regular speech what he has learned, is probably the best procedure. Continual nagging as to faulty speech will ruin all the joy and all the spontaneity to be had from the experience. Speech training, therefore, should be a separate process, the teacher setting a high standard by her own speech and commending evidences of improved speech in her pupils.

Such points as these, then—characterization, the development of plot, the enriching of dialogue and action, ensemble work, and tempo—are to be emphasized in class criticism, with voice and diction understood to be vitally important but less often criticized. Every suggestion, every criticism, should concern the most vital aspects of the dramatization; and as the pupils grow in insight, they will become increasingly independent of the teacher's guidance in the matter. After the essentials have been grasped, after the big things have been worked out, the smaller points of technique may be developed if there is time, so that the dramatization will be a finished piece of work.

THE CLIMAX

Children are eager to play a scene again and again until they have exhausted all the possibilities they are capable of working out. As long as they feel that there is something more to be accomplished, they are interested. Even after they have gone on to a new scene, they are anxious to come back to this one from time to time and play it again. It is desirable in every way to review their stories occasionally, and finally to present them for another class, an assembly, or a mothers' club meeting. The emphasis in educational dramatics is decidedly not on the exhibitional side; but the sharing of their play with some other group is a climax which always gives a class much satisfaction. The dramatization is seldom a polished piece of work, but it is distinctly a creation of their own, and, as such, it is worth more in their education than the smoothest performance of any formal play which they might present.

VALUE OF A FORMAL DRAMATIZATION

A formal dramatization differs from an informal one in that the dialogue of the latter is free and extemporaneous, varying with every playing, while that of the former is fixed by being written and memorized.

A formal dramatization is usually made when the story is to be played before a public audience. An extemporaneous performance can never boast real finish, and it is far safer to depend upon memory than upon the thinking out of speeches as the play proceeds. So, if a dramatization is to be given for the public, it is advisable to fix its form and require the children to memorize their parts.

Much of the value to the class is lost, it is true, by thus formalizing the play. The informal method, which requires them to think on their feet, to use their own vocabularies, to be alert and original has far greater educational value than the memorizing of a set play. The play, too, loses in spontaneity and charm when the form is fixed.

On the other hand, an occasional formal dramatization is worth undertaking. The early part of the process may be identical, so that the dramatization may truly be the work of the entire class. The knowledge of structure gained from the experience in writing a play, the creating of dialogue which is more carefully worked out than in an informal dramatization, and the experience of doing a more or less finished piece of work in the performing of it—all these things make a formal dramatization worth while. The amount of time necessary to prepare such a play creditably, however, does not justify a continual use of this method, even when the finished product is good.

MAKING A FORMAL DRAMATIZATION

After a story has been dramatized informally, as suggested for *King John and the Abbot of Canterbury*, the several scenes may be assigned to various members of the class to be written. In the lower grades the teacher occasionally writes the scenes as the children dictate, but junior high school pupils are capable of writing the play themselves. Best results are obtained if the children are given a chance to choose the scenes they wish to write. Several versions of each scene will then be forthcoming, and the final version of the play will be richer by the collaboration of the various pupils. Sometimes a formal dramatization is written without the preliminary step of the informal acting of the story, but for children the experience is more vital if the acting comes first. The next step is the reading in class of the scenes by their authors, followed by a brief discussion and criticism by class and teacher. When all versions of the first scene have been read, the best points of each may be suggested for a further version, and one or two of the ablest writers may be chosen to prepare it. The same process may be followed for each of the other scenes, or, if the class is large, the teacher may choose only the best two or three to be read in class. When all have been re-written and discussed again, they may be handed over to the pupil who has shown the most ability in writing for a final and unified version.

The real test is the actual production of the formal play. This is the time when all the unsuspected flaws will show themselves. There will be awkward gaps in the dialogue during a long cross, or while some of the characters eat supper. There will be unexplained entrances and obscure actions. Comedy situations which seemed very funny when done informally in class will fail to win more than a polite smile because they are not managed skillfully.

Such a production should be followed by a thorough discussion of what was good and what should be improved. And to make the experience complete, one more version should be made by the best writer, who should put into effect every possible suggestion for bettering the play. This version should remain on file in the school,

and be read occasionally to future classes to give them
a model for their dramatizations.

A DRAMATIZATION OF "BEAUTY AND THE BEAST"

One of the formal dramatizations developed in a class
in creative dramatics in the School of Speech of Northwestern University was based on the old fairy tale,
Beauty and the Beast. The experience was a complete
one, following in detail the process stated above, except
that it was never acted informally. The play was produced in the Children's Theatre of Evanston.

The problems attached to the dramatization of this
story are practically the same as those which would be
met in any traditional fairy tale. The scenes are so many
in number that selection was very difficult. Almost no
dialogue is given in the story, so that nearly all of it had
to be originated. Incidents which made up a whole scene
were told in a sentence or two, so that the students had to
draw largely upon their own imaginations for detail. The
supernatural happenings in the story had to be thought
out carefully in order to make their execution possible.

The problem of the two jealous sisters was a difficult
one. According to the story, they are changed into
statues at the palace gate, and the dramatization was so
written. But in rehearsing it, the players invariably
burst into laughter at the absurdity of it, for the sisters
had been made humorous in their very hatefulness, and
the punishment did not seem suitable. So it was agreed
to modify their punishment to what suited their offense,
and they were, instead, condemned to live always in
poverty in the village which they hated.

One of the most difficult of the problems was the opening of the play. Should it begin with a scene showing their rich home with a ball in progress? And should the news of their misfortune be brought into this festive scene? Half the class thought this a far more interesting opening than the scene in the cottage showing their poverty. The opportunity for a dramatic scene, they contended, was too good to miss. Furthermore, they wanted to show the creditors coming for their pay, and not receiving it, carrying off the furniture and the family jewels. This would afford a rare opportunity to show the contrast in the characters of Beauty and her sisters, they thought. The rest of the class objected to this because it made too many scenes before the climax was reached.

Since the class was divided, and since each side felt strongly that it was right, every student was allowed to write the scene as he felt it should be. The result was that the mansion scenes did not strike the right note, and the cottage scenes were too drab. At last one of the students wrote a scene which met the favor of the whole class. The play opened with a festival in the village, and even though the occasion was a merry one, it showed the family in humble circumstances and made clear the discontent of the sisters and the loveliness of Beauty's character.

THE EXPOSITION

The manner of introducing the exposition is always a question which requires thought. A crude and obvious soliloquy is inevitably the beginner's way of telling the audience what has been happening, but a question or two from the teacher will lead a class to see readily that there are far better ways. The natural introduction of exposition into the dialogue comes to be the ideal of every group dramatizing a story, and the pupils often become rather ingenious in managing it. Later, a class learns to make use of other more subtle means also, such as setting, lighting, pantomime, to tell the audience what has happened between scenes.

In *Beauty and the Beast* the exposition was very simple. A bit of conversation between Beauty's brother and some of the villagers, the father's story about his adventures, the mirror which showed Beauty what was happening at home—such exposition scattered throughout the play was simple and easily managed.

DIALOGUE

The writing of dialogue is by far the most difficult part of a dramatization. A class which bristles with ideas for the working out of the plot will often bring in the most mediocre dialogue imaginable, admitting with chagrin how surprisingly baffling the task was.

Such a class should read other stories of the same nature in order to become thoroughly familiar with the speech used by the characters. If it is an Irish story, the class may be set to reading Seamus McManus's stories, Lady Gregory's *The Dragon,* and perhaps Yeats' play, *The Pot of Broth.* If it is a *King Arthur* tale, Howard Pyle's *Arthur* stories should be read. In the case of a fairy tale like *Beauty and the Beast,* the reading of many other fairy stories will be a distinct help in the writing of dialogue. Saturation in the mood of the period

or country in which a story belongs, observation of the
speech of its people, and careful analysis of the characters and situations of the particular story in hand, are
the best of all preparations for making a good dramatization.

THE FORMALIZING OF AN INFORMAL SCENE

In contrast to the process used in *Beauty and the
Beast* is the more informal and less technical method
which was employed in the first dramatization in the
next chapter. *Beauty and the Beast* was from the outset
designed for a public play. It was written by young
adults who were later to direct children's dramatics.
The experience of writing and producing a play for children was a valuable part of their training. But the
building of the following little scene suggested by the
study of *A Midsummer Night's Dream* was a more significant experience for the children who developed it
than the other would have been, for they originated the
idea of their scene, planned it, played it many times,
and finally wrote it.

CHAPTER IV

CLASS DRAMATIZATIONS

THE following dramatization was developed by eighth-grade pupils in a dramatic class taught by Miss Belle Kennedy in the Haven Intermediate School of Evanston, Illinois.

The class had been given an excellent background for the study of Shakespeare during the first week of the course. They had heard about Shakespeare, the boy; his life in quaint old Stratford; the plays and playhouses of London, the manners and customs of the times. The story of *A Midsummer Night's Dream* had been told, and several of the scenes of the play read to them by the teacher.

In order to know Quince and Bottom and Snug and Flute and Starveling, in order to interpret them from the inside, this imaginary scene was developed as an introduction to their study of the artisan scenes in the play. The dialogue was originated by the pupils, the scene being played informally many times, and finally written down exactly as they had played it.

A MIDSUMMER NIGHT'S DREAM

An Imaginary Scene

Characters

Peter Quince, *a carpenter*	Snug, *a joiner*
Robin Starveling, *a tailor*	Francis Flute, *a bellows*
Tom Stout, *a tinker*	*mender*
Leonidas	A Fruit-vender
Mother of Leonidas	A Woman of Athens
Petrio, *a friend of*	A Herald
Leonidas	Some Passers-by
Nick Bottom, *a weaver*	Another Woman

A Young Girl

SCENE: A street in Athens by the public well.

TIME: Early morning, three days before the wedding of Duke Theseus.

FRUIT-VENDER [*entering*]. Pomegranates, figs, and olives. Figs from Smyrna! Best figs in all Athens! Who'll buy, who'll buy? [*Puts down his basket and wipes a perspiring brow.*] Heigh ho, nobody up yet. Not a soul stirring!

[*An* ATHENIAN WOMAN *comes out of her house, water jar in hand, and unseen by fruit-vender, crosses to the well.* FRUIT-VENDER *picks up his basket again and crosses left, calling his wares, and seeing the* WOMAN'S *door ajar, peeks in curiously in passing. The* WOMAN *turns from the well and catches him in the act.*]

AN ATHENIAN WOMAN. Ye inquisitive fellow, peeking in at strangers' doors! Know ye not that that is a vulgar habit? Begone with ye—yet, stay a moment, have ye any ripe pomegranates?

FRUIT-VENDER. Aye, mistress, see ye here. Fine, red, rosy ones!

[*The* WOMAN *bites one, makes a wry face, and spits out the seeds.*]

AN ATHENIAN WOMAN. Ugh, it is sour. I'll none of these!

FRUIT-VENDER. Here is a sweet one. Try it, mistress!

[*She nibbles the second, the* FRUIT-VENDER *watching her face anxiously. The second pomegranate is approved, but she refuses to pay the price demanded by the* VENDER.

[*Enter* LEONIDAS *and his friend, steal some peaches from the* FRUIT-VENDER'S *basket while he is quarreling with the* WOMAN *over the price of the fruit, and seat themselves on the curb, down stage left, where they furtively dispose of the stolen booty.*]

VOICE OFF RIGHT. Leonidas! Leonidas!

[TWO WOMEN *enter left and hail the* FRUIT-VENDER, *who is calling his wares again. They squabble over the price of olives. Enter* LEONIDAS' MOTHER *with a jar.*]

LEONIDAS' MOTHER. Leonidas! Oh, there thou art, thou rascal! The laziest urchin in all Athens, I'll warrant! Get thee to the well and fill me this jar with water!

[*She boxes* LEONIDAS' *ears and sends him scurrying off to the well. Enter* PETER QUINCE *with* STARVELING.]

QUINCE. Now, as I was telling thee, I am making a carved oaken coffer for the Duke, and am on my way to the palace.

[*Every one is talking at once, when amid the general hubbub enters the* HERALD *with a bell and scroll. The* WOMEN, *the* FRUIT-VENDER, LEONIDAS' MOTHER, *the* SMALL BOY *and the* WORKMEN *gather around to listen.*]

HERALD. Hear ye, hear ye, O people of Athens! Our most gracious Prince, Duke Theseus, will marry the Lady Hippolyta, Queen of the Amazons, on the third day from now. On that day there will be merrymaking in all Athens, feasting and entertainment at the palace. All Athens will be on holiday and all are invited. Hear ye, hear ye! [*Goes out.*]

QUINCE. Didst hear the news? The Duke is going to be married!

STARVELING [*mistaking the good news*]. Buried! Oh,

poor man! Why didst thou not say it was a coffin and not a coffer thou wast making for him?

QUINCE. Why, man, how deaf thou art! No, not buried, man, but *married!!*

STARVELING. Oh, *married!* Ha, ha, a joke on me that time! Who's the lady?

QUINCE. Why, now, the woman he captured in battle, that savage queen—thou knowest the name—Hippo—Hippo—

STARVELING. Oh, Hippolyta!

QUINCE. That's right, Hippolyta!

STARVELING. Well, I cannot say that I approve of the match. If they fought before, they will quarrel after!

QUINCE. Nay, Master Starveling, ye are mistaken. 'Tis my opinion he captured her because he loved her, and now he's going to marry the lady. And, hark ye, there is going to be great entertainment at the palace on the day of the wedding and all Athens is invited to take part.

STARVELING. Are *we* invited?

QUINCE. Indeed we are. Now, I have been wondering if we could not do something to entertain the Duke. He has always been very kind to us, and we should like to show our appreciation.

STARVELING. Aye, but what could we do, two old men crippled with rheumatism and old age?

[*Enter* BOTTOM *singing.*]

BOTTOM. Good day, masters!

QUINCE AND STARVELING. Good day, Nick. Hast heard the news? Hast heard the news?

BOTTOM [*puzzled, but unwilling to admit it*]. Why, yes, I hear all the news, but . . . what is it?

QUINCE. Why, our most gracious Duke is to be married!

BOTTOM. Yes, yes, of course, I knew that, but . . . whom is he to marry?

QUINCE. Why, the Lady Hip—Hip— What was her name, Master Starveling?

STARVELING. Hippo—

QUINCE. Hippo—*Hippopolyta!!!*

BOTTOM. Oh, that warlike woman he captured in battle—
Well— When is the wedding to take place?

QUINCE. In three days' time. And there is going to be
entertainment for the Duke and his guests at the palace,
with feasting and merrymaking, and oh, Master Nick,
I have an idea!!

BOTTOM. Out with it, Peter.

QUINCE. The Duke has always been most gracious and
kind to us. Now, why can't we show our appreciation by
helping to provide some entertainment for the Duchess
and the guests?

STARVELING. Yes, but what could we do?

BOTTOM. I could sing.

QUINCE. Now, thou knowest thou never could'st carry a
tune!

BOTTOM. I could juggle. [*Takes a couple of balls of
twine from his leather apron pocket and demonstrates.
Drops a ball, is much discomfited.* STARVELING *sniggers.*
BOTTOM *is somewhat abashed*]. Well, we could run a
race.

QUINCE. Thou forget'st that Starveling and I are stiff
with rheumatism.

BOTTOM. Aye, that's true. Now, what could we do?

[*All think hard. Finally* QUINCE *bursts out.*]

QUINCE. I have it! Let's give a play!

BOTTOM. A play! That was an excellent idea I had! Yes,
let's give a play . . . a play!

QUINCE. Yes, but there are only three of us!

BOTTOM. That's all right. I could play two or three parts
at once—hero, heroine, and villain—

QUINCE. No, I think we should invite our friends Snout
and Snug and the young boy Flute to join our company.

STARVELING. Now, what play shall we give—

BOTTOM. Oh, I know a play about Ercles. I could play
Ercles rarely. . . .

[*He makes a lunge with an imaginary sword, at an imaginary dragon, but* PETER QUINCE *restrains him.*]

QUINCE. Nay, Master Bottom! I have a play at home in which we and our friends can all take part. Meet me at my workshop this afternoon and—I'll give out the parts. . . .

BOTTOM. Mind ye have a good one for me!

STARVELING [*thinking of the joys in store*]. Did he say feasting? Why, I have not had a good meal since the Duke's last victory!

BOTTOM. Oh, that reminds me—I have not had my breakfast yet. Why, I must go eat at once or I shall not have the strength to play Ercles!!!

[*Goes off left.* STARVELING *and* QUINCE *exit right chuckling over* BOTTOM'S *gluttonous habits. Enter* SNUG *alone, yawning and dragging along a bag of tools, looks about, sees no one in sight.*]

SNUG. Heigh ho, what a hot day! Well, where is Master Quince? He told me to meet him here. [*Spies a* YOUNG WOMAN *filling her water jar at the well.*] Good morrow, mistress. Perchance ye have seen Peter Quince, the town carpenter.

THE WOMAN. He was here half an hour ago. Had ye been here in time ye might have seen him!

SNUG. Aye, I admit I slept late, but we all have our weaknesses.

[*Absentmindedly takes the* WOMAN'S *jar from her hands and lifts it to his lips. The* WOMAN *snatches it from his hands and tells him exactly what she thinks of him.*]

THE WOMAN. Ye lazy sluggard. Ye good for nothing fellow. Fetch your own water!

[*She makes an angry exit.*]

SNUG [*looking after her*]. Whew, what a temper! I'd hate to stumble on her for a wife! What a hot day! Oh, for a bench to rest for a little while. That is the one thing Athens is lacking at the moment as far as I am

concerned. [*Spies the stone bench.*]   Ah, good morrow,
Master Bench, thou art certainly inviting. [*Thinks of
his appointment, and is torn between his duty and the
invitation held out to him by the bench. Finally, puts
down his tools and yields to the temptation. Caresses
the bench as he stretches himself out on it.*]   Ah, a
friend in need! [SNUG *is snoring as* PETRIO *enters.*
PETRIO *tickles* SNUG'S *ear with a straw and hides.* SNUG
wakes, seizes the kerchief covering his face.]   Plague on
these Athenian flies!   Gone!   By the saints, I thought
I had him!

[*Turns over and sleeps again.* PETRIO, *hearing the tinker
in the distance, moves* SNUG'S *heavy bag of tools directly
into the middle of the street and awaits developments.*]

[*Enter* TOM SNOUT, *carrying his pots and pans, and crying
his wares from door to door. He does not observe* SNUG
who is fast asleep.]

SNOUT.   Pots and pans!   Pots and pans!

A WOMAN [*opening her door*].   Aye, Master Snout.   If
ifs and ans were pots and pans, there'd be no need for
tinkers!   And if this pan had been well made the bottom
would not have fallen out!

SNOUT.   The bottom fell out!   Nay, that could not have
been of my making.   See, this is strong and will serve thy
turn.

THE WOMAN.   Thank ye, Master Snout—   A fair exchange
is no robbing.

[*Turns with the new pan in her hand, goes into her house
and bangs the door.*]

SNOUT.   Hi!   Hi!   That pan is worth half a crown, that
pan. . . . [*But the door is barred. He shakes his head
over this bad beginning to his day.*]   So that is how she
replenishes her household wares!   [*He picks up his store
of pots and pans.*]   Pots and pans!   Pots and. . . .

[*Crying his wares, with his eyes on the house doors, he
does not see* SNUG, *and falls over* SNUG'S *bag of tools.*

The pots and pans roll merrily down the street, and
SNOUT *picks himself up, bruised and dusty, shakes the*
sleepy SNUG *and scolds him roundly.* PETRIO *dances*
with glee.]

SNOUT. Thou lazy good-for-nothing! Sleeping on the
street in the middle of the morning. Look at my good
pots and pans, dented and ruined!!

[*He shakes* SNUG *again. Enter* FLUTE.]

FLUTE. Hey-hey, what's all this, what's all this?

[*He separates the men, while* SNOUT *storms and wails over
his spilt pans. Enter* BOTTOM *running.*]

BOTTOM. The Duke is going to be married, and we are
going to give a play on his wedding day to entertain him!

SNOUT AND FLUTE. A play!

BOTTOM. Aye, Peter Quince is to choose the play, and we
are to meet at his house this afternoon.

SNOUT. Are we all to be in it?

BOTTOM. Aye. And I have had a grand idea—after the
play we shall all dance the Bergomask.

SNOUT. The Bergomask! Why, I have forgotten it. How
does it go?

BOTTOM. Why, in this way—first one foot and then the
other!

[*He demonstrates the steps of the Bergomask, and he and*
FLUTE, *and* SNOUT *with his pots, humming the tune, go
dancing down the street.* SNUG *stands, looking after
them; then, slowly picks up his tools, and murmurs to
himself, "First one foot, and then the other. . . ." He
begins a clumsy and laborious imitation of* BOTTOM's
*performance, till overbalanced by the weight of his tools
he falls flat on his face as the*

CURTAIN FALLS

The next dramatization was made by a class in creative
dramatics in the School of Speech of Northwestern Uni-

versity, and played in the Children's Theatre of Evanston. The entire class planned the play and every member wrote at least two scenes. Margaret Fuller, however, did the larger part of the final assembling and revising of the text.

BEAUTY AND THE BEAST

A Play Based on the Old French Fairy Tale

The People of the Play

Javotte | Bettine } *Village girls*
Henri, *Beauty's youngest brother*
Beauty
Suzanne | Marie } *Beauty's sisters*
M. Ribot, *Beauty's father*
Pierre | François } *Beauty's older brothers*
Godmother

M. Raoul | Baron de Mouzon } *Suitors to Beauty's sisters*
Messenger
The Beast
Witches
Jacques, *a small boy*
Gossip
Lisette
Julie
Villagers

SCENE I.   Outside the cottage of M. Ribot, the merchant.

As the curtains open on the bare little walled garden of the Ribot family, gay laughter is heard—the laughter of HENRI *and* BETTINE, *who are seated on the ground, pelting each other with flowers.* BETTINE *gives a little shriek as one of the flowers strikes her face. At that,* JAVOTTE, *who has been drawing water from the old well, runs over, kneels between them, and snatches the flowers they are about to throw.*

JAVOTTE. Bettine! Henri! Foolish ones! Those blossoms—give them to me! I need more for my jar. Do not waste them!

BETTINE [*throwing a blossom at* HENRI]. 'Tis my last.

HENRI. Why not be merry on All Saints' Day?

JAVOTTE. If your sisters [*looking toward cottage*] find you are wasting your time instead of decorating the place as they directed, you'll not be allowed to join the party when the guests come.

BETTINE. Henri, there is not another blossom to be found, and we haven't nearly finished. When will Beauty be back?

HENRI [*seeing* JAVOTTE *struggling with the bucket, and rising to pour the water into the jar for her*]. She has been gone a goodly hour. She should be back ere now.

JAVOTTE. Did she go to the woods for blossoms?

HENRI. Oh, no. Madame Jodelet offered to give her flowers from her garden.

BETTINE. Madame Jodelet's garden! It's quite the finest in the village.

JAVOTTE. Beauty must have won the heart of Madame Jodelet, as well as the hearts of the villagers, for Madame Jodelet does not give her flowers to any but those she fancies.

BETTINE. Indeed, you may be proud of Beauty, Henri. She's quite the favorite in the village.

HENRI. At our home in the city Suzanne and Marie were more courted than Beauty.

JAVOTTE. The whole village thinks they are—

BETTINE. Sh! Javotte! [*To* HENRI.] The villagers think they are—fastidious, that's all.

JAVOTTE. How I should love to see that gay, far-off city of yours, Henri!

BETTINE. Were you very grand before you came here to live?

HENRI [*slowly*]. Yes, we lived in fashion before father lost his fortune.

JAVOTTE. How did he lose so great a fortune?

HENRI. Six ships of cargo were lost at sea. Oh, well, for

myself I am not sorry—[*To* BETTINE, *who has tickled his nose with a broken flower stem.*] You little saucebox!

[BETTINE *runs away from him and jumps on a bench by the wall as he chases her.*]

BETTINE. Look! Here comes Beauty! Oh, what flowers!

BEAUTY [*outside*]. Are they not exquisite, Bettine?

BETTINE. Lovely!

[HENRI *opens the gate and* BEAUTY *runs in, her arms full of blossoms.*]

BEAUTY. Such gorgeous flowers in Madame Jodelet's garden —marigolds, larkspur, mignonettes—I should have liked to pick them all! But there was not one rose, and I did so want some for the party!

[*The girls have been exclaiming over the flowers as they take them from* BEAUTY *and use them in jars and garlands.*]

JAVOTTE. Roses do not thrive here in the village, Beauty. My father has tried, oh, so many times to raise them!

SUZANNE [*calling from house*]. Beauty, come and help me. This stupid gown is giving me no end of trouble.

BEAUTY. In a moment, sister.

SUZANNE [*appearing in doorway, a funny sight, her hair in curl papers, one sleeve out, the other ill-fitting*]. Whatever is the matter with this hateful sleeve? I loathe needlework! It makes me ill!

BEAUTY. What's amiss? You have probably gotten the left sleeve in the right armhole.

SUZANNE. I did just what you told me to do.

BETTINE. I wish I had a silk dress. They are so rich. Don't you love city fashions?

[SUZANNE *snubs her*].

JAVOTTE. What is your dress made of?

SUZANNE [*haughtily*]. This is cashmere.

JAVOTTE [*aside to* BETTINE]. I should have held my tongue!

[*The village girls exchange grimaces and slip out the gate.* HENRI *soon goes into the house.*]

MARIE [*entering languidly from house*]. Beauty, have you ironed my ruffles?

BEAUTY. Yes, and your petticoats, too.

SUZANNE [*pointing to* MARIE'S *feet*]. My slippers! The one presentable part of my wardrobe which I was able to save in the claptrap of moving to this loathsome country hut. Everything else I have to wear is homemade!

MARIE. You shall have them when I choose to give them to you, not until then.

SUZANNE. You lump of indolence! How dare you think you can wear my slippers?

MARIE. You've taken the lion's share of everything else. You took the goods out of which I intended to make my dress, so I shall wear these slippers.

SUZANNE. Sit down and take off those slippers, you greedy thing!

MARIE [*calmly*]. I will not.

SUZANNE. You shall!

BEAUTY. Sisters, why make such a fuss over trifles? Suzanne, you may wear my slippers.

SUZANNE. Yours! Imagine me wearing your slippers! The family must keep up appearances. This is my one opportunity of making an impression on Baron de Mouzon before he returns to the city. Marie, I refuse to content myself unless you give me my slippers!

MARIE. Oh, fiddle! What difference does it make to me! Since you have taken everything else, you may as well take the slippers also. There, go get your slippers! [*Throwing slippers toward her.*]

SUZANNE [*making a move toward her*]. You wretch!

BEAUTY [*who is working on her dress*]. Sister, do be more peaceable. You'll be in no mood to enjoy your guests.

SUZANNE. Do you expect me to enjoy them when I'm dressed in homemade clothes? I am not expecting, nor do

I wish to enjoy the peasants, but I should like to interest the Baron. Marie, you get those slippers which you tossed with such a high hand or I shall tell father of your preposterous conduct!

MARIE [*ignoring her*]. If our city friends knew what a stupid crowd we had to invite as an excuse for asking the Baron and Raoul—Ugh! Disgusting!

BEAUTY. Instead of complaining, you had better finish dressing, or our guests will be here. [*Listens.*] Here comes father now.

[SUZANNE *picks up her slippers, glaring at* MARIE, *and stalks into the house.* MARIE *follows languidly. The father and two older sons enter from the field.*]

RIBOT. A fairyland! Who would have thought our bare little garden could be so transformed!

BEAUTY. Is it not enchanting, father?

PIERRE. You have done well, little sister. But these are not from our garden!

FRANÇOIS. You have been robbing every garden in the village, I'll wager.

BEAUTY. It will be such a lovely party! Prithee, father, make haste and freshen up before the guests arrive! [*She urges him into the house.*] Pierre, François—André, the fiddler, has promised to come!

FRANÇOIS. André? How he does play!

[*Starts to dance as laughter and talking are heard at a distance.*]

BEAUTY. Quick, lads! They are coming! [*Boys hurry into cottage.* BEAUTY *opens gate and* VILLAGERS *swarm in laughing and chattering.*] Right welcome are you, my friends!

[HENRI *enters from house.*]

VILLAGER. Long live Beauty!

[*General greetings and laughter.*]

BEAUTY [*seeing fiddler*]. André! You are indeed welcome!

JULIE. André, a dance!

VILLAGERS. A dance! A dance!

[*Fiddler strikes up a lively folk dance. They choose partners and dance, with much laughing and chatting.*]

BEAUTY [*after the dance*]. Come into the house for cakes and wine, my friends!

[*They go off, talking gayly. After a moment* SUZANNE *and* MARIE *come out.*]

SUZANNE. I cannot endure those low-minded peasants. All they do is dance and shout, "Long live fair Beauty!" [*She apes them as* RAOUL *and the* BARON *enter the gate. At once she assumes her most gracious manners.*] Good evening, Monsieur Raoul!

RAOUL. Good evening, fair ladies. May I present my friend, the Baron de Mouzon?

MARIE. This is a great pleasure.

BARON. Charmed, my ladies!

RAOUL. And where is your delightful sister, Beauty? I have been telling the Baron about her and he is all impatience until he meets her.

MARIE [*sweetly*]. Indeed, I fear you will be disappointed, Baron. She has eyes only for the villagers.

BARON [*complacently*]. What care I so long as I may bask in the light of your fair eyes!

SUZANNE [*jealously*]. Will you come in and join our company? Perhaps the Baron will find them amusing.

[*They go in, talking. After a moment a* MESSENGER *enters the gate. He goes to door and knocks but because of the gay talking he is not heard.*]

MESSENGER. Hello! Hello in there! [*Knocks again.*] Let me in! I want to speak to you!

HENRI [*entering*]. What means all this noise?

MESSENGER. Is this the house of the merchant, Monsieur Ribot?

HENRI. It is. What tidings bring you?

MESSENGER. I wish to speak to the merchant.

HENRI. I will call him. [*At door.*] Father, a messenger to see you.

RIBOT [*appearing in a moment*]. What purpose brings you here?

MESSENGER. I bear you good news. One of your ships which you thought lost at sea has come to port with a rich cargo.

[HENRI *goes into house to give news to sisters.*]

RIBOT. This is too good to believe! The ship is in port, you say?

MESSENGER. It is, and your friend, Monsieur Dulac, sent me to tell you to come without delay lest your agents sell without profit.

[HENRI *returns with the others.*]

SISTERS. A ship come in! A ship come in! Father, then we shall return to the city to live!

[*They are so excited that they both talk at once.*]

RIBOT. Not so fast, my daughters. However, I shall leave immediately for the city.

BEAUTY. I will go and get your cloak and what money we have saved, father. [*Exit.*]

SUZANNE. Oh, father, bring me dresses, velvet ones and silk ones, capes, headdresses, and all the fancy attire you can find.

MARIE. I want necklaces, silver orna—

SUZANNE. Bring me bracelets. Slippers to match every dress!

RIBOT. Yes, yes, I will bring you all you wish if this news is true. [*To* BEAUTY *who has come out.*] Beauty, is there nothing you wish me to bring you?

BEAUTY. My only wish, father, is to see you come home safely.

MARIE. The little minx! She only wants to win his praise!

RIBOT. Is there not one thing which would make you happy?

BEAUTY [*hesitating*]. As you are so kind as to think of

me, father, I pray you bring me a rose, for there are none in all the village.

RIBOT. It is little enough, but I will bring it gladly. Good-by, my dear ones. I shall return at the earliest day possible. Take care of your sisters, Pierre. Farewell!

ALL. Farewell, father! Return soon, etc.

[*He goes off.*]

SUZANNE. Friends, friends, come out and hear our happy news! [*They come out exclaiming.*] One of our father's ships has come to port and we shall recover our fortune. We shall be going back to the city soon, I fancy.

VILLAGERS. Come, André, a tune! A dance to celebrate the good fortune of our friends!

[*Laughing, excitement. All join in a merry dance, as the*

CURTAINS CLOSE

SCENE II. The Beast's Palace.

The curtains open on a dark stage. Outside, the merchant's voice is heard calling.

RIBOT. Help, I pray you! Help a poor traveler who is lost in the forest. Just shelter for the night, I beg of you! If I leave, the beasts of the forest will devour me. Help, I beg of you!

[*The curtains noiselessly slide back from a very wide triple arch in the rear, revealing very dimly the interior of a rich palace, with M. RIBOT silhouetted against the moon-lit garden.*]

RIBOT [*after peering in for a moment.*] Oh, I thank you, my friend, but it is so dark—where are you—I cannot see!

[*As he finishes speaking the iron candelabra at either side of the center arch are lighted, though the room is still dim. The MERCHANT looks about him in astonishment at not finding any one. He shivers and draws his thin cloak tightly about him. As he does so, the brazier at his right becomes lighted. He starts in surprise and sudden fear; then he goes to it and warms his hands. He takes out of his pocket a small package which he carefully unwraps. He begins to eat hungrily the crust of bread which it contains. As he does so, the table left lights up, and a silver service containing a delicious feast is seen. The* MERCHANT *is frightened at first, and again looks all around the room. Then he goes to the table and begins to eat. After a moment he stops, rises and speaks.*]

RIBOT. Oh, I don't know who you are nor why you have treated me so generously, but I thank you from the bottom of my heart! You are making it possible for a father to return alive to his family. [*He catches sight of the rose trellis on the terrace at the back, goes up and begins to examine the roses.*] Beauty's gift! No one would care!

[*He picks a rose, and as he does so there is a clap of thunder, darkness, and then the* BEAST *appears in a shaft of light.*]

BEAST. Wretched man! I gave you shelter, warmth, and food, and you repay my kindness by stealing my roses. For that you must die!

RIBOT [*on his knees*]. Pardon! Pardon, my lord! I meant no harm!

BEAST. I am not a lord but a beast. I do not like false compliments. You have tried to rob me of my dearest treasures, and for that you must die! You have only time to say your prayers!

RIBOT. Let me but explain. I am a poor merchant, living in a cottage on the edge of the forest. It was reported that a ship of mine had been found, and I went to the city to find if it were true. The ship had indeed come in, but I had to go to law about the cargo, and I lost all I had. I was returning home empty-handed when I became lost in the forest and came upon your castle. It was my youngest daughter, Beauty, who asked me to bring her a rose, and I had not the money to buy even that in the town. You had so many I thought you would not miss just one.

BEAST. You say that you have daughters? Send one in your place to-morrow—one who will offer to come in your stead—and I will set you free.

RIBOT. Never! Beauty would offer to die for me, but I love her more than my life. I would rather you killed me now.

BEAST [*after a pause*]. You may go free on one other condition. Send me as a gift—to-morrow night—the first living thing that greets you as you reach home.

RIBOT. My dog? He always meets me after I have been on a journey.

BEAST. I want the first living thing that greets you! Do you promise?

RIBOT. I promise.

BEAST. Then go! You will meet at the end of the garden path a huntsman who will guide you safely through the forest; and when you reach home you will find there a chest of gold which will compensate you for the ship that you lost. Now go!

RIBOT. Oh, thank you, thank you, kind sir!

[*The* BEAST *sternly raises his hand, and the merchant backs out. The* BEAST *stands motionless for a moment; then from a distance is heard a harsh, cackling laugh, and soon the* WITCH *enters from off left.*]

BEAST. You? Where have you come from and what do you want?

WITCH

> On a crow as black as the darkest night,
> From morn 'til eve I have kept my flight;
> All the way from the Cave of the Seer
> I have traveled, O Beast, to find you here!

BEAST. But what do you want of me? Your coming can mean no good!

WITCH

> As I stirred up a brew with a black cat's ear,
> I saw the merchant coming here.
> I followed swift to capture him,
> But now he has gone through the forest dim.

BEAST. I am glad that he has escaped you—and just in time! What did you want with him?

WITCH

> Ho, ho! Ha, ha! Just to try a spell,
> To see if he'd change to a tinkling bell!
> I wanted one over my bedroom door
> To tell me to rise at half-past four!

BEAST. Well, you may as well go back to your den of darkness, for he has gone.

WITCH

> Aha! You may never outwit me!
> 'Tis Beauty, his daughter, you wish to see!
> But I shall chant and I shall brew,
> For to have her here will never do!

BEAST. Why should you interfere? Beware, O Witch of Knoor! You may go too far! If you lose—if you are at last beaten in one of your wicked enchantments by some one who works against evil-doers—you will lose every ounce of your power, and become merely an ugly old woman!

WITCH .

> Nothing can overcome my power!
> Beneath my spells all creatures cower!
> Now, Beauty is fairest of the fair—
> Soon as a toad she shall grace my lair!

BEAST. You cannot harm her! You gave me this hideous form, but you did not know how much of magic power came with it. I shall protect her!

WITCH [*screaming and dancing grotesquely about*]

> Her sisters are not as good as she,
> And they shall first the merchant see!

BEAUTY AND THE BEAST (*Scene II*).

BEAST. Away with you! The power of evil can never conquer.

WITCH

> You may wish 'til day is done—
> I will fight 'til I have won!

[*As she speaks, she turns and faces the back. A dim picture is revealed through a gauze curtain—three figures circling about a black pot that is set on logs. The* BEAST *sinks almost to the floor as the* WITCH *slowly recites.*]

> See, the flame burns brighter now—
> They have added a dying cat's meow!
> The three fat worms I have put to bake
> Will finish the charm I wish to make!

BEAST [*slightly raising himself*]. You can't overcome me like this! Your wickedness has gone too far!

WITCH [*laughing*]

> Eye of a toad and a nightingale's heart
> Made thee into the creature thou art!
> A brew stirred up by the Witch of Knoor
> Shall keep thee so for evermore!

BEAST. Stop! Stop, I say! [*Picture fades and he rises.*] Leave this palace!

WITCH

> I call on the gods of the midnight air—
> From the Imp's dark den and the wild beasts' lair!
> By whatever makers of evil there be,
> O we shall see! O we shall see!

LIGHTS DIM OUT

SCENE III. Same as Scene I.

The gate opens slowly, and JACQUES, *a small boy, enters cautiously, bringing a dog on a leash. He closes the gate, then tiptoes to the door and calls softly.*

JACQUES. Beauty! O Beauty!

BEAUTY [*coming to door*]. Is it you, Jacques?

JACQUES. Sh—!

BEAUTY. Why, Jacques, what troubles you? And why do you have our poor Paulo on a leash?

JACQUES. Sh—! Beauty, I have a surprise for you!

BEAUTY. A surprise? But why all this mystery?

JACQUES. Monsieur Ribot is returning home, and should be here this very day.

BEAUTY. Father—coming to-day! O Jacques, tell me, where did you get such happy news?

JACQUES. Mother met Father Michel in the village this morning when she was trading our cabbages for bread. He said he passed your father on the highway two days past. Monsieur Ribot was walking towards home. Father Michel was riding and he did not think who it was until he had gone by.

BEAUTY. Two days past? Why, Jacques, he should have been here ere this. I wonder what could have detained him?

JACQUES. Father Michel was surprised when my mother told him that Monsieur Ribot had not come.

BEAUTY. Jacques, let us tell my sisters.

[*She starts towards the house but* JACQUES *pulls her back.*]

JACQUES. Beauty, it would please your father more if you met him first! Come, let us race down the road and watch for him.

BEAUTY. No, Jacques, we shouldn't keep it from the others. First we shall tell Suzanne and Marie, and then we'll race to the field to tell the lads. [*Goes to door.*] Suzanne! Marie! I have tidings of father!

SUZANNE. Father? Is he coming?

MARIE. What have you heard?

BEAUTY. Jacques has just told me that Father Michel passed father on the road two days ago. He should have been here long since. He must have stopped to see a friend.

SUZANNE. Father returning? This is indeed most fortunate!

MARIE. Why does he not hasten? I am so weary of these rags.

SUZANNE. What think you he will bring us? How unkind of him to tarry in this manner! Does he not know that our social position is most embarrassing until he returns with our fortune?

BEAUTY. I am sure father is as eager to see us as we are to have him return. [*Patting the dog.*] Why *do* you have Paulo on the leash, Jacques?

JACQUES. He was chasing rabbits near the brook, and I was fearful that he would wander away and be lost as my dog was. Have I told you about him, Beauty?

BEAUTY. Yes, Jacques, but mayhap Paulo was starting off to meet father. Let us take off the rope.

JACQUES. Not yet! Let us take him to the field first to tell Pierre.

BEAUTY. Very well, Master Jacques!

SUZANNE. Look, some one is coming!

MARIE. The dust cloud is so dense I cannot tell who it is.

JACQUES. See, Beauty, there are two of them.

BEAUTY. Alas, that is not father!

SUZANNE. One of them is too tall, the other too short to be father.

MARIE. O Suzanne, 'tis the Baron!

SUZANNE. And Monsieur Raoul!

JACQUES. Let us be gone before they arrive, Beauty!

BEAUTY. Agreed! We will run and tell Pierre and François and Henri that father may be here any moment.

JACQUES. I'll race with you to the field!

[*They run out the gate.*]

MARIE. My dress—how faded it is!

SUZANNE. How fortunate that I wore my green gown! Raoul is so fond of green!

MARIE. Think you they have heard the news? Suzanne, is this lock in place?

SUZANNE. Sh! They are here!

[*They run and seat themselves gracefully.* RAOUL *and the* BARON *enter, and the sisters rise with exclamations of surprise.*]

BARON. Ah, good day, mesdemoiselles!

RAOUL. Fair ladies!

SUZANNE. How you startled me, Monsieur Raoul!

BARON. We wish to rejoice with you, fair ladies! We have heard that monsieur, your father, is returning on a fine palfrey, with bridle and saddle set with gems!

SUZANNE. A bridle set with gems!

MARIE [*calmly*]. At last we shall return to our proper station. This news is most pleasing to us.

BARON. We, too, are pleased to hear of your good fortune!

RAOUL. This very afternoon we had wished to seek your answer to a most important question. And now, alas, we fear that you have little time to give us!

SUZANNE. Indeed, you are mistaken, monsieur! Our father may not arrive within the day.

BARON. Properly, we should seek his consent ere we spoke to his fair daughters.

MARIE [*exchanging glances with* SUZANNE]. Our father is most lenient, Baron. Whatever we answer pleases him.

SUZANNE [*to* RAOUL]. Sit you down, monsieur.

[*They sit on bench left, and* MARIE *takes the* BARON *to a seat right.*]

RAOUL [*clears throat*]. My fair lady—

BARON [*at the same time*]. Mademoiselle—

GOSSIP [*outside*]. Mademoiselle Beauty! [*Bursts in and is surprised.*] Pardon! But I have good news for you! Your father—

SUZANNE. Yes, we have heard—

GOSSIP. 'Tis said in the village that your father is coming in a carriage drawn by six gray horses. And he is carrying trunks of jewels, and wearing a rich coat of velvet!

SUZANNE. The story grows!

GOSSIP. 'Tis said he is far richer than before!

MARIE. You are most kind to tell us! And if you will go but a short way down the lane [*takes her to gate*] this way—you will meet Beauty and give her the news!

GOSSIP. Not that way! I might miss seeing Monsieur Ribot! He will come through the village. Many are watching for him! [*She starts off, but calls back.*] Now there will be dowries a-plenty! Dowries a-plenty!

[*She laughs as she disappears down the road.*]

SUZANNE. Ugh! Let us walk to the edge of the forest; it is most noisy here.

MARIE. Those common villagers! Come, this way.

[*She leads the way out right.*]

[*There is a pause. Then a whistle is heard in the distance, and again nearer.* MONSIEUR RIBOT *opens the gate and looks about, distressed.*]

RIBOT. Paulo! Paulo! Where are you?

[*He comes quickly down right, looks about, then starts for the gate. Laughter is heard, and suddenly* BEAUTY *dashes in, and runs directly into her father's arms.*]

BEAUTY. Father!!

RIBOT [*backing away in terror*]. Beauty! Come not near me. [JACQUES *enters with the dog still on a leash.*] Oh, why did you not let my dog run to meet me?

BEAUTY. Why, father, are you not glad to see me?

RIBOT. Alas, my poor Beauty! [*Sisters and suitors enter.*]

SUZANNE. We *thought* we heard you!

MARIE. Father, you have come at last!

SUZANNE. Why, what is the matter?

[*Father goes to bench, sinks down and buries his head in his hands. They gather around, and the brothers come in, and at once feel that some calamity has befallen their father.*]

PIERRE. Father, what has happened?

RIBOT [*taking the rose out of his cloak and handing it sorrowfully to* BEAUTY]. Here is what you asked me to bring, my child. You little know what it will cost us all.

SUZANNE. I knew it! I knew that bad fortune would follow such a foolish request! Did it take a whole fortune to buy it, father?

RIBOT. I would the cost were in money! Would to God I could have bought it with the last penny in my purse!

BEAUTY. Tell us, father, quickly!

[*They gather about him as he sits on the bench. The suitors have gone out.*]

RIBOT. Listen; I must tell you from the first. When I reached the city I found that my ship had indeed come to port with a rich cargo. But I found, too, that my agent had disposed of it at once and fled with the gains, giving out that he had acted under my orders and was carrying the money to me.

PIERRE. Could not Monsieur Dulac prevent it?

RIBOT. He tried, indeed, but since he had no authority from me, he was powerless.

MARIE. Was nothing left to you?

RIBOT. Nothing. But Monsieur Dulac and others of my friends advised me to bring trial against those who had purchased the cargo, since they were clearly dishonest. Not only had they bought the cargo for much less than it was worth, but they had bought it without evidence that my agent had proper authority to sell.

SUZANNE. And did you lose your suit, father?

RIBOT. No, I won. But only to find that the expenses of those long months of trial amounted to more than could be gotten from the buyers.

BEAUTY. Father! How dreadful!

RIBOT. I started for home, thinking my misfortunes were great. But I met with misfortunes so much greater that I thought these were nothing.

HENRI. Tell us, father!

RIBOT. As I came home, I lost my way in the forest, and being weary, cold and hungry, I was almost ready to give up, when a great palace loomed before me. I sought shelter, and as no one answered my call, I entered. To my amazement the brazier suddenly glowed with flame. A table appeared laden with food. Then, alack, came evil fortune; for when I saw that rose growing near the door, I plucked it for Beauty. Suddenly the room became dark. There was a peal of thunder, and before me appeared the most hideous beast I had ever seen. [*They exclaim: "O father! How terrible!" etc.*] He threatened to take my life. I pleaded with him, and at last he agreed to spare me if I would immediately bring to him the first living creature that greeted me. Thinking it would be the dog, I promised. It was Beauty instead.

JACQUES. Oh, I would that I had let him go! [*Weeps.*]

HENRI. We shall not let Beauty go. We will seek the beast and destroy him.

RIBOT. That, I fear, is impossible, my son. He has a magic power against which you are helpless. And I have given my promise. I shall return to the palace and give up my life.

BEAUTY. No, father, that you shall never do! I shall go.

RIBOT. No, my child. Do you think that I could ever be happy again if you were to go? It is better a thousand times that I make the sacrifice.

BEAUTY. Father, whether you return or not, I am determined to go. The fault was mine.

PIERRE. You shall not die! What matters it to the beast if I go in your stead?

FRANÇOIS. We could defend ourselves, Beauty. Let one of us go.

BEAUTY. The promise was made. I shall go.

MARIE. O Beauty, dear, we shall be desolate without you.

SUZANNE. If you *will* go, I will bring your cloak, as you must start at once, I suppose. [*Goes into house.*]

RIBOT. Will nothing avail to make you give up this foolish purpose?

BEAUTY. Father, do not be so down-hearted. Methinks I shall plead with him so earnestly that he will set me free to return with you.

SUZANNE [*entering with cape and some gold coins*]. There is a chest of gold within! Why did you not tell us that you brought it?

RIBOT [*dazed*]. A chest of gold? The beast's words! He said I would find it, but my mind was too full of my misfortunes to give thought to it.

PIERRE. If the beast is so kind as to send gold, he cannot be cruel enough to keep Beauty!

BEAUTY. Pierre is right, father. He will set me free again! Come, let us go.

HENRI. Take some of the gold, then father, that you may travel in comfort.

[*He takes what* SUZANNE *has and gives it to his father.*]

RIBOT. I would that we might remain with you.

[*They go toward the gate.*]

SUZANNE. Farewell, Beauty! Adieu, father!

[*The sisters hurry them off, so eager are they to count the gold.*]

FRANÇOIS. May good fortune be with you!

[*Farewells are said, as* BEAUTY *and her father go off. As soon as they are gone, the sisters rush to the house.*]

SUZANNE. You would not *believe* how much there is!

MARIE. Quick, let us count it! Come, Pierre!

FRANÇOIS. Of what avail is gold, with Beauty gone?

HENRI. I shall not touch it!

PIERRE. Brothers, I think that nothing will harm our little sister. But that we may be near if she needs us, let us follow them at a little distance and wait near the palace. Will you go with me?

FRANÇOIS. Aye, that I will!

HENRI. Aye! A word to Suzanne and Marie, and we'll be off. [*Runs to house.*]

PIERRE. Come then—quickly!

[*They go out as the*

CURTAINS CLOSE

SCENE IV. The Palace of the Beast.

As the curtains open, BEAUTY *is sitting in a large, carved chair, embroidering. The room is bright and cheerful. There are flowers on the table and a bird in a cage to the left. Soft music is being played by an unseen orchestra. After a moment* BEAUTY *sighs, puts down her work, goes to the door and looks out into the garden. The music stops. She turns and looks at the bird from the doorway.*

BEAUTY. Are you lonely, too, little bird—shut up in your cage all the day? [*She goes to the bird.*] Do you wish you had some one to sing with?—O I know that I am ungrateful! The Beast is so good to me, and everything is so beautiful! But methinks one cannot enjoy loveliness when there is no one to share it. I am glad that I have you to talk to—I *have* to talk to some one!— Would you like to see my new book? It is such a beautiful one! [*She runs to table and gets a large book which has* BEAUTY *across the cover in letters of gold.*] See, here is a picture of the fairy queen and her court! Is she not beautiful? And over here [*laughing*] see, the funny little goblins are playing a trick on the fat old man. —But this one is best of all—here are some villagers dressed for a festival! They make me think of my own dear village! See this pretty girl in the blue dress— how like she is to my Bettine! How she does dance! She whirls and whirls and whirls! [BEAUTY *whirls about the room.*] I want to dance—*with* some one! [*She*

turns suddenly to the bird.] I know what we shall do—
we shall watch a dance!

[*She rings a little bell. The room darkens and the terrace
lights up. Several delicate figures are posed in a graceful
group, motionless as statuary. They may be dressed in
Louis XIV costumes of white, with white wigs, or some
other type of fanciful and beautiful costume. To the
soft strains of music they enact a little pantomime or
dance, and at the last, return to their last pose.*]

BEAUTY [*calling out to them as the terrace becomes dim
and the room bright*]. O do not leave me—please
come in and dance with me—or let me come there!
I want some one to talk to—I am so lonely! [*They are
disappearing.*] Must you go? Then thank you for the
dance!

[*She sits for a moment, then determinedly dries her eyes
and turns to the bird.*] I will not weep! [*Rising.*]
Even if I cannot go to my father, I can look in my
magic mirror and see him. [*She goes to table and takes
an odd mirror from a box.*] It was kind of the Beast
to give me this so that when I grow so lonely that I can
no longer be happy, I can look in it and see my father
and sisters and brothers. [*She takes it over to the bird.*]
Do you remember the last time that we looked, little
bird? And saw Marie and Suzanne getting married? It
was funny, wasn't it, when the Baron kept them all
waiting while he curled his hair again! [*She laughs.*]
And then Marie and Suzanne quarreled over whom the
priest should marry first—and poor, funny little Raoul
got in every one's way and tried to boss everything! I'm
afraid they will lead rather a quarrelsome life—it will
be hard for poor father! Let us see first what Marie is
doing. [*She holds up the mirror.*] Why, Marie and the
Baron are living in a house in the village! I thought they
would stay with father!— O look, they are quarreling—because the Baron has cut up Marie's claret-

colored velvet gown to have a new coat made for
himself! I wonder what Suzanne is doing. Why,
Suzanne is living in the village, too. She and Raoul
look ready to throw things at each other! Let us see
quickly what father is doing with no one to take care
of him. [BEAUTY *becomes greatly agitated upon seeing
the picture of her father*.] O poor father! He is lying
in bed—he is ill—and there is only Henri to wait upon
him! I wonder why he still lives at the cottage, without servants! O Henri is trying to make him some
broth—and I know he cannot! I know just how father
likes his broth— [*She puts down the glass and begins to
sob*.] I must go home—I know that my father needs
me more than the Beast does. [*She weeps*.]

[*The* BEAST *enters*.]

BEAST. Beauty, why are you unhappy? Do not weep—
I would do anything to see you smile.

BEAUTY [*rising*]. You are so kind to me, Beast—I cannot tell you—you are too good to me. [*She tries to
smile*.]

BEAST [*motioning her to a chair*]. I am glad to see that
you cry no more. Beauty, you think me very ugly, do
you not?

BEAUTY [*hesitating*]. Yes, Beast. But I think you are
very kind; your goodness of heart makes me happy.
When I think of that, you no longer appear so ugly
to me.

BEAST. I am very grateful to you. Beauty, promise me
that you will never leave me.

BEAUTY [*bursting into tears*]. O Beast, I wish I could
promise you that, but I must ask you to let me go
home. I did not mean to ask you, but my father is
ill, and I shall die of sorrow if you refuse to let me
see him.

BEAST. I had rather die myself than give you pain. I
will send you home to your father and you will stay

there, and your poor Beast will die of grief at your absence.

BEAUTY. No, no, I would not cause your death. I will return, Beast.

BEAST. I need you. I will be lonely without you. You must return if I let you go. You must return in a week's time.

BEAUTY. O yes, I will return in a week. Just let me show my father that I am alive and happy.

BEAST [*taking ring from pouch*]. Take this ring and put it on your finger before going to bed, and you will be with him to-morrow morning. When you wish to return, you have only to put on the ring at night and wish that you were back at the palace.

BEAUTY [*taking ring*]. O Beast, I thank you—   [*She runs to door.*] I must hurry to him.

BEAST. Farewell, Beauty. Remember your promise— [*He stands at door looking after her.*]

BEAUTY [*faintly, at a distance*]. Farewell!

CURTAIN

SCENE V. Interior of the Ribot cottage.

The tenth day of BEAUTY'S *visit. When the scene opens,* BEAUTY *is just entering the door.*

BEAUTY. Come in, Julie and Bettine. Do come in, Lisette, and rest awhile before you go on.

[*The girls peer around the corner of the door.*]

BEAUTY [*laughing*]. No one is here. Do not be afraid.

[*The girls enter with baskets on their arms.*]

BETTINE. O I am weary! I could sleep a hundred years!

JULIE. Fie, Bettine, such nonsense—such exaggerations!

BETTINE. Well, I could. Couldn't you, Beauty?

BEAUTY. I am weary, yes, but I hadn't thought of it before.

LISETTE. Let us divide the mushrooms while we are resting.

BETTINE [*who has draped herself over the settle*]. I'll not bestir myself for anything. I'm too comfortable.

LISETTE. You mean lazy.

BEAUTY. Come, Lisette, we'll do it. Julie, fetch me the little blue bowl from the cupboard.

JULIE. Truly, Beauty, I do not see it.

BETTINE. For shame! Fie, but you are helpless! I see it from here. It is right under your nose.

JULIE. Is this the one?

BETTINE. Yes, silly, is it not blue?

LISETTE. Beauty, why do you look so sad?

BEAUTY. I was thinking that I must soon leave here.

JULIE. You will surely stay until after the party on Saturday?

BEAUTY. Julie, I must not. Now that father is better, I must go back. Already I have stayed ten days instead of seven.

JULIE. But just two more days—what will it matter?

LISETTE. Yes, Beauty, do stay. We planned it especially for you.

BEAUTY. There is nothing I should like to do better—

JULIE. Then you will stay?

BEAUTY. I did not say I would.

JULIE. But you would if you knew how much we wanted you!

BEAUTY. It is indeed delightful of you to want me. Suzanne and Marie have urged me to stay, too. Maybe another day or two wouldn't matter so much! What think you, Bettine?

BETTINE. Indeed not! And pray think how wretched your father and sisters will feel when you go!

BEAUTY. That is true. Alas, I fear father misses me sorely. And he has not the means to get the comforts he should have.

BETTINE. If he hadn't been so foolish as to give his money all away in dowries, he could have servants!

JULIE. You *will* stay to care for him a little longer, won't you?

BEAUTY. Maybe I will stay—just a little longer.

[*The girls exclaim with joy.*]

LISETTE. What jolly fun we shall have!

JULIE. It is growing quite dark. We must go. But we will come to-morrow.

BETTINE. My brother will soon be out looking for me— and if he does, O—!

LISETTE. Good-by, Beauty. And thank you for going with us! I am glad you are going to stay!

BEAUTY. Good-by! [*She stands at the door watching them, and then puts the mushrooms away. She goes to the door of the next room and calls to her father.*] I thought he would be here. [*Pauses.*] How tired I am! I think I'll go and rest until father comes in.

[*She goes over to the table and gives the cloth a little jerk to straighten it, then goes into the next room. Soon voices are heard coming nearer.*]

RAOUL. Stuff and nonsense, who ever heard of such a thing! Suzanne, I am surprised. But I suppose I couldn't expect it!

SUZANNE [*entering*]. Expect what?

RAOUL [*following*]. Expect to have a wife with any brains.

SUZANNE. O I think you are horrid! [*Begins to cry.*]

RAOUL. You forget, Suzanne, to whom you are speaking! You forget how I raised you from a peasant to a lady.

SUZANNE. That is not true! I was always a lady. [*Continues crying.*]

RAOUL. Listen to your voice, Suzanne. It doesn't sound like a lady's. Cry, cry, that is all that you can do. I thought I married a wife, but I find I have married a loud-crying selfish baby!

SUZANNE. I am cross, am I? How can I help being cross when you torment me all the time?

RAOUL [*reading calmly*]. Suzanne, your voice—it is terrible.

[*At this moment* MARIE *enters.*]

MARIE. Suzanne—what ails you?

SUZANNE [*pulling herself together*]. O nothing—nothing.

MARIE. But there are tears in your eyes—has Raoul been treating you badly?

SUZANNE. No—O no, not at all.

MARIE. Suzanne, has Beauty said whether or not she will stay?

SUZANNE. I haven't seen her to-day. She isn't back from that absurd expedition to the woods.

MARIE. Yes, I saw Lisette and the others returning as I came along the road. I am sure Beauty must be here.

SUZANNE. I'll see. [*Starts for door.*]

MARIE. Wait. We must plan how we can keep her if she refuses.

SUZANNE. She will stay if she thinks father needs her.

MARIE. Then we must convince her that father is still sick and needs her.

RAOUL. My faith, it won't be possible for you to pretend you love her for another week!

SUZANNE. Indeed it will! She always gets the best of everything, and if the Beast punishes her terribly for her disobedience, it will be no more than she deserves.

MARIE. She has had more than her share of good fortune. She will grow selfish if she doesn't have to suffer a little.

[*The* BARON *enters.*]

BARON. Marie, my love, why did you not wait for me?

MARIE. You *would* spend so much time dressing! And it was necessary that I see Suzanne at once.

RAOUL [*dryly*]. In order to plan a merrymaking for Beauty!

BARON. A merrymaking? Delightful! I myself will be

her escort. My dear, how think you that this color becomes me?

MARIE. Raoul was joking, as usual. There is to be *no* merrymaking. [*Calls into next room.*] Beauty!— Beauty!

[BEAUTY *comes slowly in, looking distressed.*]

BEAUTY. O—!

SUZANNE. Sister dear, what ails you?

BEAUTY. I fell asleep for what seemed but a moment. And I had a most terrible dream!

MARIE. My little sister must tell Marie.

BEAUTY. I dreamed that I was in the garden of the palace and—O I am wretched!

SUZANNE. I pray you, sister, do not feel badly. It was only a dream.

BEAUTY. You are very kind to comfort me, but I cannot forget the dream. There in the garden the Beast lay dying, and with his last breath he said, "Beauty, you forgot your promise; now I shall die." But he must not die! I must go to him!

SUZANNE. You cannot go and leave father so soon. He needs you.

BEAUTY. I must! Am I not wicked to behave thus to a Beast who has shown me so much kindness? He shall not be wretched any longer on my account. He asked me to marry him. I will do so!

MARIE. Marry him!!

SUZANNE. A beast in our family!

MARIE. Impossible!

BARON. Nonsense!

RAOUL. Unbelievable!

BEAUTY. I shall. I will make him happy. He has been so kind to me— [*Just then the father comes in.* BEAUTY *runs to him.*] Father, I must go back to the palace. The Beast is dying!

RIBOT. Beauty, my daughter, I shall miss you.

MARIE. She is going to marry him.

SUZANNE. Marry a beast!

MARIE. I have a beast for a brother? Never!

RIBOT. I wish to speak to Beauty alone.

MARIE. You won't let her!

SUZANNE. Come, Raoul, we are not wanted.

MARIE. Such nonsense!

[*They flounce out.*]

BEAUTY. Father, I must go. He needs me. I will come again soon.

RIBOT. I shall miss you, Beauty—but you shall go if you wish.

BEAUTY. I should be so happy if you could be with me!

RIBOT. Perhaps I shall be some day.

BEAUTY. To-morrow morning I shall be gone.

RIBOT. Good-by, Beauty—I shall leave you now. [*Kisses her.*] Remember, my home is always yours.

BEAUTY. Farewell, father. [*He goes out.* BEAUTY *takes a ring from the chain around her neck. She looks at it a moment and puts it on her finger.*] I wish to go back to the palace!

[*She drops down on the floor, on a big rug, where she soon falls asleep. Rapidly the lights grow dim until the stage is dark.*]

CURTAIN

SCENE VI. The Beast's Garden.

The BEAST *comes in slowly as if each step were his last. He looks about the garden. He goes to the large gate in the center and looks out sadly. He comes back and sinks to his knees beside a rose bush. The* WITCH *has been stealthily following him, and when he sinks to the ground she silently dances up and down in glee. Then she goes and stands over him as she speaks.*

WITCH.

> You've lost, O Beast!   Now what to do?
> I knew she'd ne'er come back to you.

BEAST.   She promised me that she would come back.   I
thought she would keep her word.

[*He sinks lower and the* WITCH *dances about him.*]

WITCH.

> So now you see that I have won!
> The Witch of Knoor can't be outdone!

[*Runs and calls.*]

> Come, Grenalda, Hack and Zend!
> Our victim's very near his end.

[*The three spirits come slinking in, and she leads them to
where the* BEAST *is lying.*]

WITCH.

> I'm glad I let you try your spell,
> For you have done right well, right well!

[*They stalk about the* BEAST, *chanting together.   The*
BEAST *groans.*]

> The spirits of evil surround you now—
> Before our power you must bow.

GRENALDA.

> Disappointment I let fall
> In his glass; he drank it all!

HACK.

> Three drops of bitter grief I gave.
> None but Beauty his life can save.

ZEND.

> Loneliness intense I brewed
> While three new-born kittens mewed!

[*Together they chant.*]

ALL.

> Down, down to earth he goes;
> Soon his life will reach its close.
> When the nightingale sings his song
> We will know that it is gone!

> We are makers of evil charm,
> We are ones who cause all harm!
> With cats and bats, with knots and pots,
> We chant our spells and brew our plots!

GRENALDA.

> Lower he sinks and lower yet—

HACK.

> Victory goes to the charms we set!

ZEND [*slowly*].

> Lower he sinks—under spells—of ill—

WITCH.

> Lower—and—lower—

[BEAUTY'S *voice is heard calling in the palace, faintly.*]

BEAUTY. Beast! O Beast! Where are you?

WITCH.

> What's that? Be still!

BEAUTY [*coming nearer*]. Beast! Beast! O dear Beast!

WITCH [*fiercely*].

> Just as we had almost won!
> Hurry now, you three! Begone!
> I will see what I can do—
> A little time and we'll be through!

[*They slink off. The* WITCH *notices the fountain.*]

> If he does not drink to-night
> All will still come right, come right!

BEAUTY. O Beast, where are you? It is I, Beauty! I
have come back to you!

[WITCH *runs to fountain, terrified.*]

WITCH.

> She comes—no time to freeze the fountain!
> And I must hide me, or—

[*She hides behind a bush, muttering as* BEAUTY *enters.*]

BEAUTY [*running in, seeing the* BEAST *and kneeling beside
him*]. Beast! Beast! It is I, Beauty! I have come
back to you! Speak to me! O please speak to me!—
He is dead! Why did I not return sooner! You have

needed me, and because I did not return as I said
I would do, you are dead! [BEAST *groans and moves.*]
He moves! He is still alive!

[*She runs to the fountain. The* WITCH *silently makes
a spell. It holds* BEAUTY *for a moment, but she over-
comes it and gets the water. As she holds it to his lips,
he moves again and says,* "BEAUTY!"]

BEAUTY. Yes, Beast, I am here. I have come!

BEAST [*moaning*]. You forgot your promise.

BEAUTY. My family wanted me, and I didn't realize that
you were suffering. Forgive me—O forgive me!

BEAST. It doesn't matter now. In my grief at losing you,
I determined to let myself die of hunger. But I die
happy since I have had the joy of seeing you once
again.

BEAUTY. No, no! You shall not die! I have come back
to stay! You shall live to marry me!

[*The lights go out.*]

WITCH [*screams*].

Alas, alas, the spell is broken!—
My charms shall never more be spoken!

[*She goes off. When the lights come on, they reveal a*
PRINCE *standing smiling at* BEAUTY.]

BEAUTY. What has happened? Where is my Beast?

[*She looks wildly about.*]

PRINCE. Beauty, I was the Beast. A wicked witch condemned me to live in that form until some good and
beautiful maiden should be found who would love me in
spite of my ugliness. You alone, dearest Beauty, have
judged me by the goodness of my heart, and in return I
offer you my hand and my crown, though I know the
reward is much less than what I owe you.

[BEAUTY *offers him her hand, and he kneels and kisses it.
At this moment the gates at the back swing open, reveal-
ing the* FAIRY GODMOTHER *in a blaze of light. The* GOD-
MOTHER *comes in.*]

PRINCE [*going to her*]. Godmother! I thought you had forgotten me!

GODMOTHER. Foolish boy! I have been watching over you all the time. I could not fight the Witch myself, but I sent Beauty to you. [*Holds out her hand to* BEAUTY.] Because she cared more for a true heart than for a pleasing appearance, she made it possible to break the power of the Witch. Now the Witch can no longer harm you. All happiness shall be yours! What do you desire?

PRINCE. Since Beauty loves me there is nothing that could bring me more perfect happiness.

BEAUTY. Gracious lady, I am completely happy; but I wish that my dear father could share my joy with me. He was so sad to have me leave him!

GODMOTHER. Your wish is easily granted, dear Beauty.

[*She waves her wand and the gates swing open, revealing* BEAUTY'S *family, who come in, a little dazed.*]

RIBOT. Beauty—my child!

BEAUTY. Father, I am so glad to see you! We shall never be parted again!

RIBOT. But Beauty, I do not understand! How did I reach here? And where is the Beast?

SUZANNE. You did not tell us there was a Prince!

PIERRE. Beauty, what has happened?

BEAUTY. The Beast was not a real Beast, you see, father, but a Prince who was enchanted by a wicked witch. Now, with the help of his kind Godmother, the spell has been broken, and I am to wed him.

MARIE. And live here in the palace? O Beauty dear, I shall visit you.

SUZANNE. I will come, too!

GODMOTHER. No, Beauty, you broke the spell. I only watched and guided you. This palace shall be yours to live in always. [*Turning to the father.*] Because you have always been a kind father, you shall share your daughter's happiness, and live here also. [*Turning to the sons.*] And you shall be given positions of high honor and wealth. [*To the two sisters.*] But you, selfish and ungrateful girls, shall go back to the village you hate and live there in poverty, nagging and quarreling all your lives. Now go!

BEAUTY. Oh, Godmother, I am sure they did not mean to be unkind—

GODMOTHER. Nothing but unselfish love can change their fate, Beauty.

[*The sisters go. She waves her wand again and two little pages enter, with two crowns on cushions.*]

GODMOTHER. Kneel, my children. [*They kneel and she places a crown on the head of each, as she speaks. To the* PRINCE.] May you rule wisely and well! [*To* BEAUTY.] May your goodness and kindness bring happiness to all the land. [*They rise and she takes both their hands.*] And may you live happily ever after!

CURTAIN

CHAPTER V

A DRAMATIC COURSE FOR THE SEVENTH GRADE

THE FIRST SEMESTER: ELEMENTARY COURSE

CREATIVE activity of every kind requires great freedom if it is to accomplish the amplest realization of its purpose. A course in creative dramatics, therefore, is always essentially flexible. It has certain aims, plans, and content, but so much plasticity that it can be guided by each successive class.

The course suggested in this chapter has been planned for beginners in the seventh grade. It can easily be adapted to the fifth or sixth grade if dramatics is begun there. In such cases, the seventh grade may start with folklore or balladry. No class should be plunged into the dramatic study of classics, however, without some acquaintance with the fundamentals of creative dramatics. By introducing pantomime, dramatization, voice and diction training with simple, familiar material, by encouraging free self-expression and natural dramatic impulses, the teacher paves the way for an intelligent dramatic study of literature. The child learns to use the tools, as it were, so that he acquires ease and a certain amount of skill in this form of self-expression before venturing to build an ambitious structure. The course is planned for a class which meets three forty-five-minute periods a week for eighteen weeks.

Technique is, of course, taught indirectly, all attention being centered on content. While the children are having a most delightful time being somebody else and playing a kind of glorified charade, or making up absorbing plays from stories, they are unconsciously gaining not only a wider knowledge of people, but a considerable amount of skill in interpreting character. They are growing in power to think through a story and play it so that it has point and effectiveness. They are accumulating a wider vocabulary, which they find must be constantly enlarged to fit each new characterization. They are beginning to gain freedom in expressing ideas without words and to realize how greatly pantomime can aid the spoken word. They are becoming faintly aware that a pleasing voice and careful diction are desirable acquisitions. And with all this, they are gaining wider experience—pushing out the limitations of their own environment and stepping forth into a broader understanding of themselves and others.

PANTOMIME

Pantomime is the form of dramatic expression which has proved to be the most natural point of departure into the general field of creative dramatics. It has the charm of being a new study; it is simpler than dramatization which requires original dialogue as well as action; and it stimulates natural, spontaneous expression far better than does the study of a formal play. To this study of pantomime is later added the accompaniment of speech; and a step toward dramatization is taken when bits of story grow out of the original situations.

Just what pantomime is, of course, will be the first

discussion to follow the general introduction to dramatics. The teacher will explain and illustrate the expression of thought and emotion without the use of words. She may walk across the room first as one character, then as another, the class guessing whether she is a haughty princess, an aged beggar, a bully, or a timid countrywoman. She may react to imaginary situations calling forth fear, impatience, admiration, and other emotions.

The relation of pantomime to motion pictures will, in all likelihood, come up for discussion in one of these first lessons, and the teacher will explain that in true pantomime we imagine that people do not have the use of language at all; that their only means of communication is the body. Hence, there is no lip movement as in motion pictures. Then she goes on to tell a bit about the time when man had no language, and about the way he made his wants known. How might he ask his neighbor to lend him his horse? What would he do if he wished to spread the news of an attack by a hostile tribe? Demonstrations of primitive man's ingenuity in making himself understood will always be forthcoming in a seventh grade class; and their study of pantomime is started.

FIRST LESSONS IN PANTOMIME

The kindergarten teaches pantomime with music. The rhythms played on the piano suggest to the children all manner of fascinating plays. First they are prancing horses, and then suddenly they become lumbering bears or impish brownies, or fairies, perhaps, light as thistledown. In the school of the dance, pantomime is but a form of dancing. In place of being imitative, it becomes an interpretation of the mood of the music.

Pantomime in this seventh grade dramatic course is neither an imitative rhythm nor a dance. It is not done with music, nor is it purely the expression of a mood. It is, rather, the interpretation of character and situation without the use of words, and is used more as a step in the process of free dramatic expression than as an end in itself.

Many experiments have been made to determine whether first lessons in miming should concentrate on accurate movements based on careful observation, or whether characterization should start at once. The results have been overwhelmingly in favor of the latter procedure. Fine coördinations are impossible at the start, and definite, clean-cut pantomime can be developed most successfully after considerable experience in large, general movements. Characterization, too, is more interesting to seventh grade boys and girls than is action for its own sake, and it offers, besides, a stronger motivation for accuracy, since the pupils are anxious to make their impersonations so definite that they can be recognized by the class.

The first assignment, therefore, may concern characteristic walks. "You are to be some one quite different from yourself," the teacher may say, "some one who is on his way to a fair. And as this person walks down the street, we should be able to see just what kind of an individual he is. If you decide to be some one you know, notice carefully how this person walks. What does he seem to be thinking about? Is he erect or stooped? Does he walk rapidly or slowly? We want to know whether he is young or old, strong or feeble. We want to know something about his disposition—whether he is kindly or ugly or thoughtful. See how much you can make us know about him as he walks down the street."

GROUP PANTOMIME FIRST

The attention of the entire class to the pantomime of a single child sometimes proves so disconcerting that self-consciousness ruins his first attempt, and he finds it impossible to lose himself in his characterization. For this reason it is advisable to do the first miming in groups. Indeed, if the class is small, every member may be in the passing stream of pedestrians. Thus there will be no onlooker except the teacher, and since her attention must be divided among the various members of the group, no child feels himself the center of attention.

And so, down the street will come a motley crowd of kings and beggars and lame old women and haughty heiresses and plodding farmers! And there will be people in the crowd who are just people, with no more distinction than the mass of humanity one would really meet going to the fair. For the most part, however, this is an interesting and varied stream of passers-by, for every child wants his character to be an interesting one.

From this group the teacher may pick several especially distinct characterizations, and ask these people to walk home from the fair. "See if you know who they are," she may say to the class. And as the characters pass across the room, the pupils in their seats guess what kind of a person each may be. All the other children are then given a chance to have their characters guessed, and profiting by their bit of experience, as well as by their observation of the others, they improve their pantomime so that their characters, too, may be recognized.

After each pupil has achieved a characteristic walk, he is given the problem of putting his character into a situation. He may look for a lost book, try on hats, miss a train, get weighed, go to the movies, stand in a crowded train, cross a muddy street, go to a fire, or do some other pantomime which seems natural to his character.

These pantomimes are commented upon by teacher and class, the first question being always, "What did you like about it?" and then, "How could he make it better?" Children are remarkably observing, as a rule, and with a little guidance, they soon develop the ability to pick out the really good points and suggest the needed improvements. As time goes on, more and more definiteness, and careful observation of actual happenings, are required by teacher and class alike.

Following this assignment, the pupils may be allowed to originate situations in which two characters appear, first playing them in pantomime and then adding language. They will bring in such scenes as the meeting of two friends who do not recognize each other at first, a clerk showing goods to a fussy customer, a camping expedition, and other familiar happenings. And unless they are gently discouraged, the vivid imaginations of the boys will often concentrate on hold-ups, fights, and even murders. In such cases it is well for the teacher and class to suggest a variety of good situations, thus crowding out rather than forbidding the bloodthirsty tendencies of the minority!

As speech is added to the pantomimes, attention may be called to the diction of the various types of people impersonated. The speech of refined, educated folk is contrasted with the slovenly language of ignorant people. Their voices, too, are commented upon, the class noting that harsh, shrill voices suggest a lack of education (though, alas, no such criterion exists as yet in America!) and smooth, cultivated tones indicate refinement and culture.

"How careful are we in our own character?" the teacher may ask. Then she may write on the board such words as *education, character, president, history, believe, gentlemen, Tuesday, comfortable,* and the pupils may test their pronunciation and suggest other words which are often pronounced carelessly. A study of the correct manner of articulating vowels and consonants is the logical beginning for training in diction. This should be followed by word and sentence drills. Along with the study of diction there should be careful voice training, emphasis being placed always on relaxation of the throat. Several class periods may well be taken for voice and diction alone, and, thereafter, five or ten minutes at the beginning of each period should be devoted to varied and interesting drills. For this is largely a technical matter, and nothing but constant drill will be of any value. Gradually, the improvement accomplished in this short period will carry over into the speech of the dramatic lesson, though it must never be forced, or all spontaneity of expression will be lost. References for the study of voice and diction will be found in the appendix of this book.

THE INTRODUCTION OF DRAMATIZATION

By the sixth week of the semester it is time to introduce the dramatization of stories. And just what is dramatization? How does it differ from what the class has been doing? As with pantomime, the teacher explains and illustrates. In the work from now on, there will be stories to start with. The plot, dialogue, and characters are used, and new dialogue or conversation, which will go well with that in the story is added. If the people use quaint, old-fashioned language, for instance, the pupils will, of course, use that manner of speaking in the dialogue they create.

In almost every dramatization there will be need to use characters who are barely mentioned, or not spoken of at all in the story. Perhaps some of the characters who have been brought into class recently will fit into the dramatizations which are to be made. And there will doubtless be many new ones which the class will create. But the dramatizations, though original, will be based upon stories with plots instead of being merely imaginary situations.

The method of dramatization will be demonstrated by starting at once on a story. This story—an exceedingly simple one—is best told rather than read by the teacher, and the dramatization proceeds in the manner suggested in the chapter on dramatization.

For this first study, such a story as *The Boy Who Cried Wolf* might be used. It is short, simple, and familiar, and children can find much use for their characterizations in the persons of the villagers. Other possible stories are *The Old Woman and the Tramp, The Three Wishes, To Your Good Health.* Care should be taken to avoid plunging the class into an elaborate dramatization. Stories which require only one or two scenes are better to use during the first semester, so

ALADDIN.

that each dramatization may be carefully done. If a dramatization of five or six scenes is attempted it will require so long for its completion that the class is likely to lose interest. In lower grades the ideal material to use is Mother Goose, out of which all kinds of charming dramatizations may be made, from the simplest to the most elaborate. In the seventh grade, some of the fables and many of the simpler folk tales may be used as material. But since much foundation work is to be done in pantomime, voice, and diction, there will be time only for two or three simple dramatizations, each one involving much planning and analyzing, individual and ensemble pantomiming, the creating and enriching of dialogue, and many repetitions to give all the pupils a chance to play various parts. A few dramatizations thoroughly done are infinitely preferable to many played superficially. Pupils learn how to do thorough work; they gain experience in careful analysis of character and situation; they find many ways of improving their dialogue; they acquire some skill in playing varied parts; and they heartily enjoy extracting every drop of meaning from the story.

THE SECOND SEMESTER: FOLKLORE AND HERO TALES

After one semester's work, the dramatic course may well be built around one unified body of literature. This plan will give it more value, educationally, than a smattering of many things; and it will have all the interest attaching to the project method of study. Pantomime, dramatization, speech work, will all draw on the same body of material for content; and when the course is ended, the class has gained not only skill in interpretation, but a richer background in some specific field of literature.

Choosing this literature is a process which is determined by some three or four considerations. Besides having intrinsic worth, it must suit the age of the children; it must be of the kind which lends itself readily to dramatic treatment; and it must be chosen with regard to the previous dramatic training of the pupils. Much of the literature studied in the seventh grade is not suitable for dramatic work, and some of it is too difficult to use unless the class has had more than one semester's work in creative dramatics.

Hero tales have a strong appeal to children of this age, though stories which have a romantic glamour are beginning to be attractive to them. They are still in a realistic period, but they baffle the psychologist who may wish to catalogue their interests, for they are eager to dramatize stories of any kind whatever, as long as the teacher introduces them in an interesting way. Seventh grade children have been known to take the keenest delight in dramatizing Mother Goose rhymes, fairy stories, realistic hero tales, and romantic ballads. The reason is, doubtless, that their interest in dramatics is so genuine and so strong that they take any opportunity which presents itself to enter into a dramatic activity.

Nevertheless, the choice of material for dramatic study this semester may preferably be that which is realistic and adventurous. It will include one or more hero stories, sturdy and full of action, with possibilities for stressing not only physical but moral courage. Because the twelve-year-old child likes Robin Hood's bold, adventurous spirit, he is the more influenced by his finer qualities: generosity, good sportsmanship, gentleness to women, kindness to the unfortunate. Because he admires Arthur for his courage in the face of desperate adventure, he may also regard him as an ideal in chivalry, courtesy, and standards of honor.

FOLKLORE

Experiments with classes beginning dramatics in the seventh grade have proved that one body of material which fulfills all the requirements is folklore. The term is a broad one, and it may be restricted or not to the folklore of a particular country. Abundant in quantity, rich in dramatic possibilities, and familiar as one's own hearthstone, it is a veritable treasure house for a class beginning dramatization. In schools having dramatic training throughout the grades, folklore would be used earlier. That there is a large number of old folk tales which fit admirably into seventh grade interests, however, is easily proved by the enthusiasm which they arouse, the earnestness with which they are discussed, and the delight the children take in impersonating the familiar characters. Even when stories new to them are chosen for study, the characters are familiar, for folk tales grew up among people whose outlook on life was that of children. A twelve-year-old boy or girl feels a strong sympathy for their attitude toward life, with its clean-cut virtues and vices, its simple justice, its pure democracy.

Hero tales have grown out of this mass of folklore. They may almost be considered part of it, for the traditional hero tales are only the old sagas unified and enriched by the hand of an artist.

The material of this course, then, may include varied tales from the great body of folklore, or it may center on one of the hero cycles, with occasional relief in the way of a short comic folk tale. *King Arthur, Siegfried, Ulysses,* offer possibilities for concentrated study if the material for dramatization is carefully chosen. *Robin Hood,* though the most popular of all, should be saved for the balladry course, for it fits perfectly the spirit of the old ballads.

BACKGROUND FOR HERO CYCLES

Each hero cycle needs a background of collateral material if it is to be highly successful. Both history and literature should contribute to the store of knowledge the children must have in order to feel thoroughly at ease in dramatizing the stories. Tennyson's *Idylls of the King* is much too mature for seventh grade, though bits of it may be read to the class to illuminate their study of the *Arthur* cycle. Malory and *The Mabinogion* will furnish a background for the teacher, while the pupils will find great interest in Howard Pyle's *King Arthur,* in Lanier's *The Boy's King Arthur,* and in *Knightly Legends of Wales.* Many of the stories are too romantic for use in the seventh grade, others too full of violence. The scene of the drawing of the sword from the stone, part of the Gareth-Lynette story, the tale of the testing of Sir Gawayne by the strange woman, and an occasional story of one or another of the knights have all been used with success.

Sigurd the Volsung by William Morris offers the best

material for the study of the *Siegfried* legend, though a much larger background is necessary for the teacher. The *Volsunga Saga,* the operas, and some of the old romances offer rich possibilities for material, though none of them can be used directly for class work.

The *Odyssey* can be used more easily than can either of the other two hero cycles mentioned. Both the poem and Palmer's prose translation are interesting to the children, and the epic would make a fascinating project, not only for the classes in English and dramatics, but for history, geography, and art as well.

VARIED FOLK TALES

Infinitely more valuable for purposes of self-expression, however, is the dramatization of varied folk tales. Concentration on a single cycle means a distinct gain in scholarship, but the dramatic experience is, as a rule, less rich than when time is spent on stories of several types, all chosen for their literary excellence and dramatic values. The widely different themes and plots, the varied characters, the changing points of view—all these are more stimulating to the imagination, more productive of growth and versatility than is the best of the cycles.

Suppose, then, the literature of this semester is to be chosen from the store of folklore and traditional hero tales, each story being entirely distinct from the others. Out of the great mass of folklore, the teacher selects ten or twelve stories, from which about four will be used for actual dramatization, according to those which seem best to suit her class. They are chosen with reference to the tastes of the children, the standards of life and art which the stories exemplify, and their dramatic possibilities. One of the stories may be a familiar droll, as *The Parson and the Clerk, The Squire's Bride, Why the Sea Is Salt.* Most certainly there will be one Arabian Night's tale, for in dramatic possibilities, *Aladdin* and *Ali Baba,* especially, are among the richest to be found anywhere. An old mythological story, such as *The Golden Touch* or *Baucis and Philemon,* is often used in this course, and sometimes a good modern tale, too excellent for dramatic purposes to be passed by. *Old Pipes and the Dryad* or *The Bee Man of Orn* by Stockton, scenes from *The Prince and the Pauper* by Mark Twain, *The King of the Golden River* by Ruskin, *The Knights of the Silver Shield* by Alden, and *The Nuremberg Stove* by Ouida, offer fine opportunity for dramatization. A choice made from these stories, with a tale from one of the hero cycles, will make a most interesting and valuable semester's work.

A complete course for the dramatic study of literature extending through the grades would provide for more thorough study of each type of tale included in this semester's work. But until the time comes when this is possible, the course in folklore may include an example of each.

At the close of the year a delightful program may be given by the dramatic class, at which time the pupils will play for the school the best dramatizations which have been made during the year. One short story may be done entirely in pantomime after an introduction by some member of the class. The story of another may be told up to a certain point, the curtains opening on the final scene. And if a frame story is to be acted, such as Ruth Sawyer's *The Voyage of the Wee Red Cap,* which is supposed to be told by an old man to a group of Irish folk, the whole group may listen to the story, as they sit on steps at the side of the stage, watch the scenes when the curtains open to show incidents of the story, and comment on the plot and characters as if they were just a part of the old tale. Such programs make an excellent close to the year's work in creative dramatics, for they should be well enough done to afford real entertainment for the school, and at the same time give the players an experience which will bring them both satisfaction and encouragement.

CHAPTER VI

A DRAMATIC COURSE FOR THE EIGHTH GRADE

The First Semester: Balladry

BALLADRY is an ideal subject for the first semester of the eighth year. It grows naturally out of the previous course; it suits the tastes of both boys and girls; and it is difficult enough to demand their best efforts. The old ballads have the vigor of youth, they are red-blooded, they deal with adventure and heroic deeds. The boys like them for these reasons, while the girls are even more attracted by their romantic element. Ballads run the whole range of human emotions, from sturdy humor, through love and hate, to dark tragedy. In working out plays with this material, horizons are widened, vicarious experiences provide an outlet for the rising new emotions of growing boys and girls. Feelings which seek expression find a wholesome and satisfying escape through the reading and dramatizing of these old stories in verse.

Here, as in folklore, the teacher will make a careful choice, rejecting many ballads in which the tragic or love element is strong, and choosing those which have either a jolly humor or a dramatic plot with no harrowing element. *King John and the Abbot of Canterbury* has proved one of the strong favorites, and *Robin Hood and the Widow's Three Sons* another. These are good ballads for the early part of the semester. Other old ballads, such as *Sir Patrick Spens, Saddle to Rags, Get Up and Bar the Door, The Heir of Linne,* and several others from the *Robin Hood* cycle have been used with success, as well as modern ballads like *Lochinvar, King Robert of Sicily, The Lady of Shalott, Lady Clare,* and *Alice Brand.*

PRESENTATION OF THE SUBJECT

In this course the building of a background is highly important. Such references as Olcott's *Story Telling Ballads,* Allingham's *Ballad Book,* and Edward's *A Book of Old Ballads* (which has a very good preface by Hamilton W. Mabie), will prove of immense benefit to the teacher, both because of the many ballads they contain and because of their excellent introductory material on the subject of balladry. Indeed, the shelves of a good library contain numerous books of ballads worth examining. A talk about balladry will create a lively interest in the class for it is a fascinating subject. The great halls where the minstrel was a welcome guest; the singing of the ballads to the accompaniment of the harp or bagpipe, with the household listening eagerly, and perhaps joining in the refrain—such things make good storytelling. Then a word will be said about the gradual dropping of the refrain, and finally the dropping of the music, until a ballad came to be considered merely a simple story told in verse, sometimes merry, oftener sad.

After the mood is created, it is time to read one of the ballads to the class. No commonplace reading will do; it must be given with spirit and enthusiasm. The rhythm must be strongly marked; it must have a lilt and a swing which the hearers cannot resist. If the reading is well done, it will carry the class so thoroughly into the spirit of the story that they will be eager to try reading it themselves.

One of the older ballads will be chosen for this first reading, and it need not be one which will be played. *Sir Patrick Spens* is a good choice, for it not only is one of the best examples of this type of verse, but it also has an unusually strong appeal to children. Others may be read from time to time, in order to acquaint the class with a larger number of ballads than they will have time to study. In the reading the children will note certain characteristics of the ballad, such as its quaint language, its swing, its frequent change of accent to suit the rhythm, its gaps in continuity, its characters, its theme. One ballad, such as *The Cruel Brother* or *Binnorie*, may be read by the teacher, while the class chants the refrain. The pupils may dramatize the situation, the teacher or a member of the class impersonating the minstrel, with the others gathered around as if in an old baronial hall. As the minstrel speaks the lines, the guests chant the refrain, which is an echo, perhaps, of the sentiment of the story, deepening and intensifying the mood.

Following this introduction to ballads, copies of one of those which have been read may be given out, and the pupils may try their skill in reading it. This one has been chosen with reference to its possibilities for class dramatization. Such a ballad should have the following characteristics:

1. Its story must be one that appeals to the class. A highly romantic ballad, such as *The Gay Goshawk,* or a deeply tragic one like *Lord Randal,* will hold interest for a single reading but lack sufficient appeal for continued

study. *King John and the Abbot of Canterbury,* though not one of the finest ballads, has good opportunities for characterization, a broad humor which appeals to boys and girls of this age, and a plot on which the class will be keenly interested to work for many a day. This ballad has been used as an illustration in the chapter on dramatization.

2. The action must be of the kind that can be worked into a play. *Sir Patrick Spens,* though greatly liked by balladry classes, has considerable action which is unsatisfactory to manage. The imagination of eighth graders is vivid, but it is scarcely adequate to suggest satisfactory action for the following stanzas:

> They fetched a web o' the silken claith,
>   Another o' the twine,
> And they wapped them round that gude ship's side,
>   But still the sea came in.
>
> O laith, laith were our gude Scots lords
>   To wet their cork-heel'd shoon;
> But lang or a' the play was played
>   They wat their hats aboon.

The drowning of Sir Patrick Spens and his "gude Scots lords" is far less satisfactory for a dramatization than the action in the following stanza from one of the *Robin Hood* ballads:

> Thrice Robin shot about,
>   And away he sliced the wand,
> And so did good Gilbert,
>   With the white hand.

Even though the shooting is no more actual than the drowning, it can be much more easily imagined and suggested.

3. Some theme other than love must be the dominant idea of a ballad suitable for children. Adolescent girls are interested in reading about love, but both girls and boys are painfully self-conscious if the love element is strong in a dramatization. *Lochinvar,* in some classes, is hard to handle, even though the students enjoy reading about the bold lover who carries off his lady; while *Lady Clare,* which is also romantic, has been used very successfully because the situation requires no love-making.

As a first dramatization, either *King John and the Abbot of Canterbury* or a *Robin Hood* ballad would be a wise choice. An interesting preliminary to the *Robin Hood* ballads is an imaginary scene in Sherwood Forest, introducing the men of Robin Hood's band. Some little incident suggested by the reading of the Pyle stories could be used as a basis, or no special incident at all. The gathering of the men around the fire at night after a day of adventure, each relating something of what had befallen him, would serve to introduce the characters and make them the children's own. A dramatization of the story of how Robin Hood became an outlaw and how he gathered his band around him would be even better if a cycle of the ballads was to be used.

As a contrast to the bold, vigorous spirit of these bluff tales, a widely contrasting ballad like *The Lady of Shalott* or *Alice Brand* will be welcome for a second dramatization. The mystery, the atmosphere of chivalry, the romance in the fate of the unhappy Lady of Shalott provide an outlet for the imagination which makes it excellent material for use in the dramatic class.

One of the favorite modern ballads which may be used in this course is *King Robert of Sicily*. Here is a story which is more complex in the working out than most of the others. Consequently, a considerable amount of time must be allowed for the dramatization. Its story is understandable and appealing to eighth grade pupils, it has almost unlimited possibilities in its action, and its only difficult problem is the church ceremonial, with the chanting and processional. Rightly managed, however, this is simple and dignified, suggesting rather than illustrating the ritual of the church.

In the course of a semester, with three meetings a week, not more than three ballads can be dramatized with any degree of thoroughness. One week is spent on the background and the reading of the ballads, and about five weeks apiece on the dramatizations. Each dramatization will have, as a rule, three or more scenes, each requiring much time for planning, executing, judging, and polishing. Individual work in pantomiming the characters and situations takes a week or more after the initial discussion, with twenty or more pupils to be considered. The polishing of certain scenes for the final demonstration requires more repetition than would be necessary for ordinary class work.

A BALLADRY PROGRAM

It is highly desirable that as a climax for the semester's work, the best scenes should be given in assembly. This demonstration makes a valuable incentive for superior class work, and at the same time it sets a standard for the children in the lower classes. Delightful variety in the way ballads may be used in a dramatic class makes it especially interesting to work toward this final program. For such a culmination of the semester's work there might be a little talk about balladry, several scenes from dramatizations, one ballad mimed, and the story of another told as if by one of the characters, and to complete the program, the singing of several ballads with a chorus giving the refrain. It would be a fitting close for the course, a charmingly varied yet unified program, which would give the class the opportunity of sharing with the rest of the school the interesting new experiences they have gained.

THE SECOND SEMESTER: SHAKESPEARE

The original dramatization of stories reaches its climax when, in the eighth grade, the classes dramatize tales from Shakespeare's plays. Of all material which has been used for experimentation in the dramatic courses in the Evanston schools, the Shakespeare stories have proved not only the favorite material but also the most successful in accomplishing their purpose.

The children enter this advanced course with eagerness, partly because of their pride in studying Shakespeare, but chiefly because they have seen and heartily enjoyed in assembly the Shakespeare scenes of the preceding class. Through the whole semester the interest is keen because of the surprising possibilities for varied experience in the stories. The richness of plot, the depth and variety of characterization, the very complexity of action fascinates the class, and the pupils plunge into the playing of the stories with a zest which can be realized only by those who have watched eighth grade children in the midst of such a dramatization.

THE AIMS OF THE COURSE

The course is planned to accomplish the following purposes:

1. To give to the pupils an appealing introduction to Shakespeare, so that they will approach with interest their later, more detailed study of the plays.

2. To afford opportunity for rich dramatic expression.

3. To widen horizons by the study of Shakespeare's characters.

THE MATERIAL

The stories of some of Shakespeare's plays, with certain scenes from the plays themselves, are used as the material for this course. Lamb's *Tales* have been superseded by several well-written modern books of Shakespeare stories, more interesting and stimulating to the imagination than the older book. McLeod's *Stories from Shakespeare* has proved especially successful. So little dialogue is given even in this version, however, that the scenes to be dramatized should always be read to the class from the text of the plays in order to give the players a model for their original dialogue. In this way the flavor of the scene is made truer, the dialogue is kept more fitting, and a stronger link is formed with the play itself.

For use in this course, two of the plays best suited

to the eighth grade may be selected, and several scenes from each of them chosen for dramatization. Study may be limited to one play, the class dramatizing as many as eight scenes; or four or five plays may be used, with the dramatization of but one scene from each. Several years of experimenting, however, have proved the superiority of the plan first mentioned. Every Shakespeare play contains much that is too mature in idea for pupils of the eighth grade. Therefore, a limited number of good scenes in each play are available. The fairy and artisan scenes from *A Midsummer Night's Dream* make the best of dramatizations; but the love scenes between Hermia and Lysander, Helena and Demetrius are impossible to use. The study of but one scene from each of several plays means a superficial acquaintance with all of them. To choose only the wrestling scene from *As You Like It*, the court scene from *The Merchant of Venice*, the witches' scene from *Macbeth*, and the homecoming scene from *The Taming of the Shrew* would mean that the class would have time for only a slight acquaintance with the characters—not nearly enough time to characterize from the inside. When they dramatize several scenes from the same play they get to know the characters as real people, and as a result, their characterization shows far greater understanding.

On the whole, it would seem wiser to introduce a class to two contrasting plays, choosing the scenes which will give them the widest experience, rather than to limit them to one play or to introduce them to a large amount of new material which they will have time to use only superficially. Some scenes which have proved especially good material for either pantomime or dramatization are the following: from *The Taming of the Shrew*, the Katherine-Bianca scene, the arrival of Petruchio and Grumio at the gate of Baptista, the homecoming and the final scenes; from *A Midsummer Night's Dream*, all three of the artisan scenes and the fairy scenes; from *The Merchant of Venice*, the two casket scenes combined and the court scene; from *Macbeth*, the witches' scenes; from *Julius Cæsar*, the scene before the murder of Cæsar and the forum scene; from *The Comedy of Errors*, the succession of little scenes which center around the summoning of Antipholus to dinner; from *As You Like It*, the scene between Rosalind and Celia, the wrestling scene, the Audrey, William and Touchstone scene.

WHY DRAMATIZE?

The question may be asked, "Why dramatize Shakespeare stories rather than act the plays? Why not use the beautiful Shakespearean language, since it is so infinitely better than what the children can invent?"

The answer lies in the fact that with children the reading or memorizing of these same beautiful lines stands in the way of free, spontaneous dramatic expression. With books in hand the class becomes instantly a formal group, centered on the text rather than on the characterization. Free expression is impossible when pupils are struggling with lines which are as difficult as are Shakespeare's. Even when lines are not difficult, children are far less free and natural in reading than in original dialogue. Read the text to a class and it will quite naturally adopt much of the language and give the spirit of the rest; but do not allow children to read their lines from a book while they are on the stage if you wish to accomplish creative dramatic work. Everything depends upon the pupils feeling thoroughly at home with their material. They must know the characters personally, they must let them take possession of their bodies and speak with their voices. Now, if the language which these characters use is so different from their own that they feel ill at ease in using it, they will flounder helplessly. The difficulties are too many for successful achievement.

The flavor of the Shakespearean language, however, is quite easily attained. Words, phrases, sometimes whole sentences from the text appeal to the imagination of the pupils, and they adopt them for their own. As a result, they achieve not only a joyous and spirited playing of the scenes but a taste for the language which will help them in their later Shakespearean study.

THE BACKGROUND

Most eighth grade children have a certain amount of knowledge about the Elizabethan period, but even a good background needs much enriching before they are ready to launch into a dramatization of the Shakespeare stories. The project may start with a talk about the boy, Will Shakespeare; his life in the quaint old town of Stratford; his family, his school, his boyhood pranks. Stories of the year he went up to London, and held horses outside the theaters for lack of better employment, always interest the boys and girls, as well as accounts of the time when he became a great and influential figure in the theaters of London. In preparation for such a talk as this, the teacher will find *The Facts about Shakespeare*, by Neilson and Thorndyke, most useful.

Along with these stories about Shakespeare will naturally come a discussion of Elizabethan England. The great pride of country resulting from the defeat of the Armada, the explorations in the New World, and the widening commerce; the increased scientific knowledge, improvement of living conditions—all these things help to give the spirit of the times. Court life will be pictured, with its magnificent show, its colorful pageants and tournaments. The celebrations at Kenilworth Castle, with their masked revelers, bloody spectacles, coarse farces and feats of skill, will be mentioned. Accounts of the great interest in the theater will be given, with descriptions of the playhouses and the showing of pictures of playhouses and costumes.

Sometimes, however, the teacher touches but lightly on the life of the Elizabethan period, preferring rather to trace the history of the theaters in England, from the miracle and morality plays in the churches, through the performances in the inn yards by the strolling companies, down to the theater of Shakespeare's day. Whatever is said, the purpose will be to build a background which shall give the boys and girls the feeling of the times, so that they may be more intelligent and more eager in the study of the plays of Shakespeare.

THE DRAMATIZATION BEGINS

The class is now ready for the telling of the story of one of the plays. The teacher has chosen a play which she believes is suitable for this particular class. A group of keen, high-spirited boys in a class suggests, for instance, the desirability of using the artisan scenes from *A Midsummer Night's Dream*. Along with these, she might use for the girls the Oberon-Titania scenes, though, indeed, many girls delight in playing Nick Bottom, Snug, Flute, and the rest of the comic band. Other classes might have more aptitude for *The Taming of the Shrew, The Merchant of Venice,* or *As You Like It.*

The story may either be read or told to the class. A good telling is preferable to a reading, though there is no serious objection to the latter if well done. A discussion of this story follows. Is it a good story? What parts do you like best? Which characters interest you especially? Why? These questions and others will bring out the points of interest and often guide the teacher in choosing scenes to dramatize.

A scene having been chosen by the pupils with the guidance of the teacher, it is read to the class from the text of the play. The purpose of this reading is twofold: it helps the players to gain a more definite conception of the situation and characters, and it serves as a model for the dialogue. Far more vivid than the telling of the story is the reading of the dramatic version of the scene, particularly after the class is familiar with the whole story; and if the teacher clarifies difficult passages as she reads, the class will come to feel familiar enough with the language to use many of the expressions. From time to time, during the process of dramatization, the scene may profitably be read to them, so that they may come closer and closer to the Shakespearean language.

"Suppose," some one may ask, "the children memorize the lines of their own free will?" The answer is, let them if they wish to do so. But they seldom do. Playing different parts from week to week, not knowing what characters they will have the chance to play, few children make a conscious attempt to memorize lines. Dialogue will have a strong Shakespearean flavor, however, and many apt expressions will be taken over. "Are we all met?" asks Nick Bottom in the words of the play; and Peter Quince, beckoning in the others, answers, "Pat, pat; and here's a marvelous convenient place for our rehearsal." Petruchio, finding Shakespearean language far more picturesque than his own, will, if he has a spark of genius in acting, exclaim with gusto when Kate brings in the obstinate wives, "There's a wench!" The witches in *Macbeth* cannot be imagined without their "Double, double, toil and trouble!" This taking over of Shakespeare's language should be encouraged, commended, for in the measure in which the children make it their own, they come nearer to a future enjoyment of Shakespeare.

THE IMAGINARY SCENE

The class has heard the teacher read the scene and explain difficult words and expressions. Now they are to get really acquainted with the characters. They are to view them from all sides; imagine their appearance, their manner of speaking; note how much light is thrown on them by their conversation, and how much by the other people of the scene; consider what they think about, and why they act as they do.

Suppose the scene chosen is the first artisan scene from

A Midsummer Night's Dream. The pupils want to know Quince, Bottom, and the others as real people. They imagine how they look, how they are dressed, what their ages are, and what their trades. In order to get acquainted with them individually the class may develop an imaginary scene, introducing the characters one at a time, and leading up to the play itself. Such a scene is the one given in Chapter IV, which was developed by the pupils in one of the Shakespeare classes.

By working out such a scene as this the class has come to feel thoroughly at home with the people of the play. Having met them one at a time instead of all at once, the children have learned their individual characteristics so well that their work on the real scenes will be vastly superior to what it would have been without this preliminary study.

As this scene is developed for *A Midsummer Night's Dream,* so may "leading up" scenes be built for the other plays with as good effect. Small units, whether imaginary scenes or not, are well worth the time spent on them, for they prepare the children for really surprising achievement in any dramatization.

THE REAL SCENES

Now the class is ready for the actual scene from the Shakespeare story. They know the characters and their relation to one another. They have played several of the parts. They are thoroughly prepared for the real scenes, and eager to work them out.

As the text of the scene is read to them, they are planning the setting, visualizing the action of the characters, and storing in their memories the gist of the speeches. And when the setting is agreed upon and the teacher asks for volunteers, there are plenty of applicants for every part.

With greatest care she chooses her first cast, for these people will set a standard for the work which is to be done on the scene. Not all the best players in the class will be used; but the important parts will be cast with the people who have best interpreted the characters in the imaginary scene. The scene must go successfully if it is to hold class interest; and starting on a high plane, it will eventually reach a degree of excellence impossible without such a beginning.

The first playing may be done either with or without words. A scene involving much action is usually better done first in pantomime. One with little action should be dramatized at once. The reason is obvious. Excellent results are best obtained by thorough preparation; and the pantomime serves as a step toward the complete dramatization. On the other hand, a scene which depends mainly on speech (as the wager scene in the last act of *The Taming of the Shrew*) loses so much in pantomime that it is unsatisfying to the class if interpreted in this way.

From this point, the procedure is the same as in all other dramatizations, except that the scene which the class is dramatizing is occasionally re-read to them, together with other scenes which throw light on the characters involved.

Four weeks, with three periods a week, will be necessary for the background and imaginary scene, and two or three weeks apiece for the real scenes, according to their degree of difficulty. The first five minutes of each period should be given to voice and diction training, which should have been going on steadily throughout the preliminary courses. Frequent reviews of the scenes are well worth the time spent on them. The children never tire of repeating them, and their fertile imaginations continually devise enrichment of characters and action, so that by the time the scenes are presented for the school at the close of the semester, they have developed into remarkably interesting little plays, entertaining and really Shakespearean.

A SECOND SEMESTER OF SHAKESPEARE

No provision has been made in this program for a second semester of Shakespeare, yet such a course is heartily recommended. By introducing dramatics before the seventh grade, or by combining the elementary and folklore courses, a year could be devoted to this study. During the first semester, the class has been introduced to Shakespeare; has acquired some knowledge of the time in which he lived and wrote; has become acquainted with perhaps two of his plays; and has gained some experience in analyzing and interpreting characters far more complex than those in the ballads and folk tales.

With this background, a second semester's work is productive of results highly gratifying to both teacher and pupils. The class is ready to plunge into the study of a new play with no preliminaries. The pupils start out with zest and with confidence, and they accomplish really fine results. They have grown in analytical power, in ability to plan the scenes intelligently and play their parts freely and sincerely, and they are now ready to do superior work.

In this second semester, the class should use the text of the play to a greater extent than before. A small school edition of the plays to be studied, such as *The Tudor Shakespeare*, edited by Frederick Tupper, should be provided, with copies enough for the whole class. After the story of the play is told, the scene to be dramatized is read by the pupils from their seats, but after the discussion, those picked for the cast will play their parts on the stage without books. Why not allow them to read the lines on the stage? One experiment will be enough to prove how incredibly wooden they become. Shylock, Rosalind, Katherine, Peter Quince, Dromio, all lose their characters at the hands of pupils who are trying to do too many things at once, and any teacher who tries both methods will see the superiority of the informal method in an eighth grade study of Shakespeare. The value of the books is to bring the pupils nearer to the text of the play by familiarizing them with the Shakespearean language. The reading of the scenes will improve their diction, if the teacher develops their appreciation of well-spoken lines. There should be careful and detailed analysis of character and situation, discriminating criticism and more intelligent use of criticism, independence of interpretation, better vocabularies, more responsibility in teamwork, for the study should go deeper than in the first semester. But the class work should still be chiefly dramatization.

One of the scenes studied should be dramatized first, later memorized and given on the assembly program. The process will have some of the disadvantages encountered in rehearsing plays given for exhibition. That is, attention will be centered on the finished product instead of on the process. The preliminary dramatization, however, will do away with much of the unfortunate stiffness which usually results from rehearsing with books in hand; and the class will gain much benefit from the careful and repeated reading of the lines. Some of the rehearsing, after the cast is chosen, should be done outside of class, so that no period is monopolized by a few pupils.

The final program given by the advanced class in Shakespeare will prove the worth of a second semester of work with this material. The pupils' growth in ability to appreciate well-made plays, to understand and interpret character, and to speak the English language in a clean-cut and pleasing manner, will be a convincing argument for the inclusion of such a course in the school program.

CHAPTER VII

A DRAMATIC COURSE FOR THE NINTH GRADE

First Semester: One-Act Plays

THE ninth grade is the time to change from the informal building of plays from stories to the study of formal plays. The pupils have had at least two years' experience in dramatization, and they have now reached the age and the stage of development when they are ready to begin the formal study of drama.

This change does not mean that dramatic study is no longer to be creative; but it is to be creative in a different way. The pupils will not originate their scenes and dialogue, but they will work creatively in developing a play, from the study of theme, plot, and characters, to a finished production. They will analyze character and situation as they have done heretofore. They will plan the scenes; work out the action of the play; act the parts, using first original dialogue, then the words of the play; criticize, and work over the action again and again.

This class study will be entirely different from the ordinary rehearsing of a play for the public. It will be a much slower process, because it will be accomplished by the combined efforts of the class rather than by the teacher. It will require much more thinking on their part; and in the end it will be their production rather than hers. In that sense it will be as truly created by the class as were the story dramatizations. True, the pupils will use, finally, the speeches written by the author; but the experience they have gained in their original work will have formed in them the habit of thinking as they speak. Their imaginations will have plenty of exercise in the creation of character, and because of their own experience in originating dialogue, they are better prepared to appreciate lines which have literary worth. It is now possible, too, to carry over into speech more completely than ever before the voice and diction training which they have had for two years.

AIMS

The aims of this year's work will be to gain:

1. A knowledge of the structure of well-made plays.

2. An appreciation of the way characters are drawn in plays, and a deeper appreciation of people and their points of view.

3. Some skill in playing before an audience. The exhibitional aspect of the work is still secondary, but the pupils should now have the consciousness of getting over to an audience the ideas of their plays.

4. A definitely better use of voice and diction, with a growing appreciation of style in the dialogue of plays.

THE MATERIAL OF THE COURSE

The material chosen for this semester's study will be one-act plays of good quality. Compared to the Shakespeare course, the material will be very simple. But the type of study is to be entirely different. There was no

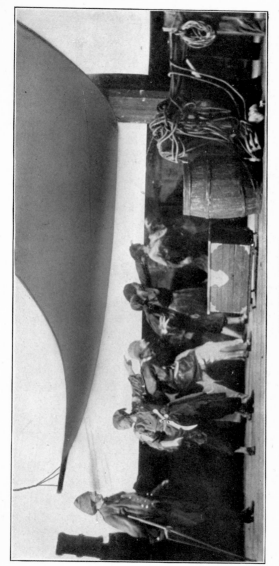

TREASURE ISLAND.

thought of a complete and thorough study of Shakespearean plays. A delightful introduction to Shakespeare, with intensive study of a few short scenes was as much as could be hoped for in such a course. But this semester's work is to be a study of two or three complete plays. The material, therefore, should be very simple, for it is the student's introduction to formal drama.

The choice of material for this course is not easy, for the plays must have high enough literary and dramatic merit to justify a careful study; and the theme and characters must be of the kind to interest the class deeply. If three plays are chosen, it will be well to pick three of decidedly different types; one, perhaps, with an excellent plot; another, with fine character study; and a third, with dialogue of exceptionally high quality. Whether two or three plays are used in a semester, one should be a comedy. In the list of plays which are worth the careful study of such a course as this are the following: *The Fifteenth Candle* and *Three Pills in a Bottle* by Rachel Lyman Field; *A Pot of Broth* by W. B. Yeats; *Spreading the News* by Lady Gregory; *The Birthday of the Infanta,* dramatized by Stuart Walker from the Oscar Wilde story; *The Golden Doom* by Dunsany; *What Men Live By,* adapted by Virginia Church from Tolstoy; and the first act of *The Romancers* by Rostand, and the Dutch scene from *My Lady's Dress* by Knoblock, both of which are virtually one-act plays.

THE DEVELOPMENT OF THE COURSE

By the time they have had two years of dramatics, pupils naturally expect certain things of the courses.

They expect to make their own plays from literature, to originate scenes, to use extempore dialogue. Now that the aims and type of material have changed, they need a new understanding of what dramatics is to mean.

Unless care is taken to insure a true understanding of the course at the start, the class will inevitably believe that the production of the plays—the exhibitional side—is the important thing to be accomplished. This, they are led to see, is still of secondary importance. The study of these plays is to be their own project, just as the panto-mimes and dramatizations were theirs; and if their work is of high quality, the best play will be produced. With some such brief preparation, the teacher is ready to present the first play to them. And as a rule, some introduction will be necessary in order that the mood may be right.

Suppose one of the plays chosen is that well-written little play by Rachel Lyman Field, *The Fifteenth Candle*. It is a particularly good play to use during this semester, for it is written around an idea which they can all understand and appreciate: child labor. It concerns a fourteen-year-old girl whose talent in art promises a real career for her if she can but finish her art course in a city high school. Her sister, who has had no chance in life herself, offers to make any sacrifice in order to keep Rosa in school, but the father, an ob-durate Italian cobbler, signs a contract which binds the child to make artificial flowers in a city factory. As the elder sister contemplates the fifteenth candle on Rosa's birthday cake, she says in pathetic resignation, "And one to grow on. I wonder what she will grow into—maybe—" It is a sad little play, probably more suited for the second study than the first; and the class should be prepared for it. But it is so sincere and so well written that it never fails to make a strong appeal to the pupils whose own age makes them feel a special sympathy for Rosa.

The introduction in this case has to do with the child-labor law. Illustrations of the way children are allowed to work in factories; specific instances of pale and stunted children making artificial flowers, picking out nut meats, carrying huge bundles of clothes from the basement sweatshops to the factories—such information, based on actual facts, will be of the best kind to invite the mood for the play.

To strengthen the impression, Mrs. Browning's *The Cry of the Children* may be read to the class, unless the teacher feels that it would be too depressing. Boys and girls from comfortably situated families, well fed and cared for, need to have their sympathies aroused for the less fortunate, however, and such an introduction will set them thinking, to the end that they will be keenly alive to the theme as worked out in the play.

THE STUDY OF THE PLAY

The play will then be read to the class in its entirety. The teacher's preparation has enabled her to read it effectively, and the imagination of the pupils will be stimulated in a far greater degree than if they had read it themselves. It may be objected that the teacher's interpretation will limit the imagination of the students in the same way that the illustrations of a story often limit the visual images. If the teacher were a poor reader, this would be true. Even the best reading will have a tendency to suggest a certain interpretation. But the object of the teacher's reading is to stimulate rather than limit the imagination of the pupils—to stimulate them so that they can go much further than would otherwise be possible. And she does not attempt impersonation; she merely suggests the characters. She opens the way for the understanding of the stubborn and ignorant Vedetti, who is a victim of conditions which ought to be changed; the patient and wistful Stella, who is the most finely drawn character in the play; Goldstein, the crude and common "boss"; the happy, confident little Rosa, all unconscious of having reached the parting of the ways; and Miss Roberts, the art teacher, who suspects the situation, and tries in vain to change it.

The reading over, the play is discussed. "Is it a good play? Why?" "Because it seems so real, so true," some one may answer. And then there will be numerous comments and questions. Is it convincing? Does the author make us see the evil of child labor? Does she do it in a natural way or does the play sound like a preachment? And the class is quick to respond that the play is altogether natural; that it is like a section taken from life.

"What do you think of Vedetti?" The pupils are unanimous in condemning him. "Do you think he realizes just what he is doing?" They are divided on this point. Some think his desire for money is so strong that he does not care if he ruins Rosa's life, so long as she can bring him her wages. Others believe that he is so ignorant that he cannot see ahead; else why should he not realize that if Rosa were allowed to go on with her schooling she would be capable of earning much more? They finally come to the conclusion that the kind of life he has led is largely to blame for his attitude. He probably knows nothing else but grinding poverty, and now that he has a chance for a little better living, he is determined to take it. But Stella's pleading—he must be very hard not to be moved by it! He *is* hard, and we dislike him intensely. But we cannot help thinking that he might have been different if his lot had not been such a hard one. The discussion is here likely to touch upon the immigrants, and the high hopes with which they come to this country, only to find, in many cases, a life as hard as the one they left.

Concerning the other characters in the play there will be more unanimity of opinion. But each one will be so carefully analyzed that the class will know them better by the end of the discussion than they know most of their classmates.

"How," the teacher may ask, "do you know the people in this play?"

"From what they say," will be the response.

"How else? Think of Rosa. Do you know her only from what she says?"

"No, from what is said about her by the other characters, too."

"How else?"

"From the description given by the author as to her looks; and from what she does."

"You see we have many ways of getting to know a character: the things he says, and sometimes fails to say; the manner in which he talks, using few words or many; the way in which the other characters react to him. If we watch all these things we get to understand our characters, and we can play the parts far better when we know them thoroughly."

After the discussion of the characters, points concerning which will come up again and again as the interpretation goes on, the copies of the play will be distributed, and the play read by the pupils. The setting will not be planned until the class has become more familiar with the play, in order that it may be designed so as to make the action smooth and effective.

THE READING BY THE CLASS

The reading of the play by the members of the class is not for the purpose of trying out for parts. It is a part of the study of the play, and at first there need be no effort to have the pupils read the characters for which they are best suited as to type. In fact, it is not even necessary that the girls read only the women's parts, nor the boys the men's parts. They read without action, trying to interpret the people of the play—trying to make them live. The reading will stop often for discussion of character. The teacher may suggest that they look for new light on the characters, and report as they see something which better explains any one of them. They will attempt to suggest the sound of the voices and the quality of diction used by the different characters. The dialect of Vedetti will offer some difficulties, but it is so well suggested by the spelling that it can easily be mastered. More difficult than dialect always is the understanding of foreign temperament. To city children, however, the Italian organ grinders, fruit dealers, and cobblers are so familiar that they have the opportunity of studying them at close range.

As the class reads, the teacher calls their attention to certain aspects of the play which, because the study is new to them, they would not notice for themselves. The beginning: how much would we as an audience get before anything is said? We see the poor room. We know it is a basement because of the window. We see Stella sitting there, sewing, and hear her singing, with a touch of foreign accent, the popular American song. And almost immediately we hear Vedetti call, "Stella! Stella! Stella! What for you maka so much noise?" We have thus gained at once a fairly good idea of what their life is like. Is it an interesting beginning? Do we want to know what is going to happen?

The high points of the play are noted as the reading goes on. Where do we first know what is to happen? What starts things moving? Where is the most suspense? What is it that we want to happen? Are there places where we think this may be possible? What is the climax, the turning point in the play? Is *The Fifteenth Candle* a good name for it? Why? Such questions will stimulate thought and discussion, to the end that the play will be clarified and made real and vital to the class.

After the study of one play, the class will begin to notice these points for themselves, but the first must be used somewhat in the nature of a model. The discussion should be left to the class in so far as possible, the teacher encouraging them to continue taking the responsibility to which they have become accustomed in their previous courses. If the creative spirit is to be retained, the teacher, while guiding them, will yet cause them to feel that it is their own project.

THE PLANNING OF THE SCENE

The play having been read and studied with care, the class begins to plan the setting. They are guided by the author's description, and in their first attempt will plan a setting which looks like such a room as that in which the Vedetti's might live, with a high window on the alley, a door into the shop and another into the bedroom. Some of the class will have a feeling for balance and proportion, which may lead them to plan a scene appearing in all ways satisfactory. But have they remembered the way in which the characters are to use the room? As Stella sits at the small table up by the window, will she be cut off from part of the audience by the table in the center? Is there sufficient space for effective entrance from the shop door, or is the table too near? Where is the stove to be?

The most difficult problem will be found to be the placing of the table which is somewhere near the center of the room. It must not hide Stella, nor must it be too near the door; and it must have some special relationship to the other parts of the setting, because there are scenes when one person sitting at the table will converse with another person sitting elsewhere in the room. In other words, the scene must be so planned that all the action will not center around the table. Much depends, in this little play, on the exact way in which the furniture is arranged. The simplicity of scene and action makes it seem an easy matter, but it is not so easy.

Much of the dramatic effect may be lost by careless planning; and it is an absorbing study in itself to work out a perfect arrangement.

THE ACTION OF THE PLAY

After a thorough study, a group from the class may volunteer to do the first scene with extempore dialogue— the play dividing into scenes, of course, only according to the French manner of beginning a new scene with the entrance of each additional character. The reason for starting with the pupil's own version of the dialogue is that it forces him to think, to know his character, to imagine how he feels and what he does. He works from the inside, and if his understanding is superficial, it is at once evident, and he is set to thinking more deeply. Pupils may remember some of the lines of the play, and they are free to use them if they choose. Characterization, however, is the significant thing to be achieved just now, and evidence of insight into character is to be commended above exact representation of the scene.

At the end of the playing there are many criticisms and suggestions, for every one has been keenly alive to what has been going on, and eager to sugggest improvements in characterization and action. "Vedetti would be bent from working year after year at mending shoes." "He would be older." "He would be a more obstinate sort of person in the way he talks and acts." "Stella would move about more, for she must lay her work aside, put on her hat and coat, look in the mirror, show her father the cake and the sweater which she has made for Rosa, plead with him"—these suggestions and more will be made, for the first playing, like the first playing of the previous dramatizations. will be more or less barren of action.

If the class objects radically to any of the action, the matter will be discussed, and either decided or experimented upon in another way. Then the scene will be played again, with a different cast. As many pupils as possible should be given a chance to work in each period, for a loss of interest is inevitable unless there is frequent change. When a scene is rather long, a break may be made in the middle, in order to give more pupils a chance to take part. In any case, the best results will come from working with small units of the material.

As the scenes are worked out, the class may find that it has made a bad mistake in the matter of setting. The teacher, perhaps, knew from the start that they were wrong, but she wished them to find it out for themselves. If the class is keen, they may discover it with no help from her. If, because of their inexperience, they do not recognize what the trouble is, such a question as, "Would a change in the position of the shop door help to make the action more effective?" is advisable to ask rather than to allow the class to flounder. An experiment will then show them that the action all the way through will be improved by the change. But it will also mean that the previous scenes will have to be gone over. Such changes, however, are likely to be discovered in one of the first scenes, so that the readjustment is easily accomplished.

CASTING THE PLAY

Every member of the class is thoroughly familiar with all of the characters before the casting is done. Each has had many chances to play the various parts, and the class has virtually learned the lines, so often has the play been reread. Some boy will be so far superior to the others in playing Vedetti that when the time comes for the class to decide on the cast—and the class can be depended upon to decide wisely—the decision is unanimous. The other characters are less definitely decided, as a rule. Goldstein is sometimes outstanding, but several girls could play Rosa and Miss Roberts. Stella is by far the most difficult character to cast. Occasionally, a girl may be found who is so sensitive and understanding that she strikes the right note at once. As a rule, though, a Stella must be searched for, and often developed from material that seems at first most unsatisfactory.

If the class is small, all of the members will be cast in one or another of the semester's plays. The danger in casting three plays is that all the most able members of the class will be chosen for the first play. To avoid this, the teacher may remind the class of the distribution of parts for three plays, and subtly guide the class by so commending the work of a less outstanding pupil who seems to fit a part that they will realize his worth. One of the plays should have a cast large enough to include those in the class who are not capable of carrying successfully any leading part.

REHEARSALS

The play may be developed only into a walking rehearsal, to be presented for another dramatic class. In this case, two outside rehearsals will be sufficient, since the play is already thoroughly familiar. If the cast prefer to memorize the lines completely they may do so, though it is not really necessary. Each of the three plays studied may be managed in this way, and then the best one chosen for a finished production.

Even the rehearsals are to be conducted in a manner different from regular play rehearsals, where the director is dictator of interpretation and business. The best student director is appointed, and he or she will have a considerable amount of authority. But the cast must do independent work on characterization if the ideal of the course is to be lived up to. The work will be less finished than if the teacher stepped in and directed, but it must ever be kept in mind that the exhibitional side of the work is to be secondary, the pupils' development being the chief consideration. The teacher will, of course, be present and make suggestions when there are difficulties, but her chief duty will be to stimulate thought and imagination.

The business has all been planned and learned before the cast was chosen, and the pupils know the characters thoroughly. The outside rehearsals are for the purpose of giving smoothness. The play should be gone through at least twice without a stop, in order that the players may have experience in sustaining the characterizations throughout the performance.

This performance will not be a finished one, but it should be sincere, intelligent and interesting. If this happens to be the play chosen for the final production, the lines will be memorized at once, and the teacher will rehearse it thoroughly, so that when it is produced it will be smoothly and beautifully done.

THE SECOND PLAY

Immediately following the casting of the first play, the second one is introduced into class, and the work proceeds as before except that each play brings a fresh discussion, with many new points to be considered. The class is initiated now, too, and they will approach this play with some knowledge of what to look for, some idea of what constitutes a good play. This second play should be a strong contrast to the first, not only in type but in setting and characters. There should be freshness in the way it is introduced, and variety in the manner of developing the characters, action, and dialogue.

As soon as the walking rehearsal of the last play is given, the class chooses the one it considers best for production. The pupils will base their choice on two things: the play itself and the acting. More than likely, their favorite play will not be the one best acted. In such a case, they should give the preference to the play which is better done.

Stage, property, and costume committees will be appointed for this production, and the duties of each clearly outlined by the teacher. Their work will, of course, need supervision, but they will be made responsible for as much as can be expected of inexperienced people. The play may be given for one of the assembly programs at the close of the semester, or it may even be given on a public program; and it should be of a high degree of excellence in every respect, not only for the sake of the school and teachers who will see it, but more especially for the pupils who are to see in final form the play which they have had a share in creating.

SECOND SEMESTER: THE STUDY OF A LONG PLAY

With the preparation of the first semester, one of the best possible projects for this last semester is the study and production of a full-length play. It is a logical and a fitting climax for the dramatic work of the junior high school. Nothing will awaken so much interest on the part of the class, and nothing, perhaps, will be so valuable to them.

As in the first course of this year, one of the chief aims of the work is to build a greater appreciation for good drama by cultivating a discriminating taste based on understanding of its principles. The freedom and poise gained from the acting are still important, though less to be stressed than the appreciation of the art of the drama.

MATERIAL

The choice of this play is of even greater importance than was the choice of the one-act plays, for on this one play is based the work of the whole semester. It must have unquestioned literary and dramatic merit; it must be within the power of the class to do well; and it must arouse their enthusiastic approval from the start.

A Shakespeare play is possible, but a public performance of Shakespeare would be better left to the senior high school. Many of the really good modern plays are too mature or too difficult. It is not easy to find a play which is neither too old nor too young in idea.

In a school which sponsors a children's theater, this ninth grade project might well find its climax in one of the regular productions for children. No better incentive could be found for enthusiastic and purposeful work than the prospect of giving an ambitious production in a well-established children's theater. The project would be within the sphere of interest of ninth graders, and worthy plays could be found for this purpose, with opportunity for careful study. Even if the school had no children's theater, this play could be produced for an audience of children.

To begin with, there is Molière's richly humorous comedy, *Le Bourgeois Gentilhomme*, which would be suitable to present either for children or adults. With some adaptation, it could be done amazingly well by ninth grade classes who had had two years of dramatic training. It is broad and farcical, with characters who could be thoroughly understood and beautifully acted by older children. The situations are such as appeal most gloriously to boys and girls of fourteen and fifteen. Consider the dancing, fencing, and spelling lessons; the scene where the maid laughs until she tumbles over on the floor at the ridiculous figure her master cuts in his absurd new suit; the clever scene in which Jourdain is duped by the swindler, Dorante; and best of all, the wildly fantastic and ludicrous Turkish initiation!

As presented in the Children's Theatre of Evanston, this play, adapted from the Curtis Hidden Page translation, and called *The Make-Believe Gentleman*, was one of the favorites of the season. Even the younger children appreciated the comedy of the lines and situations; they found the characters deliciously funny; and they readily understood the central idea of the play—the absurdity of trying to be something one is not.

If this were the play chosen for the semester's study, it should be adapted and mimeographed for the members of the class, for it is long and confusing to use as it is. The scenes concerning the intrigues with Madame Dorimene should be omitted, and several other scenes cut. It is probably wise to change the form from many scenes to three acts, to which it can easily be reduced. Let the class read the translation of the play in its original form for their preliminary study, but work it out in the simpler arrangement.

THE PROCESS OF STUDY

As a background for the study of this play, the class will need to know something about Molière and his plays, one or two of which might be read in class. They will be interested, too, to hear about the production of this play at the court of Louis XIV, where it was performed, in 1670, as an entertainment which united music, dancing, and comedy.

The play will, of course, be considered first as a whole, being read to the class by the teacher, and then discussed as to characters, situations, and dialogue. Though it is a farcical comedy, the characters are unusually well-drawn, and will repay careful study. The plot, though less important than the characters and the comic situations, is interesting to trace for the way it builds up to the climax.

As soon as the pupils have a good general knowledge of the play, intensive work begins on the individual scenes. For this purpose, the acts will again be broken into the short French scenes, that the study of them may be thorough and effective. Reading without action, followed by pantomimes of individual characters and short dramatizations, will precede formal rehearsal of the acts.

The great amount of action in this play suggests a most interesting experience in pantomime. Whole scenes may be worked out without words, the players concentrating on the broad comedy of character and situation, and finding out how much they can say by action alone. Gradually they may add words, again improvising at the start and eventually using the lines of the play.

No one scene will be finished for some time, as every character must be interpreted before casting can begin. Enough scenes, therefore, to introduce all the characters are considered during the first three or four weeks, and, gradually, the members of the class will fit themselves into the various parts. Fifteen characters besides the dancers were used in the Evanston production, and if a class were large enough, the play could have a double cast for the main characters, at least, as the play should by all means have more than one performance.

Now, after the cast is chosen—probably by the class guided by the teacher—and the scenes are in rehearsal, it will be almost impossible for every pupil to rehearse in each class period. The other activities connected with the production, therefore, should be started in time to keep the entire class busy. The costumes will require careful research work in the library, and several of the girls may be interested in designing them under the teacher's supervision. If the art teacher is interested in coöperating, some of the more artistic members of the class can, under her supervision, make most effective tapestries out of dyed Turkish toweling. Dancers are needed, and the gymnasium teacher can, if she will, be of wonderful help in working out the Turkish ceremony. If some of the boys are on the stage staff, they may be experimenting on the lighting for the play, while others are occupied in such positions as stage manager, prompter and property committee.

The entire action of the play requires but one setting, and this setting can, therefore, be done with unusual care. A study of pictures of Molière's day will be of help in planning it to suit the period, the imitation tapestries giving, perhaps, the best touch, and the Louis XIV furniture (adapted, perhaps from secondhand store wares, and gilded to suit Monsieur Jourdain's taste!) carrying out the seventeenth century ideas.

Some of the final rehearsals will need more time than a class period, and will, therefore, be held after school. In polishing the play for public presentation, the teacher will, no doubt, be forced to be a bit arbitrary at times in order to insure an effective performance. To the greatest extent possible, however, she should use the ideas of the pupils, for it is their play and should be the product of their own experience.

The presentation of the play for the eager audiences which always throng to a children's theater will be nothing less than a thrilling experience for the players, and the experience will be the more rich and satisfying if not one but several performances are given.

OTHER PLAYS

Unless the teacher knows her class well, it will be both wise and generous for her to give the pupils a choice in the matter of plays. Suppose she reads several to them, any one of which is possible for them to do. The discussion of merit which would follow such a reading could be highly profitable to the pupils if skillfully guided by the teacher into an actual criticism of drama.

Of the plays which might be included in such a list, the following are worthy of consideration:

Sherwood, by Alfred Noyes; *The Dragon,* by Lady Gregory; *Treasure Island,* by Jules Eckert Goodman; *Make-Believe,* by A. A. Milne; *The Little Princess,* by Frances Hodgson Burnett; *The Chinese Lantern,* by Laurence Housman; and *The Blue Bird,* by Maurice Maeterlinck.

CHAPTER VIII

DIRECTING A PLAY

A program is to be presented for the parent-teacher association by the music and dramatic departments of the junior high school. The occasion will be worthy of some note, for hundreds of guests will come, not only to be entertained, but also to judge the quality of the wares offered by these two departments. The orchestra will play, the combined glee clubs will sing, and, as a climax to the program, the dramatic department will present a short play.

The choice of this play will not be an easy one for the dramatic director. High literary and dramatic quality, a worthy idea, popular appeal—all these must characterize the play she chooses for this important occasion. The audience will be made up of all classes of society, and, with the exception of the few parents who will see their own children take part, the people will be interested in the excellence of the program rather than in the showing off of their children. Furthermore, the play chosen must be one which is possible for the pupils to act and stage with distinctive excellence. Such a play as Dunsany's *The Golden Doom* will be rejected because of its lack of popular appeal; Wilde's *The Dyspeptic Ogre,* because its farce does not fit this particular occasion; Meig's *Helga and the White Peacock,* because of its length; Oliphant Down's *The Maker of Dreams,* because it is too mature; and Minchin's *The Jester's Purse,* because, though attractive, its idea is of little consequence, and the number of its costumes and scenes is prohibitive.

On the other hand, the director may consider seriously such plays as Stuart Walker's dramatization of Oscar Wilde's story, *The Birthday of the Infanta,* because of its high literary and dramatic worth, its beauty and its appeal; his *Six Who Pass While the Lentils Boil,* which is unusual and attractive; Perry Corneau's *Robin Hood and the Widow's Three Sons,* with its ever popular hero and its lively action; Rachel Lyman Field's *The Fifteenth Candle,* which stimulates thought about a serious problem; her *Three Pills in a Bottle,* because of its quaint message; or Marguerite Merington's *The Testing of Sir Gawayne,* which is dramatic and colorful.

The method of producing this play will differ widely from that used in building the original plays of the classroom. There it is the process which is most significant; here it is the result. There the ideas used are those of the students. Here the teacher, instead merely of stimulating the pupils and coöperating with them, produces the play according to her own ideas. She must be the controlling influence if it is to be a really artistic achievement, for her pupils are too immature and too unskilled as yet to be capable of accomplishing artistic results themselves.

The value to be had from taking part in such a play is not inconsiderable. At best, it is less than the pupils derive from the creative work of the classroom; but a conscientious director will never make her players mere puppets, trained to do her bidding. She will require them to think, to imagine, to contribute as much as they are capable of contributing to the production. The greatest good, however, that they will gain from the play will be the experience of having a part in something which is extremely well done. To take part in any activity which accomplishes a highly finished result is to have a better model for future work. It is to do something which brings one a step higher in accomplishment, and often it means that a student will so improve the caliber of his work, so gain in skill and confidence, that always thereafter he will maintain a higher standard than he had reached before he went into the play. It is this aspect of the work which makes it worth while for the players. For the students who only see the play, it will be a standard and inspiration for future work in the classroom and the assembly, as are the plays they see from time to time at the Children's Theatre.

PREPARATION OF THE TEACHER

Having chosen a play which she considers both worthy and appealing, the teacher should make such a thorough study of it that she is perfectly familiar with the characters and dialogue; sees the stage exactly as it should be; understands all the light changes; and visualizes the working out of the entire action. She knows just what the qualities of each player should be, what difficulties will hinder the working out of the production, and how she will go about it to overcome them. She has studied the action of the play so carefully that she knows exactly what arrangement of doors, windows, and furniture will allow the most effective stage business. If it is a room in a house, she should know the general architecture of the house, what it looks like from the outside, where the street is, what rooms adjoin this one. Suppose the play chosen is *The Birthday of the Infanta*. The scene must show a striking contrast between the heavy formality of the palace and the brilliant beauty of the garden which is seen through the grim stone arch of the royal balcony. It must be so managed that it exemplifies the shut-in, smothered life of the Infanta, and suggests the free beautiful life which is forever out of her reach.

THE STUDY BY THE CLASS

Players from a dramatic class are to present this play; therefore, it will be started in the classroom, and all members of the class may try out for it. Two casts are to be chosen, and there will be several performances, so that both casts will have a chance to play if they are sufficently good. By choosing a double cast, the director will not only give opportunity to more players, but she will safeguard her production from the disaster which might come from sickness or from players who proved disappointing after the rehearsals were well under way. Furthermore, if a player knows that in order to hold his place in the first cast, he must live up to rehearsal requirements; if he knows that some one is waiting to step into his place if he fails, he can be held to his best efforts.

The teacher's introduction of the play to the class is most important. Momentary enthusiasm is easy to stir, but it is a different matter so to inspire a class that they will work like Trojans for weeks to make their play really superior. The director will speak first of the occasion—how important it is, how many people will be there, what a fine chance it is for the dramatic department. Then she will tell them about the play. Whatever, in her estimation, will make the strongest appeal to the group before her is what she will choose to say about it.

Suppose the play were Alice C. D. Riley's satirical comedy, *Ten Minutes by the Clock*. The fact that it is a satire will not interest them, and so she will barely mention that point. Nor will she talk about meaningless conventions, for the term suggests little to children of this age. It is the plot and the characters that will appeal to them, and so perhaps she says, "The play tells of a queen who was so fascinated by a gypsy's song that she ran away from the court and became a gypsy herself. But her life of ease had spoiled her for the hardships which she met, and she was glad to come back to the routine of the court. The play pokes fun at people who senselessly follow customs which have no reason for being. The fat king, the tall, lean cook, the pudgy councilor, and the two funny little servants, Dux and Dox, all believe that the only right way to cook an egg is to boil it exactly six minutes. Eggs always have been cooked that way, and therefore it must be the right way. By accident the king's egg boils ten minutes, and when I read the play, you will see what came of this unusual happening, and what it all had to do with the queen."

Now is the time to read the play to the class. The first reading should be by the teacher, for the class is sure to be far more enthusiastic about it if it is well read than if they stumbled through it themselves. Besides, they will be able to discuss it more intelligently if their attention during the reading has been undivided. The characters in this reading should be suggested rather than impersonated, but the rhythm and tempo should be perfect, the climax built high, and the central idea made very plain.

Next comes the class discussion and analysis. Suppose the play were *The Birthday of the Infanta*. Some questions such as the following would stimulate thought and start discussion: Do you see clearly every detail of the scene as it is described? Does it suggest what the Infanta's life is like? What do you think of her? What side of her character do we see first? Where do we get another side of her? How does the little Fantastic look as he comes in? In the dialogue between him and the Chamberlain, what do we find out about the character of each? What does the Fantastic think when the Infanta laughs at him? Why does she throw him a rose? What are the Fantastic's different moods as he stands before the mirror? How do you feel toward the Infanta at the end of the play?

Many of these questions will not need to be asked, for the discussion will lead from one point to the next. One class period will not afford enough time for a full discussion, and therefore the analysis will be continued at the following meeting. At this second session a mimeographed copy of the play should be given out to each pupil, and the parts read around the class. As the reading goes on, frequent stops should be made for discussion, and, by the time this period ends, the class should have a very clear idea of plot, character, dialogue, and setting.

At the third meeting the tryouts should begin. It is understood that the parts are to be given to the pupils who can play them best. Here, obviously, the method differs from that of the classroom, where the teacher is constantly assigning parts to the pupils who need them most. In a public performance the audience should be given the best which the school can offer, for even the most talented players are unskilled and amateurish. Besides, it is no more than fair that the brighter students, often the most neglected in the public schools, should be given an occasional opportunity to put their natural ability to its hardest use.

Interpretation should come first in casting a play, but size and type are important. If a child is cast for a part for which he is physically unfitted, he has much to overcome in order to create the right illusion. For this reason it is wise to try first the ones who are best suited in type. In *The Birthday of the Infanta*, for instance, a rather small girl with a certain dignity and poise should be considered first for the Infanta, while a thin little child (either a boy or girl, but preferably a boy) should play the Fantastic. If there happened to be in the class an imaginative boy who was not like other children in physique or in temperament, he, naturally, would be the one that the director would think of trying first. Taller children should be cast for the adult characters. It is difficult at best for children to play such parts, and size does help to create illusion.

Aside from type, the director should consider the voice
—whether it suits the character, and whether it will
carry well; the diction—whether it is sufficiently good
so that with minor corrections it can easily be understood; and bodily freedom—whether the player seems
likely to act the part as well as speak the lines.

Understanding of character is more important, however, than any of these things, and understanding depends upon observation and imagination. A child who
cannot imagine such a creature as the little Fantastic
cannot play the part even though he may look extraor-
dinarily like him. He may come to understand him
after the teacher and the class have discussed him, even
though he did not at first, and if he reads the lines
poorly, he may be questioned in order to find whether
or not his imagination can be stimulated. If he responds
satisfactorily, it would be wise to give him a thorough
trial to ascertain whether he is imaginative enough and
flexible enough to be a possible candidate for the part.

A method which has proved satisfactory in trying out
children for parts in a play is the following:

First, choose a short scene in which at least one of
the most difficult characters appears. In *The Birthday
of the Infanta* it might be the scene between the dwarf
and the Chamberlain. In *The Fifteenth Candle* it would
be the second scene between Stella and Vedetti. Assign
the characters to children who seem naturally most
fitted to play the parts. Have them stand and read,
characterizing as best they can. Suggest changes at
times to find out how flexible they are. "Make Vedetti
older." "Remember that Guinevere must have queenly
dignity." "Sir Kay should be more blunt and harsh."

When the director is satisfied that these children are either possible or entirely unsuitable for the parts (and she should be able to determine this in their reading of only a few speeches), she should ask another group to read on. Before repeating any of the children who have read, she should try all the possible pupils. She may jot down the names of those who read certain characters well, but as a rule, she will remember the ones to whom she wishes to come back. After she has tried all who seem possible for these particular characters, she may ask, "Does any one else wish to try this part?" She may find that she has overlooked some one who is good, and at all events, she will have satisfied the children.

After she has made the rounds once, she will go back to the pupils who are likeliest to suit, and starting with those who seem the most possible, she will try out this selected group. This time she will probably find one or two characters who are really satisfactory. There will be doubt as to others, and she will want to have them read some other scene and do a bit of the action. At once this will decide some of the doubtful cases. But unless she is extremely fortunate, there will be parts which no one seems to fill satisfactorily. She will listen critically to their voices and inflections, judge the amount of intelligence and imagination in their reading, and look over them searchingly, trying to see them costumed as their characters will be, moving about with the other characters in the setting she has planned. She will watch a group walk through bits of action, or she will have them put aside their manuscripts and try characteristic postures and walks. In such plays as *Six Who Pass*

While the Lentils Boil and *Three Pills in a Bottle* she will find this a very valuable method of tryout because of the great variety of character. Unless she is remarkably fortunate, however, she will not be able to decide on the entire cast at this first tryout. No characters should be announced until she can announce the entire cast, but, naturally, the class will guess her choice, for she will try all the uncertain ones in turn with those who are sure. And whether or not she is able to decide on the characters in the first scene read, she should, at this first tryout, have other scenes and characters read. This is not only more fair to the pupils who are waiting anxiously to read parts for which they are more suited, but it may clear up doubt about uncertain ones who can better prove their worth when they read another scene.

Before the next meeting of the class, the director will do well to find out from the school office the standing of the pupils who seem most likely to be chosen. Scholarship need be considered only to the extent of finding whether they can spare the time for an extra activity. Pupils who have never made themselves felt in any other field sometimes find in a play their big opportunity, and by distinguishing themselves there, gain the confidence which enables them to become leaders in other activities as well.

By the next meeting the choice will be so narrowed down that it will be possible by the end of the period to choose and announce the two casts. There will be heartaches, no doubt, but if the director has given them a fair tryout, the students will be satisfied that her judgment is good. Besides, there are offices for those who have come the nearest to making the casts. Two assistant directors, one for each cast, who will be prompters and general helpers to the director, a property committee, and a costume manager will be necessary, and, if these positions are made honors, the pupils will feel compensated to a large degree for not having made the cast.

Before the parts are actually assigned, however, the director should find out whether the players are able and willing to meet the rehearsal requirements. She should deliberately make these sound difficult. She should tell them first on what days and hours the rehearsals will be held, and she should make it clear that she does not expect any one to accept a part unless he can come to the rehearsals and be on time. If some of the children have music or dancing lessons after school, they are to tell her now when they must be absent from rehearsals, in order that she may determine whether or not she can arrange for those days rehearsals of scenes in which they have little or no part. A teacher who makes the players feel that rehearsals are so important that pleasures may have to be sacrificed for them will find that the children gain added respect for the play, and, upon going into it with their eyes open, they will expect to practice regularly and well.

REHEARSAL PLANS

The time of rehearsing, if there is no free period in school time, will probably be immediately after school. An hour four times a week for three weeks is sufficient to prepare a one-act play for public performance after it is cast. Extra time must, of course, be allowed for the two dress rehearsals, two hours for each being none too much.

A schedule of rehearsals should first be made. If the same director is to do all the rehearsing for the two casts, a double schedule will be necessary. If she is to have assistance in directing, rehearsals of both casts may often be placed at the same hour. When there is any choice as to days and hours, the cast should be consulted and an agreement made. Then the director, assistants, and casts should write down the full schedule, preferably on the back of their manuscripts. Students of junior high school age should never be asked to come to evening rehearsals. Afternoons and Saturdays should be the only times used, unless a morning period chances to be available. Minor characters should be present only at first rehearsals, and then not until the important parts are entirely worked up. If there are several long dialogues, certain rehearsals each week should be set aside for the characters who take part in them. No child should be required to waste time waiting while the director is concentrating on a long scene with two or three characters.

Time should be used carefully at these rehearsals. The director should start promptly, work steadily, and close promptly, leaving the cast each time with the feeling that they have accomplished something, and that there is much more interesting work to be done. She must always be one of them, spurring them on by her enthusiasm, setting the goal high, encouraging them to go further than they ever dreamed they had the power to go, and making them feel always the great joy of accomplishment.

EARLY REHEARSALS

At the first rehearsal of each cast, the entire play should be read without action. This is the time for special attention to the lines. Interpretation, voice, and diction should be carefully and minutely observed. The pronunciation of certain words will need to be corrected, careless enunciation criticized, voices made to respond to the requirements of the characters, and hazy points in the play cleared up. At best, the understanding of the characters by the players is somewhat superficial, and it is the teacher's business to see that this is deepened now. The players' reading will show her instantly wherein they fail to grasp their parts, and she should stop the reading again and again to help them to understand. For instance, in *The Birthday of the Infanta* she may find that the girl who is playing the Infanta is making her merely a spoiled, disagreeable child. By reminding her that the Infanta is heir to the throne of Spain, that she has been reared in an atmosphere of dignity and social grace, and that she must never be common, but must keep a certain fineness even in her petulance, the director should be able to change entirely the girl's conception of the part.

At this rehearsal, too, the players should be given an understanding of how to build to a climax. The director will have to work indirectly throughout the rehearsals for proper rhythm, for it is too subtle a thing for beginners to understand. But she can begin to make them realize how to make the big moments of the play really big, and she can illustrate the part that increasing tempo and volume have to do with climax. This is an extremely

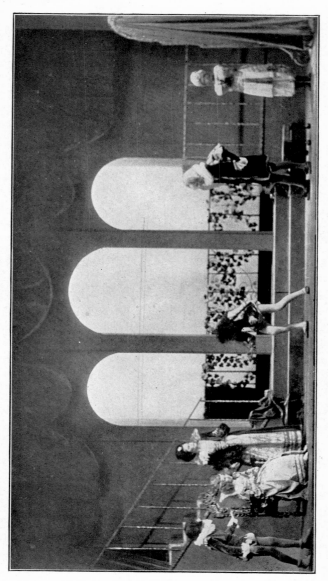

THE BIRTHDAY OF THE INFANTA.
Played by eighth-grade children.

valuable rehearsal, and it would be well, if the play were more than usually difficult, to devote two periods to it.

Next will come the first rehearsal with action. The director should show the players a well-made diagram of the stage as it is to be, with doors, windows, and furnishings exactly placed, and she should have the real stage set to correspond. If rehearsals cannot be held regularly on the stage where the play is to be produced, this rehearsal, at least, should be there, that the cast may gain a correct idea at the start. It is a decided advantage always to practice there, not only because of the stage, but also because the players will then adapt their voices and their whole interpretation to the large auditorium. If they are compelled to do all their rehearsing in a small room, they naturally fall into the habit of doing everything on a small scale. Skilled players can do this, and then suddenly enlarge their characterizations and their voices when moved to a large auditorium. Unskilled players, not being able to adapt themselves readily, have made many a director sick at heart when she heard how thin and small and amateurish her play sounded when she finally took it to the stage. A miniature painting may be a lovely thing, but hung on the walls of a great gallery, its loveliness is often lost. Just so, a play which is charming for an intimate performance may be ruined in a large theater. The larger an auditorium, the bigger must be the brush and the stronger the colors with which a characterization is painted. See to it, then, that as many rehearsals as possible be on the stage where the play is to be presented.

The rehearsal begins. The players, manuscripts in hand, are given their positions by the director, and they walk through the play, entering, crossing, sitting, and making their exits as the teacher directs. Only the big moves are made at this rehearsal. The aim is for the players to get a general idea of the action, associating it with the lines before they are fixed in mind. Little correction of interpretation should be made at this rehearsal. All attention should be given to the pattern which is planned for the production. Instead of working out any detail, the director emphasizes clean-cut, definite action in the main business of the play, insisting on exact moves rather than vague crossings in the general direction indicated.

From the first, she should use the stage terms, "up," "down," "right," and "left," in her directing. Coming from a dramatic class the pupils will have been taught that "down stage" means toward the audience and "up stage" away from it, and that "right" and "left" refer to the players' right and left.

If there is time to walk through the whole play twice, it is extremely desirable to do so. If not, only as much should be blocked out as can be done twice. A second time through always fixes in mind what is done the first time, whereas much of what the director says is forgotten if it is not clinched by repetition.

At the end of this rehearsal, the players should be asked to start memorizing their lines at once. Lines should never be memorized until they are associated with the action, and then no time should be wasted in becoming line perfect. None of the finer business can be done satisfactorily until the players are free from their manuscripts, and if they fail to learn their lines at once, a day should be set at which time no books will be allowed. And if the director makes such a requirement, let her by all means hold to it even if it means that one rehearsal is ruined by constant prompting or by her refusal to allow one or two players to practice. It will be found worth while to spoil one rehearsal if it proves to the cast that the director means what she says, and the future rehearsals will find the children enough better prepared to make up for the lost time.

At the next rehearsal no finer business will be used than before, but there will be greater care as to characterization. See to it that the players move and sit in character. Let the old man feel his age as he walks. Let him be less active, let him sit carefully, rise with difficulty. Let the duchess carry herself as becomes a duchess; let her move with dignity and deliberation. Let the girl who plays the washerwoman's soul be as dainty and light on her feet as the washerwoman herself is slow and plodding. Fix in mind during this rehearsal the broader aspects of both character and action. Commend the pupils who show that they have been studying their parts. Always encourage when possible, and always stimulate them to do more.

At the following rehearsal, which is, say, two days after the preceding one, the players should be free from their manuscripts. There will be much prompting the first time through—and this is done always by the director's assistant, that the director may be free to watch the players. Do not be exacting this time about either interpretation or business. Let them center attention on their lines. They will do better the second time, for they will have gained confidence. Now they may begin finer business. Instead of Stella's merely sitting at the table at the opening of *The Fifteenth Candle,* she should really be sewing. Instead of only walking over to the place where her wraps will be, she should really put them on. From now on the business should be worked out with properties—not the ones, probably, which are to be used in the performances, but with satisfactory substitutes.

LATER REHEARSALS

Each rehearsal henceforth should be marked by a finer degree of finish. Not only should there be great growth in character portrayal and ensemble work, but there should be more and more smoothness and polish. Every rough place should be gone over and over until it is smooth, and the rehearsal should then start several speeches back in order to connect it with what has gone before. This bridging process is highly important and should never be neglected.

During the early rehearsals the director has stopped the play often to give directions and criticisms. As time goes on, the interruptions should be less frequent, until, toward the last, the play should often be allowed to go through without a stop. Only in this way can smoothness be accomplished.

Tempo should be given much attention during the later rehearsals. The tendency with children is to take up their cues too slowly and then talk too fast. This makes a jerky, sometimes unintelligible performance which must be corrected. Every time a child is slow in taking a cue, the director should stop the play and ask for the preceding speech to be repeated. After this has been done a few times, the players who are slow begin to remember. Too rapid talking is much more difficult to correct. Work should start at the first rehearsal to overcome this fault, and never stop until the players speak at the rate their parts call for.

From the beginning, too, the director should be working to build to the high places in the play—the important entrances, the minor and major climaxes, as the entrance of La Belle Pilgrim in *The Testing of Sir Gawayne,* built to by the knocking and the discussion as to whether the door shall be opened; the minor climaxes in *Six Who Pass,* when the boy thinks the headsman is coming; the fine major climax in *The Birthday of the Infanta,* when the Fantastic sees his misshapen little body in the mirror, begins to suspect that it is himself, refuses to believe, is convinced when he sees the reflection of the rose which the Infanta gave him—"the only one in the world" —and finally dies of a broken heart.

TECHNIQUE

From first to last, the players should be led to think of the play itself; its plot, its meaning, its characters. The word "technique" should never once be used. But the director should not forget that it is a very important word for her, and that without a knowledge of its principles her play would be a failure. Indirectly she uses technique constantly, and the children learn much about it in the course of the rehearsals. Like the pattern of a dress, technique may be altered to suit the occasion, but both pattern and technique are everlastingly necessary to give style and fitness and effectiveness. Always, however, while using her best technique, she should so motivate the action of the play that there is a logical reason for everything that the players do. If she wishes to get a person from one side of the stage to the other in order to gain variety or balance, she should be able to give the player a reason for his move.

The children in Constance Mackay's *The Christmas Guest* draw apart from the tattered stranger because they are a little afraid, and the balance of the stage becomes perfect. In Graham Robertson's clever little play, *The Slippers of Cinderella,* it is necessary that Belinda get up stage before she gives the children an explanation of the fairy godmother's surprising gifts. While Myra, her older sister, is reprimanding her for having brought about all the embarrassing happenings, Belinda goes up to her, vainly trying to get in a word of explanation. By the time Myra allows her to speak, she is in the desired position up stage, and she has appeared to get there for a perfectly natural reason.

Certain simple rules of technique which the director will use continually are included in the following list:

A. *Entrances*

1. The doors should be in such a position that entrances can be made to the best advantage. Neither furniture nor players should be so near as to interfere with effective entrances.

2. Build to the entrances of important characters by the position and attitude of the people on the stage. The play itself usually helps by previous conversation about the character, by the sound of his voice outside, by a knock, or by some other device.

3. Preparation off stage. Every player should be taught to assume his character off stage, so that instead

of entering and *then* taking on his character, he may already have thought himself into his part, felt the consciousness of where he was coming from, taken on the mood, and assumed the attitude of his character.

4. Enter on time. Amateurs need much training before they will enter exactly on cue.

5. On entering, the players should be stimulated to imagine what their character would naturally do first. If one is entering a strange room, he will be likely to take in the whole room at his first glance. If it is a familiar room, he will not notice the place, but will go straight to the chair, perhaps, where he wishes to sit. His mood, his purpose or lack of it, his familiarity or strangeness, will instantly be comprehended by the audience if his entrance is right.

6. Two people entering together, talking, should be heard off stage, before they enter. The speaker may be either first or last, but children find it easier to be natural when the speaker comes first. If the guest is speaking, and the host must lead the way in, the child who plays the host must be made to feel that he is ushering in the guest, and he must have something very definite to do, such as placing a chair for his guest, as soon as he enters, else he will feel exceedingly awkward.

7. When there is a choice of several kinds of entrances, the director should study the situation to determine which is the most effective. A character may come in and announce his news at once, or he may enter, close the door softly behind him, and then turn around and begin to speak. In *Beauty and the Beast*, a player on the stage announces that she sees Beauty coming down the road with her arms full of flowers, then Beauty calls

from a distance to the girl who is watching, the other players run up to the gate and throw it open, and Beauty runs gayly in amid their exclamations of delight at her beautiful flowers. In *The Bubble Peddler,* a delightful little sequel to *Red Riding Hood,* by Alice C. D. Riley, the Peddler's entrance is unusually effective. While Granny, in bed, is directing Red Riding Hood, whom she thinks is entering, to come in and close the door, the Peddler steals in with a great bunch of gay balloons, doubles up with silent laughter to think how he is fooling her, and finally startles her by speaking.

8. Make an entrance *felt.* Even a servant or a minor character should have a personality, and each character is supposed to be felt in one way or another. In order to make a good entrance, a player needs first to assume his character off stage, and, second, to use the devices which will make him felt. This is easy enough in such plays as *The Stolen Prince* by Dan Totheroh, and *The Dyspeptic Ogre,* where the important characters enter and bow. In most plays entrances are far more difficult. In Stuart Walker's *Nevertheless,* the Boy enters, slams down a book, goes to the table, and as he takes up a bank, looks back to see that he is not observed, and then gives it an impatient shake. He must have assumed the mood off stage if his entrance is to be effective. In *Snow White and the Seven Dwarfs,* Snow White is brought in from the kitchen by a group of maids of honor, and stands in their midst, distinctive because of her rags.

B. *Exits.*

1. A player should hold his character until he is entirely out of sight of the audience. Almost invariably,

without correct training, an amateur drops his character an instant too soon. To avoid this, a player should be taught to hold it well beyond the door at which he exits.

2. Make exits definite. Unless characters are supposed to wander off while the attention of the audience is elsewhere, they should make their exits count for something. When Cassim leaves his home to find the cave of the thieves, in Louise Armstrong's pantomime of *Ali Baba and the Forty Thieves,* he throws his mantle about him with a magnificent gesture, hiding the sack he is carrying, and with a contemptuous smile in the direction of his poor brother's house, strides off to seek the gold. Most exits have no such exaggerated style as this, but they should always be clean cut.

3. As a rule, a long cross just before an exit should be broken up. Some motive can bring the character to a table, perhaps, which is not far from the door, and when it is time for his exit, he will have only a short distance to go. Often his last speech, or a part of it, is said at the door just before he leaves. This is an old and familiar device, but a very useful one with amateurs, who feel as conscious, during a cross and exit, as if the eyes of the world were upon them. Several of the characters in Tolstoi's *What Men Live By* make very effective exits by giving the last part of their speeches just before they open the door at the top of the steps leading out of the basement room.

C. *Crosses*

1. Make them definite. Go somewhere. Do not move aimlessly. Every cross should be motivated. Olaf, in the climax of *The White Peacock,* rends the web at the

window of the Troll's cottage, leaps in, crosses quickly to the Spider-Woman, breaks her distaff, and rescues his sister. Such crosses as these are strong and full of meaning.

2. Avoid crossing on a line. The effectiveness of the speech is killed if the speaker is moving. Exception should be made for a line which indicates a move, as, "Wait! I'm coming," or a line which has very little importance. A comedy line is ruined if a move is made on it, for moving always divides the attention of the audience. It is well to remember, however, that a cross made between parts of a speech often emphasizes what is said after the cross. After Stella, in *The Fifteenth Candle,* has heard the crushing news that her father has signed the contract for her sister to go to work in a factory, she says quickly, "They're coming—don't you say nothin' to her—not on her birthday." Then going close to her father, she looks so intensely at him that he shifts uneasily, and after a moment she says, "You hear me, Poppa; don't you say a word to her about this!" The very fact that she pauses in her speech and crosses closer to him makes the last sentence doubly intense.

Be very sure, however, that the speaker comes to a full stop before he goes on talking. Every amateur player will ruin the effect of his last line when directed so to break up his speech by saying it just before he stops. Much patience is required to train him to do it correctly, but after several repetitions, he will get the idea, and a very effective bit of technique will have been crystallized.

3. When A crosses to speak to B, he should swing slightly farther up stage than B before he stops if he

needs to have the advantageous position in the ensuing dialogue. In so doing, he can talk slightly down stage to B, and the audience will get his voice and the expression of his face far better than if his profile were toward them. This rule needs constant attention from the director, for, properly observed, it will help the play greatly in getting over to the audience.

A person crossing past a character who is standing ordinarily passes him on the down-stage side unless the one crossing is a servant or very minor character. This rule is often broken, but is followed in the majority of cases.

4. After a cross, a player turns toward the audience unless there is a special reason for his turning up stage.

5. In crossing to sit, the player usually turns toward the audience as he seats himself. If there is any reason, however, why he would naturally turn the other way, he may do so. For instance, if he passes on the down-stage side of a table and sits on the other side of it, he is very likely to be interested in something on the table, as a book, paper, or food, and if he has any business connected with the table, he will, by all means, turn his back to the audience as he sits.

D. *Grouping*

1. The stage pictures made by the continual grouping of the characters are of very great importance, because the visual appeal of a play is so big a part of it. If grouping is managed skillfully, it is always pleasing. Even the ugliest play may have beauty of grouping. Balance, proportion, inner meaning—everything which

makes a painted picture beautiful makes for beauty in stage picture.

2. Avoid too great regularity in grouping: even distances between people, straight lines, semicircles. For instance, the attractiveness of a picture is made greater if one of a group of three is slightly separated from the other two; if two of a group of five are a trifle apart; if several in a group are standing on different levels; if some of those in a group are standing and others sitting. In a group around the fireplace in Constance Mackay's *The Christmas Guest*, the picture is very attractive when Dame Margaret sits in the armchair, with one little girl on the arm of her chair, the oldest on a stool, facing up stage toward Dame Margaret, the smallest sitting on the floor between the chair and stool, also facing up stage; one of the boys lying flat on the floor, chin in hands, and the other standing close by her side, all listening to the story of the little old lady in the firelight.

3. Let the physical position of the group suggest the psychological. A conflict is, of course, the easiest idea to picture. A person standing alone on one side of the stage can balance perfectly a dozen or more on the other side, when a conflict of one against many is indicated. Miss Minchin, in Frances Hodgson Burnett's *The Little Princess*, balances the whole group of neighbors sheltering Sara Crewe. The scene speaks more vividly than words of the opposition between kindness and cruelty.

4. Ways of focusing attention in grouping:

(*a*) Place the person who is to be the center of attention up stage, and have the other characters turn partially up stage, facing him. By turning away from the audience, they make themselves unimportant. In

The Slippers of Cinderella, the entrance of Myra in her absurd white satin costume is twice as effective if the door is up stage, the other five children staring up at her, petrified with astonishment.

(*b*) Place the important person on a higher level. A high position always gives superiority, and this fact should be made use of to a greater extent in plays than it has been in the past. Standing on steps, platforms, hills; sitting on a table or higher chair; sitting in a chair while the others sit on the floor, centers attention on the person so elevated, and makes whatever he says seem more important. The statue of the Egyptian princess, standing center stage on a platform, in Rachel Field's *Theories and Thumbs,* makes her completely dominate the play.

(*c*) Place the character in a position radically different from all the others; as, sitting when all others are standing, or crouching with fear as Tom Canty is doing, in *The Prince and the Pauper,* when all the courtiers are erect and shouting, "Long live the King!"

(*d*) Let a person speak from the lightest spot in the room. Instead of spotting him with light, let him come naturally into the light. A character standing in front of a window through which moonlight is streaming, speaking to some one in the darkness, will take on extraordinary importance.

(*e*) Use color to center attention on a character. A person wearing silvery white, scarlet, black velvet, in the midst of neutral tones, is strikingly picked out from a crowd. And, to a lesser degree, a character in a neutral tone stands out in a crowd decked in gay colors.

(*f*) Avoid using any device which has the effect of being unnatural or artificial. Startling effects should be used only for startling plays. Keep to natural effects for realistic plays.

E. *Dialogue*

1. The first speech is very important. Be sure that it is done particularly well, for it instantly gives the audience an impression of what the quality of the acting is to be. If the speech is given in a weak or colorless manner, the audience expects the play to be amateurish, and the cast cannot easily change the impression. Because the audience is not entirely settled when the curtains open, this first speech needs to be projected exceptionally well. The director should take especial care in rehearsing several of the opening speeches. She should sit in the back of the room after two or three rehearsals to be sure that the players are projecting their voices sufficiently. If the first speeches, or any others, for that matter, are weak, she should tell the players to aim them at her, and to speak very distinctly. If this direction is not enough for some of the characters, she will need to do some private work with them, requiring them to separate their words with exaggerated slowness until they can easily be understood in the auditorium.

2. The characters should talk to one another as people would do in ordinary conversation. They should look at the person to whom they are speaking, not half at the audience, as players were trained to do twenty-five years ago. They should listen for the response to their speech rather than feel, as many children do, that their responsibility is ended when they have said their lines.

3. The characters should be trained to react not only to what is said to them, but to what is said to others.

When in *The Fifteenth Candle* the teacher talks to Vedetti about the need for Rosa to stay in school, each member of the family reacts in a different way. Vedetti's dogged expression says plainly enough that he has other plans for Rosa; Stella's anxious despairing look, from Miss Mitchell to her father and back again, shows that she clings to a forlorn hope that something may yet be done; while Rosa, ignorant that her father has arranged for her to work in the factory, glows with pride and eagerness at the thought of her future. Many of such reactions will come naturally to players who have a strong dramatic sense, but the imagination of the average child must be stimulated before he really reacts as his character would do.

4. Players should not, by unnecessary action, attract the attention of the audience from those who are speaking. Movement catches the eye and divides attention, and, therefore, should be kept to the minimum when attention is desired elsewhere.

5. Speeches should be properly pointed. Few amateurs point them sufficiently. Inflection and emphasis may be correct without being strong enough to be effective. This is especially noticeable in comedy lines. Professionals must not miss a single chance to get their comedy, but amateurs fail again and again, either because they do not appreciate the value of the expression, or because they lack a sense of humor. The dyspeptic ogre in the Percival Wilde play, in complaining because the little girls he ate always disagreed with him, works up to a climax of self-pity in a paragraph ending, "I fed them on the fat of the land; I thought nothing was too good for them! And how did they repay me? They

kept me awake nights!" Few children will point the last sentence sufficiently without help. The paragraph must build up and up, increasing in speed and volume, until, just before the final sentence, there is a pause which will help to make it emphatic. Then, fairly exploding with anger and disgust, the ogre utters his charge against little girls. Mechanically, the pointing consists in saying it much more slowly than the preceding sentences, and strongly emphasizing the two final words. But true pointing depends upon appreciation of the humor, and this the director should constantly endeavor to build. Sometimes a question will cause a player to see how to point his sentence; sometimes a paraphrase is better. When everything else fails, the director should *show* him. Often by doing this, she will illuminate in a flash what she means, and he will understand better how to give proper value to other speeches.

6. The tempo of speeches has been dealt with earlier in the chapter. The rate of speaking must always be determined by the type of character. Cues must be taken up promptly. The tempo of some scenes should be slow, others fast, according to the mood. Comedy should be played faster than serious drama, a play of adventure, faster than a poetic play. The tempo of a play is usually accelerated toward the climax.

7. Pauses are dangerous in an amateur play. A director may train her young players to make a highly dramatic pause, only to find that the audience thinks that some one has forgotten a cue. Amateur players, no matter how good, are seldom able to manage successfully more than very slight and very obvious pauses.

8. Dialogue should never be blurred. Especially in

comedy, children are likely to blur their lines by continuing while the audience is laughing. They should not only be warned, but they should also be rehearsed with laughs. Some outsiders may be invited in and told quietly by the director that they are expected to laugh at the right times! Or the director may give the players a little drill in holding their scene by gathering about her the players and staff who are not on the stage, all of whom laugh vociferously at the humorous lines. Not only does this relax the players and give them practice, but it livens a rehearsal at a time when the comedy is beginning to seem stale.

9. Dialect. Be consistent in its use. Most dialect is done carelessly by amateurs, and dialect poorly done always hurts the general effect of the play. To underdo it is far better than to overdo it. Most amateurs overdo. In *The Fifteenth Candle*, Vedetti's dialect is much easier to master than is the Italian temperament of the man. Do not let the boy who plays the part be extreme in his pronunciation, and be sure that he does not make it sound like Irish or German or Swedish!

DRESS REHEARSALS

No fewer than two dress rehearsals should be held for a public performance. In the first place, the children must get used to wearing their costumes if they are to be expected to act natural in them. In the second place, since the costumes may need to be altered, and since some may be found entirely unsuitable in style or color, there should be time to make right the things which are wrong. Two dress rehearsals insure a smoother first performance, especially when the second rehearsal is given for the school. At the first one, the usual things will be wrong. Richard will wear tan sport shoes with his king's costume because the proper footwear was not provided, and Nancy will forget to bring the rose veil which she thinks will be just the thing to go with her medieval headdress if only it doesn't clash with her gown. If there is another dress rehearsal to come, the director's peace of mind will not be disturbed by the omission of some of the details, and she can give her players the encouragement which is so real a factor in their success.

The last dress rehearsal should by all means be given before the school. Properties, parts of costumes, off-stage effects which would never have materialized at an ordinary dress rehearsal will appear for what seems a real performance. There will be infinitely more spirit in the playing of the cast, if an audience is present. Things will go wrong, but there is time to right them before the big performance, and so nobody worries. The plaudits of their schoolmates will encourage the players, too, and they will approach the important performance with a confidence which will carry them far beyond what they might otherwise have been able to do.

The production end of the play should all have been planned and made ready so that the setting, lighting, and properties may be used at both dress rehearsals. This means that the director has attended to the staging as soon as she started rehearsing the play. If she has no other member of the faculty to help her with this, she should have a student staff which she has begun training at the beginning of the year. There are always some boys in school who are both eager and capable in stage work, and they will make the best permanent stage staff.

To the stage manager the director will have given a diagram of the stage as she wishes it to be, explaining to him what is necessary in the way of setting, lighting, and properties. She should explain in detail the light changes to the electrician, giving him a list of the light cues, and she should give a list of the properties to the property chairman. All of their work should be supervised, for junior high school students are too young to be entirely responsible in such an undertaking.

The director's stage setting has doubtless been planned to utilize the actual permanent stage equipment of the school. In this case, the staging will not be difficult, and all efforts can be centered on procuring satisfactory properties and lighting effects. If setting and lighting are inadequate, as in only too many schools, she will have to use her ingenuity in manufacturing substitutes. Most stages have either hangings or flats of some sort. If there are hangings, and doors and windows are needed, the manual training department, if consulted in time, may be able to help out by constructing some frames. These the director and her assistants may have to cover with unbleached muslin, and size and paint. If a set of flats is available, but painted so as to make it utterly unsuitable, she may have to summon her crew and paint it. The director of the manual training department, however, will in most cases be able and willing to supervise this work for her. Lighting, too, may have to be devised, and the suggestions given in the chapter on stage equipment may be found helpful.

If additional lights are needed, or if the location must be changed, the work on them should be done before the first dress rehearsal. If only the regular equipment is needed, the cues are worked through at the first dress rehearsal. If the stage is ready on time, as it should be, the play can be gone through twice. No stop should be made either for the players or the staging, but the director should jot down all suggestions and corrections. After the first time through, she should give the players and stage crew her criticisms and suggestions, and then have the play rehearsed a second time. After this, she should be able to expect perfect smoothness at the final dress rehearsal.

THE PERFORMANCE

Several performances of the play are to be given, but the first will be the most important one. On the night of this performance, the players should come an hour before they are to appear in order that they may be dressed, made up, and inspected leisurely. The director should have one or two other mature people to help her, as well as the students on the stage crew and costume committee. If possible, some one besides the director should make up the players so that she may be free to give the many final directions. Since she is usually the only one who is able to make them up, however, and since the cast of a one-act play is not ordinarily large, she can manage if some one else is available to help with the costumes. The stage should have been set completely unless it must be used for the rest of the program, in which case everything should be in the wings ready for a quick change.

The director's attitude is a big factor on this last night. If she is plainly worried and excited, her cast will be worried and excited also. If she is calm, they will go into the play feeling that all is right. A director who is wise, therefore, will conceal her qualms, and encourage her players with lively and cheery words.

At both dress rehearsals, the director should, by all means, sit in the audience. In no other way can she know well enough how the play is going to criticize it properly. Seen from the audience, a performance is quite different from what it is when viewed from the wings. And if her pupil assistant has been well trained, she is perfectly capable of prompting satisfactorily. For the final performance the director will feel safer to remain in the wings in case an emergency should occur. With a more mature staff and players, she should be in the audience always, but junior high school students are young to take the entire responsibility of even a short public play, and they will feel steadied by knowing she is there.

Finally the play is over! The audience has applauded cordially, the orchestra has played the final number, and every one has gone home. The director, with one more look to see that the last costume has been taken back to the wardrobe, that the last bit of make-up has been cleared away, wonders, as directors do, whether it was all worth while. She has given many precious hours to this short production. She has put into it her imagination, her enthusiasm, her very self. No one quite understands just how much she has given to it. But she herself knows, even without all the commendations she has received, that her work has been good. She knows that her children have gained from this experience something they can never lose. And she knows that it has been worth to her all the time and thought and work she has put into it. For she has had the joy of creating something.

What has been said about the directing of a short play applies equally as well to the procedure when a long play is to be used. In addition, the following points must be taken into consideration:

1. *Choice.* This is discussed in the chapter on children's theaters. Long plays should be cut to one or one and a half hours if children are to act them.

2. *Length of time for rehearsals.* The casting of a long play should begin five or six weeks before the date of the first performance. Rehearsals should be from an hour to two hours in length. Twenty-five to thirty rehearsals are necessary for a difficult long play.

3. *Procedure in a three-act play.* The reading rehearsal should cover the entire play. The first act should then be blocked out and gotten well under way, though not perfected, before the second is begun. That is to say, the action of Act II should be started about the fourth rehearsal after that in Act I was blocked out, and the action of Act III the same length of time after Act II. As soon as possible, two acts should be taken in one rehearsal, in order to keep each one fresh in mind and the relation clear.

The tendency of amateurs is to spend too much time on the first act and to neglect the last. In order that the play may be a unified whole, of true proportion and uniform excellence, the time should be divided to give each act its share of attention. In the last week, at least, the cast should go through the entire play at each rehearsal, in order to insure smoothness and unity of effect.

4. *Dress rehearsals*. Much more time must be allowed for these than for the dress rehearsals of a short play, not only because of the acting time, but because of complications in setting and lighting, which are usually more elaborate in a long play than in a short one.

ADVANTAGES OF THE ONE-ACT PLAY

The short play has every advantage over the long one when children are to play the parts. Long plays are usually one-actor plays, giving one or two children parts which are difficult to sustain, and the others very small parts. Short plays divide the honors and the responsibilities. Instead of long, taxing rehearsals which are wearing both on players and director, the short plays, requiring less from each group of players, can be done in short, lively practices which move with spirit and dispatch. Fewer weeks of preparation are necessary because two can be rehearsed in one afternoon; and if the director has an assistant who is at all capable, two can rehearse simultaneously. The resulting performances are usually more satisfactory than are the performances of a long play done by children, because the interest of an audience at a children's play is likely to be in the players rather than in the play. Therefore, a director, if she is wise, will choose for her players, not necessarily a one-act play, but certainly a play short enough for the children to sustain to the very end.

CHAPTER IX

ASSEMBLY PROGRAMS

THE custom of holding regular assemblies in junior high schools is well-nigh universal. Schools differ as to the frequency of these meetings, and they differ as to the size. In many smaller schools, the seventh, eighth, and ninth grades meet together in one assembly. In larger schools, each grade, as a rule, holds a separate assembly. But most school principals realize the great unifying and socializing influence of these meetings, and make it possible for every student to be in assembly at least once a week.

The educational possibilities of an assembly are unlimited. Information given by experts on a wide range of interesting subjects; inspirational talks by people who have done important things in the community; the building of appreciation for the arts by the presentation of fine music, illustrated lectures on art, and good plays— these, and many other types of programs may make an invaluable contribution to the life of the school.

TRAINING AUDIENCES

Not the least of the opportunities of the assembly is the training of audiences. To educate an audience to be discriminating by presenting superior programs week after week is a worthy object for any school. It is a slow and more or less intangible process, but it will inevitably result in an improved taste in the community.

The training of audience courtesy is a far more simple achievement. Respect for the place and the occasion is the first requirement, and if this is inspired by the little ceremony of entering and opening the exercises, as well as by the program itself, the first step in the training will be successful.

In schools where the assemblies are conducted entirely by the students, a sense of responsibility is developed both in those who conduct the meetings and those who compose the audiences. A dignity having been given them, they rise to be worthy of it. The presence of the teachers gives importance and formality to their meetings, with the result that the best possible attitude is brought about for the learning of audience courtesy.

The first opportunity comes with the seating of the audience. The students enter in groups, and sit with their own home rooms. They are expected to pass to their seats quietly, say little to their neighbors, and conduct themselves in a well-bred manner throughout the period. When a student sitting next the aisle sees a teacher or an outsider without a seat, he offers his immediately, and, if it is accepted, he finds another for himself. The pupils feel themselves the hosts, and they do not hesitate to act when they see a way to make their guests more comfortable.

Another bit of training has to do with the introduction of speakers. Here in assembly the students learn the courtesy of giving, by generous applause, a cordial greeting to those who are introduced. They learn, too, that when a distinguished guest is presented, they are to rise and stand for a moment to show him special honor.

The habit of listening aggressively rather than passively is cultivated in an assembly audience by suiting the program material to the interests of the boys and girls. Such a habit formed in youth will carry over, to a greater or less extent, into the future, making more alert and intelligent audiences in years to come for church, lecture hall, and theater.

Few things so plainly indicate the culture of an audience as its laughter. To observe the kind of laughter, the things at which it laughs, and the length of time its laughter lasts, is to know precisely the spirit and the intelligence of an assembled group. Junior high school students cultivate a refined sense of humor in well-conducted assemblies, and though they express it freely and spontaneously, they take care to keep within the bounds of good taste. Hoydenish laughter, that knows not when to stop, is frowned upon by both students and faculty, and any student who offends finds himself so distinctly in the minority that he quickly changes his behavior.

Applause, too, indicates in its timing and volume the character of an audience. Assembly groups are very genuine in their applause. They are cordial to all who appear on their programs, but they are quick to recognize and give special reward to those who are distinctly superior.

All of these phases of audience training as developed in junior high school assemblies are deserving of the most hearty commendation. They point to a time when discrimination and courtesy on the part of the audiences will be the rule rather than the exception. They hold out a hope that future audiences will demand a higher type of recreation than the present affords, and that they will appreciate the best in lecture, music, and drama.

ASSEMBLY PLAYS

Among the most popular of the programs given in a school assembly are the plays. The number given each year depends, usually, on the available time for the dramatic teacher, for, naturally, it is her place to direct them. Schools which offer dramatic courses may have, in addition to the plays, dramatic programs which are an outgrowth of the class work in folklore, balladry, Shakespeare—whatever material is used in the courses. A plan of organization which has proved successful for dramatic programs is the following:

1. Occasional formal one-act plays done by pupils either from the dramatic classes or from certain "home rooms," who have been trained for several weeks by the dramatic teacher.

2. Original programs for special occasions, such as Better English and Book Weeks.

3. Several programs at the end of the semester given by the dramatic classes, as a culmination of the semester's work. These will be formal plays by ninth grade classes, and pantomime and dramatization by seventh and eighth grades.

The term "home room" denotes one of the many groups of students into which a school may be divided. Each group has its headquarters, as its name indicates, in a room of its own, though the work is entirely departmental, and one teacher is responsible for each group.

Thus, they have an identity of their own. They are a smaller unit of their class. If there are several 7B home rooms, for instance, they are numbered 7B1, 7B2, and so on.

In assigning programs to be presented in assembly, a certain number of these home rooms may be specified by the faculty assembly committee to take charge of them. Occasionally, one of these programs will take the form of a play and the dramatic teacher will be asked to direct it. Some school principals, it is true, seem to think that any one can direct a play, and when no dramatic teacher is available, they turn the plays over to the English teachers, many of whom have not the slightest knowledge of play directing. Most good junior high schools have dramatic directors, however, and it is their business to plan and direct the dramatic programs.

Four weeks is a reasonable length of time to spend on each of these plays, and they should, if possible, be trained in school time. An assembly is a regular part of the school program, and the training for it should be regular work. If the classes use the time of the assembly period as a study or "home room" period the four days of the week that they do not go to assembly, this is the best time for the special training. With four forty-five minute periods a week for four weeks, the pupils can be tried out, cast, and trained to give a one-act play for assembly in a very creditable manner. The dress rehearsal is the one time that the pupils need to be asked to rehearse after school, and that only because a forty-five minute period is too short a time in which to rehearse and get into and out of costumes.

THE CHOICE OF THE ASSEMBLY PLAY

The qualities desirable in an assembly play are as follows:

1. *Good Literary and Dramatic Quality.*—Inferior plays should never be used. Great numbers of plays listed in the catalogues of play publishers are an insult to the intelligence of the students, and a discredit to dramatic departments in general. A dramatic teacher who must supply many plays is often hard-pressed for suitable material, and sometimes she is tempted to compromise. But each time that she does compromise she is losing an opportunity to educate the taste of players and audience. The material need not always be standard, but the plays should have enough merit and enough charm to be worth playing and worth hearing.

2. *Suitability to the Age of the Students.*—If all three grades meet together, the choice is much more difficult than if separate assemblies are held, for there is rather a wide variation in the interests of seventh and ninth grades. A play that is too young is decidedly a mistake, yet one that is too mature is equally as unfortunate. Some of Constance Mackay's plays, as *Troll Magic* and *The Forest Princess*, are delightful for fifth or sixth, but too young even for seventh grade; while T. B. Rogers' *The Forfeit*, or Eugene Pillot's *Two Crooks and a Lady* would be too old for seventh grade, though interesting to the ninth.

3. *Simplicity in Setting and Costuming.*—No money is spent on assembly plays, as a rule, and therefore the setting and costuming often can be merely suggested.

A play which depends for its effectiveness upon these things would, of course, be a poor choice.

4. *Length.*—A twenty-five or thirty minute play is the best length. This gives time for the opening exercises, announcements, and a little music to enrich the program.

PRESENTATION TO THE CLASS

The dramatic teacher introduces the play to the class in their own study room, as a rule, if a home room is to present the play. All the pupils are present and ready for the tryouts. To eighth grade students she may say something like this: "Perhaps you know that your room has been chosen to give an assembly play this semester. This means an honor for you and a chance to make a name for your room in dramatics. It means a good deal of work, too—but work that most of the pupils think is really good fun. You are to give the first play of the year. It will set a standard for the others, and I know you want to set a high one. Your date is October twenty-ninth. And since it is so near Hallowe'en I thought you would like to give a Hallowe'en play. So I have chosen one for you called *The Slippers of Cinderella*. The name sounds as if it might be a fairy tale, but it isn't. It is a modern play which the author calls 'an impossibility in one act.' . . . You can guess that it is a comedy. It tells about an absurd thing that happened on Hallowe'en—an impossible thing. But, you know, impossible things are supposed to happen on Hallowe'en! And in this play we see what amazing things came about when a godmother like Cinderella's appeared and granted some children their 'heart's desire.' "

With this much of an introduction, and a brief explanation of who the characters are, she may proceed to try out this play without reading it to the class. A modern play, the characters of which are children, may easily be read first by the pupils. If the dialogue were more difficult, the teacher should read parts and tell the rest, as suggested in the chapter on directing a play.

In as limited a time as is to be given to this play, there is no chance for analysis by the class. For this reason, an assembly play should be one of only moderate difficulty. The lines and the quick explanations and suggestions of the teacher must be the only guides for the children's interpretation.

In rapid tryouts there is no time to use action. The director must depend upon quick grasp of the thought, on type and on voice and diction. Since not so much depends on the result of this play, she can afford to be less exacting than if it were to be a public performance. Among the pupils whom she may use, she will find several who are more eager and interested than the others, and they will help to narrow her choice, for it will be worth her while to give the parts to those who seem most to want them. Naturally, some children are so reserved that they will cover up their eagerness. But a sensitive teacher can read their hope in their eyes, and if she considers them good material, she will be happy to gratify that hope.

A skillful director, with a fair degree of good luck in finding material, can cast a play in one forty-five minute period. She must work fast, but she can do it if the cast is not too large nor the characters too difficult. As a rule, however, the choice is only narrowed, and she will use another period to finish. The second meeting, if she expects to try fewer than half the pupils in the class, she may take them to the practice room in order not to waste the time of the others. This time she finishes the tryout and announces her players. She does not train a double cast for an assembly play, but she may tell those who came near to making the cast that they have done so well that if any of the players she has chosen prove disappointing, they will have the chance to step in. She has ascertained before actually giving out the parts that the pupils to whom they were given were willing to work their hardest to make the play a real success.

From the group who did not make the cast she then appoints an assistant who will act as prompter, an announcer for assembly, and several property men.

REHEARSALS

At the same period each day the pupils pass to the practice room, ready to start without delay on the rehearsal. The director must work fast, as the periods are short, and every minute must count. Rehearsals are conducted as suggested in Chapter VIII, with a reading rehearsal first, then the blocking of the main action, and after that the finer business. There is less time, of course, for discussion, but the play should not be difficult enough to require a great deal of it. The teacher may need to do more specific helping and suggesting for the understanding of some of the characters, but she should always stimulate thought rather than use imitation.

To get the maximum results from these rehearsals, the director should have present only the children whom she can keep busy practically all of the time. The problem of discipline has always to be reckoned with when children are rehearsing a play, and a director who scolds is sure to ruin the spirit of her rehearsal. Children who must wait fifteen minutes for their turn to come on the stage naturally become restless, and even the best of them are likely to get into mischief. Therefore, a wise teacher will see to it that the situation does not arise. She will divide her play into short scenes, and after the first two or three rehearsals, she will begin to rehearse by scenes. In *The Stolen Prince*, for example, she may work one day on the scenes in which the fisherman and his wife appear, and the next on those with the nurse and the children. Even though minor characters belong in a scene, it is worth while when two characters have a considerable dialogue to rehearse them alone for a while, having the other parts read by the prompter. Then, when they are worked up, the scene can go fast, the director spending most of her time on the minor characters.

THE STANDARD OF WORK

Whether or not the pupils in the cast are dramatic students, the teacher should let them feel that she expects much of them. The tendency is to accept a poor interpretation as the pupil's best instead of working constantly during the first two weeks to stimulate a better one. Suppose the players are rehearsing *Lantern Light*, and the girl playing Granny is making her much too young. The teacher says, "But Granny is older—a sweet little old lady. Relax. Try to *feel* tired and old. Yes, she is a little bent. Better! Now, make her sound old. No, older. Yes, you can. Old ladies talk more slowly. And her voice should be a little quavery because she isn't young and strong, but old and feeble. Much better!" Make the players think that they *can* do things. Sometimes a dramatic teacher can get them to surprise themselves by plunging into a characterization before they quite know they are doing it.

By the beginning of the second week they should be line-perfect. Some pupils inevitably lag behind, but it is entirely unnecessary, for children can learn their lines easily in two or three days at most, if they apply themselves.

Very definite directions are necessary if children are to remember them. Inexperienced teachers often wail, "They don't remember my directions from one time to the next!" True enough, probably, but the fault was doubtless at least half hers. Either she gave them in a vague, indefinite way, or she failed to fix them in the players' minds by repetition of the action.

After the first two weeks, the director should no longer stress characterization. In those first rehearsals she refused to give up trying to get what she wanted in character interpretation. But by the third week, she must give most of her attention to perfecting the business, regardless of how far from satisfied she is with the characterization. The fourth week must be devoted entirely to work for smoothness.

To one of these last rehearsals—not the dress rehearsal

—the home-room teacher should be asked to bring the rest of the class. The play will not be new for them when it is given in assembly, in any event, and their presence at the rehearsal will spur the players to do their best. Criticisms by their teacher and class will emphasize those which they have received from the director, and after one dress rehearsal, they should be well prepared for a good performance.

The costumes for the play should be only such as may be supplied from the costume room of the school. Students should never be asked to have costumes made at home, nor should they be required to pay for material which is to be made into costumes at school. Where assembly plays are usual, the school should have some plan for providing costumes, such as is suggested in Chapter X.

The setting should be that which is on hand as permanent equipment, and the properties should be simple. This does not mean that the stage should be colorless and uninteresting. Such things as brilliant banners with effective coats-of-arms, made of cheap materials and painted; gay pillows of various colors; and old portières draped over seats, help to give color and distinction to the barest stage. And if the lighting equipment is at all good, a student electrician with an eye for artistic coloring can do much toward making the play lovely to look at.

THE PERFORMANCE

A play makes of the assembly a more festive occasion, perhaps, than do other programs. It savors of the theater, and the theater holds almost a universal appeal for children. The pupils are highly interested, too, in seeing their classmates as players. They like to watch the development of a good plot. They enjoy using their imaginations.

In keeping with the spirit of the occasion, the preliminary part of the program might well be made a bit unusual. If the school boasts an orchestra, why not make this a real little theater event? The mood for any play can best be invited by orchestra music. In case this is impossible, the best substitute is solo or chorus music. Every school has pupils who sing or play some instrument well, and they are always flattered to be invited to play for the programs.

After one or two musical numbers, the president of the assembly says that a play will be presented by 7B2, and that Barbara Davis will announce it. Barbara has been trained by the director to give a brief introduction to the play, and she now steps from between the curtains and delivers it in a simple, natural manner. Ideally, this introduction should be prepared by the student herself. But an introduction is a very difficult thing for a child to think out, and since it may do so much to prepare the audience for the play, it should be planned with care. Introductions well done will set standards for the future, thereby becoming one more part in the educational process which is going on in the assembly.

One type of introduction which might be used is the following: "We are giving for you this morning a play of Zuñi Indians written by Marian Brown. It is called *On the Tower of the Shadows*. A long time ago people thought that the only way to conquer their enemies was by shedding their blood. It is taking the world a long,

long time to find out that there is a much surer and a much more lasting way. In our play are two kinds of people: those who believe that force is the best way, and those who believe just as firmly in the other way. What happens is worth our thinking about. The scene is the roof of an Indian pueblo in New Mexico. The cast is as follows. . . ." The players are announced, the announcer disappears between the curtains, and the play begins.

OTHER TYPES OF DRAMATIC PROGRAMS

Even more interesting for assembly than formal plays are certain programs which give opportunity for original dramatic work on the part of the pupils. The following are descriptions of several which have been used successfully in seventh and eighth grades.

1. *A Book Week Program.*—Each of the twenty-three home rooms in an intermediate school was asked by the school librarian to prepare a two-minute scene from some book, to be given at an assembly for Book Week. As soon as the scene was decided upon, it was to be reported to the librarian in order that no book should be used more than once. Immediately the home rooms went into deep consultation. The liveliest interest accompanied the choosing of the book and the scene, and the greatest secrecy surrounded the choice, for the scenes were to be given in the manner of charades, every pupil writing down the name of the book from which he thought the scene was taken.

Many of the home-room teachers, knowing little about dramatics, delegated the directing of their scenes to some pupil who was studying dramatics, and the children themselves planned and carried them out. Again and again the teachers expressed their surprise at the capable manner in which the pupils assumed the responsibility, and the ingenuity with which they worked out their scenes.

When the day came, all classes gathered in the auditorium except the groups who were scheduled for the first scenes. Only the principal, one dramatic teacher, the electrician, and a boy to draw the curtains were on the stage, most of the home-room teachers remaining in the audience throughout the program, with the players passing back and forth at stated intervals.

As soon as one scene was finished, the pupil-manager removed his properties and the next manager arranged the stage for his scene. Everything was done simply, some groups costuming their characters, others acting without special costumes. No make-up was used, and only curtain settings.

In about an hour's time, all of the twenty-three scenes had been given—a record which indicated skillful management on the part of the principal. There was the windmill scene from *Don Quixote,* the drawing of the sword from the stone by King Arthur, the search for the chest from *Treasure Island,* the porridge scene from *Oliver Twist,* the opening scene of *The Christmas Carol,* and many other well-chosen and cleverly presented incidents. No one expected finished performances or fine stage effects, but every one was amazed at the effectiveness of it all. Teachers and pupils alike glowed with pride as they came out of the auditorium at the close of the program. The boy who had never taken part in a play in his life felt that he had had a real part in the success of the program even though, perhaps, he had only said, "It is he."

Such a program, a coöperative enterprise of the entire school, shows one of the possibilities of dramatic training as a fine socializing influence. Such a program could, it is true, be given without the background of dramatic training, but that it could not have been given with a fraction of the success which it did achieve, was unanimously acknowledged by the teachers of the school.

2. *A Christmas Program.*—Each December, in one intermediate school, the music and dramatic departments unite to give a very beautiful Christmas program. As the boys' and girls' glee clubs sing softly the Christmas carols, pupils from the dramatic department tell, in picture and pantomime, the Nativity story. Costumed in the lovely flowing garments which are kept for this occasion from year to year, the boys and girls enact the beautiful old story, always with a dignity and grace in keeping with the spirit of the message.

And at the very last, when the kings and the shepherds are kneeling in adoration of the Babe in his mother's arms, from afar off come the lines of the old carol, "How far is it to Bethlehem?" sung by the high little voices of young children. The voices come nearer, and a tiny girl and boy in white garments—the garments of to-day—enter, bearing wreaths and garlands for the Christ Child. And as they offer their gifts and kneel with the others in adoration, the curtains close on as touching and beautiful a scene as is to be found in any Christmas service.

3. *Dramatic Demonstrations.*—These are the programs developed in the regular dramatic classes, de-

scribed in Chapters V, VI, and VII. They consist of the best dramatizations of stories and ballads from the various classes. One program is made up of folk tales, one of ballads, one of Shakespeare scenes, one of plays. Though given without scenery or costumes, these programs are among the most enjoyable of the year, arousing interest in pupils who have never elected dramatics, and setting standards for class work. Informal as they are in seventh and eighth grades, they are thoroughly and carefully done, for they represent the whole work of the semester, and the collaboration of entire classes.

CHAPTER X

COSTUMING THE SCHOOL PLAY

A fairy godmother, appearing suddenly with her magic wand to touch the characters of a play and clothe them in ivory and crimson and gold, would be as welcome to the busy young play director as she was to Cinderella —provided, of course, that she had a good sense of color harmonies and irreproachable taste! For the furnishing of costumes for school plays is one of the most perplexing problems which a dramatic director ever has to face.

Who is to make them? Shall the mothers of the children taking part be asked to assume the responsibility for the individual costumes? Will the home economics department lend its assistance? Shall the costumes be rented? Or must the dramatic teacher make them herself?

Every play director reviews these possibilities when she faces the problem of costuming her plays. Some teachers find an entirely satisfactory solution, and thereafter have little worry. Perhaps the mothers in this prosperous neighborhood are so gratified to have their children chosen for a play that they are entirely willing to make the necessary costumes. The home economics department sometimes counts on costume-making as one of its regular projects. It may be that the income from the plays makes it possible and desirable to rent all the costumes. If no one of these plans materializes, the dramatic teacher manages in some way herself.

Of all these possibilities, the home economics department would seem to offer the best solution to the costume problem. A regular class, directed by an expert, could be depended upon to do superior work, and such a project, surely, would be of interest and value to the class. The plan can be carried out in senior high school; but few junior high school classes have the time or the skill to turn out costumes rapidly enough, since most of the work must be done after the cast is chosen. And unless a home economics course were planned to include such a project, even a senior high school class would be unable to coöperate, for such a task would be impossible to undertake as an extra.

There are many drawbacks to the plan of asking the mothers to make their children's costumes. In the first place, most mothers are so busy with home or social duties that they do not wish to undertake them, or know so little about sewing that they must hire a seamstress if they are to do it satisfactorily. They may be too poor to afford to buy the material. On the other hand, some proud mothers insist upon dressing their children in costumes far too fine for the occasion. On the whole, it would seem advisable to provide costumes, if possible, in some way other than this.

The plan of renting costumes is not at all feasible, for neither the style nor the size of most of the costumes needed for children's plays is procurable at a professional costumer's. Even if they were to be had, the custom would not be a good one, for every school needs a wardrobe stocked with costumes which can be used for plays for which no admission is charged. Assembly plays, dramatic demonstrations, plays for parent-teacher's meetings—all these must be provided for, and a school which has no costume room is at a loss when occasions arise for smaller, less pretentious plays.

For the dramatic teacher to assume the responsibility of making the costumes herself is most unfortunate, even if she has assistance from other teachers. She is under the strain of the rehearsals, and if she takes upon herself the extra burden of costume-making, she will be forced to divide her energies, with the result that both the play and the costumes will suffer.

How, then, is the play to be costumed?

Among the possible satisfactory solutions is the mothers' club. Nowadays, the parent-teacher organizations are so strong in many schools that their large memberships are divided into many working groups. Why not ask for a costume committee to be appointed from among the mothers who volunteer for designing and sewing? Such a group, headed by a capable chairman who could manage the work, might meet regularly to sew on costumes for the various plays. This would mean that the dramatic director must choose her plays early, distribute them at regular intervals through the year, plan efficiently for the designing of the costumes and the buying of the materials. There might be mothers whose artistic training would make them extremely valuable in designing and decorating costumes; and others whose experience in cutting would enable them to make their own patterns from pictured costumes. The less skilled could do the stitching and hand sewing, of which there is always a large amount.

PEASANT: FULL SKIRT, BODICE, BLOUSE, AND APRON

Another plan involves the designing and buying of the materials by the dramatic teacher, assisted, perhaps, by the home economics teacher, and the actual making of the garments by a paid seamstress—one who, necessarily, is clever enough to cut patterns from pictures, but who is a fairly inexpensive worker, sewing by the day. There is an independence and certainty about this method which gives it an advantage over a volunteer committee, but its success depends upon whether a good seamstress is available, and whether finances permit of hiring her.

Whatever the method chosen for the making of the costumes, the chief responsibility for their planning inevitably rests upon the director of the play. She it is who knows best the play, the characters, the cast; she it is who knows the limit of expense, and the practicability of costumes for future uses.

STOCK COSTUMES

In planning her costumes, a wise director always takes into consideration, not only the play of the moment, but the many plays for which the costumes may be used again. This leads her to choose somewhat more conservatively than if she were costuming this play alone. These costumes, made for *The Birthday of the Infanta,* she decides, can be used later for Shakespearean scenes. These tunics will do for the gentlemen in any medieval play. Those tights are a good investment, for they will be used in one play after another until they fall into holes.

There are certain kinds of costumes which are needed

PEASANT TUNIC AND HOOD

again and again in children's plays. The robes worn by kings and queens change little from one century to another, and one or two sets should be in every school wardrobe. A jester's costume is needed for many plays; so are pages' suits. If Nativity plays or pantomimes are given at Christmas, some long robes are necessary. For the girls, the two types of dress most used will be the long, half-fitting costume worn by ladies in the Middle Ages, with long tight sleeves, flowing skirts, and wimple; and the typical peasant dress, with full skirt, bodice, and white blouse. For the boys, no costume is so much used as the tunic and tights. A director does not wish to inflict the same set of costumes on her audiences over and over again; but fairly conservative costumes can be used many times in various combinations and for different audiences, and after they have been called into service so often that they are clearly recognizable, they can be made over—if they are not worn out! The silver trimming on a lady's gown of gray may be changed to rose, with the result that the dress is made new. The costume of a gentleman of the court may be so altered by different combinations of tunics, under-tunics, and tights, that it may serve for several seasons.

DESIGNING THE COSTUMES

Period costumes, rather than modern, are required in nearly every play for children. Consider a list of plays for junior high school: *The Silver Thread, The Testing of Sir Gawayne, The Knave of Hearts, Robin Hood and the Widow's Three Sons*, and numberless others, and note how few there are which make use of modern dress.

Even the costumes in fanciful plays are based on the fashions of some historical period. The more imaginative the designer, the less do the costumes seem to belong to any period, for she adapts them so skillfully that they seem entirely original. But examine them carefully, and they will show earmarks of fourteenth century France, of Restoration England, of early nineteenth century America. Scarcely a play can be found, even to the modern musical comedy, in which some historical period does not show through many fantastic adaptations.

Because most plays for young people are so costumed, the director finds a knowledge of period costuming to be a great advantage. True, she will have to look up reference books no matter how thorough her knowledge, but if she has made a careful study of the subject, she not only knows the best references, but she is better able to sense the feeling of the various periods. In any historical play she can visualize the costumes at once, and if she reads a play which is set in no definite period, she reviews the possibilities offered by all the periods, and fixes on the most fitting and beautiful fashion in which to dress her characters.

THE SILHOUETTE

The dress of any period is most clearly distinguished by its silhouette. Far more characteristic than color, material, or decoration, is the outline of a garment, and if a designer would plan costumes which will best express a period, she must give careful attention to the silhouette. The hoop skirts of the 1850's, the high waists and narrow skirts of the 1800's, the square effect of the Henry VIII coats, the exaggerated shape of the headdresses in the fifteenth century—such characteristics as these are so significant that they instantly place the action of the play.

Not only the dress, but all accessories as well should be planned to give the impression of the period. The headdresses, the shoes, the jewelry, the purses, the swords, are all characteristic, and should be considered as carefully as the dress itself. It is the duty of the designer to become acquainted with the distinctive features of every period. Reference books on costumes are expensive, as a rule, but several good modern ones are sold at very moderate prices, and may be in every school library. Reference to several of these is made in the bibliography of this book.

SOURCES FOR COSTUME DESIGN

Aside from the many costume books are sources of various kinds. An unabridged dictionary has many illustrations which may be of service when costume books are lacking. Prints of great pictures are of much value for certain plays. The *Infanta Marguerita* of Velásquez is often used, for instance, as a model for costuming the Infanta in the Stuart Walker play. Van Dyck's portraits are perfect for the cavalier type of costume. The Abbey pictures are remarkably fine for King Arthur plays.

Among the best of all sources of costume design are beautifully illustrated books. Many children's plays are based upon favorite stories which have been illustrated by true artists. Virginia Frances Sterrett's illustrations for *The Arabian Nights,* Howard Pyle's drawings for his *Robin Hood* tales, W. C. Wyeth's pictures in *The Boy's King Arthur* and *Treasure Island,* and Kay Neilsen's

MEDIEVAL LADY

illustrations for *Andersen's Fairy Tales* and *East of the Sun and West of the Moon* are examples of the many colorful and imaginative costume designs which the director of children's plays will find invaluable. No better

MEDIEVAL GENTLEMAN

design can be found for the costumes in Louise Saunders' charming little play, *The Knave of Hearts,* than Maxfield Parrish's exquisite illustrations in the large gift edition of the play itself.

CONSIDERATIONS OTHER THAN PERIOD

Individuality in costuming a play will heighten decidedly the dramatic effect of the characters. In ordinary life most people dress alike. Personality does not often show itself through clothes, for the reason, perhaps, that in this day of ready-made garments the effort to find distinctive clothes is usually fruitless. Occasionally a woman, as deft with her fingers as she is original in her ideas, expresses her individuality in the way that she dresses. She is rare, and she is often conspicuous. In the same way that she stands out from a group, a character in a play may be made outstanding. Since the visual appeal is so strong in the drama, it would seem in every way desirable to increase the effectiveness of particular characters by this means. Just as the grouping in a play may be made highly significant, so may the color and style of the costumes do more than fulfill the requirements of beauty and period. In a day of elaborate headdresses, a character who wore only a soft veil on her head, bound by a narrow fillet, could instantly suggest a lovely young heroine, just as an overelaborately dressed young man would suggest a fop, and a large, fussily-garbed woman, a meddlesome old dowager. Personality as well as period must be considered if the costuming is to do its part in the effectiveness of the play.

The mood of the play, too, must be considered. If it

is dignified and formal, the heaviness of the color and cut of the costumes should emphasize such formality. If it is a bright and sparkling comedy, a light touch in costumes will reflect the gayety of the plot. If it is a fantasy, the oddity of the costumes should be a part of the general unreality.

The background, against which the costumes will be seen, may or may not be a factor to be reckoned with. The setting should be a foil for the costumes, and when it is neutral in tone, as is usually the case with modern settings, it provides no problem. In a Children's Theatre production of *Aladdin* an unusually effective background was made by gold screens, against which the gorgeous Oriental costumes stood out in vivid relief. As the lights changed in color from scene to scene, the screens took on a soft lavender or golden or pinkish glow, and the costumes, bolder in color but tinged with the same hues, appeared more rich and varied because of what the background added.

Lighting is a more subtle and difficult element than setting, in the scheme of which costuming is a part. Color in lighting is necessary to beauty and significance of production, but it is also a source of great anxiety to the director, for the amount of experimenting necessary for real effectiveness in lighting is rarely possible in an amateur play, and much is left to chance. The beauty of costumes may be heightened amazingly by skillful lighting, however, and chances are worth taking. Crudeness in color and style is softened by delicately colored lights; materials take on a surprising richness; and the mood of the play is intensified a hundredfold.

Colors in costumes must be chosen with reference to

COSTUME OF HENRY-THE-EIGHTH PERIOD

the lighting if they are to be highly effective. The material for every costume should be examined under artificial light, and samples tested under lights of the colors which will be used with them. To a great extent the lights may be adjusted to suit the costumes, but certain colors are always a risk in artificial light. Pastel shades often fade into a dingy white; purple is likely to turn brown; and Alice blue looks gray. Amber lights must be used with especial care, as they have a tendency to kill many of the colors most used. Strong colors are safest on the stage, but delicate color harmonies can be used successfully if the lights are carefully handled. White is too startling to be good on the stage; cream is far more pleasing. Silvery gray costumes have more possibilities, probably, than any other kind, for they take on whatever color is thrown on them, exhibiting the most varied and exquisite hues as they move from one area of the stage to another.

THE SIGNIFICANCE OF COLOR

So dramatic and so emotional is the effect of color that a drama might almost be enacted by color alone. Producers have scarcely begun to realize its possibilities; and it is only the rare play in which color in lighting or costumes even approaches the effect of which it is capable.

Symbolism in color is carried out to a considerable extent in pageantry, and in a smaller degree in plays. Blue has always been a favored color to suggest truth as exemplified in the hero or heroine. White has always stood for purity; green for youth and freshness; black

LADY OF HENRY-THE-EIGHTH PERIOD

or dark gray, for sorrow; scarlet, guilt; purple, royalty.

But aside from the emotional values of various colors, aside from their symbolism, is the fact that certain colors belong to certain periods and countries. Gray, more than any other color, is associated with the Puritans; earth browns and bright reds with the Indians; rich heavy maroons and purple with Henry VIII and Elizabeth; red, yellow, black, and white with the peasants of southern Europe; dull, somber brown, green, and black, brightened by flashes of crimson or orange, with the northern countries; delicate mauves and tans and blues, with the 1840's; yellow with the Chinese; black with the Spanish. In some of the period costume books—Grimball and Wells' *Costuming a Play*, for instance—may be found information concerning characteristic colors as well as styles, and the designer of costumes must study one as much as another if her costumes are to look as if they belonged to the characters who wear them.

MATERIALS

Materials are characteristic, too, both of the individual character and of the period. Soft silk for the costume of Queen Elizabeth would be as out of place as rich, heavy brocade for a modern frock; and tweed trousers as absurd for the gentleman of 1800 as stockinet ones would be to-day.

Extravagant periods demand extravagant costumes. *The Prince and the Pauper*, set in the time of Henry VIII, requires elaborate costumes. So, also, do the plays set in the time of Louis XIV, and Charles I and II of England. Colonial plays which have as characters the wealthier class of people, are far more effective when costumed with rich, heavy materials. The periods of voluminous skirts, velvet coats, satin trousers, lace frills and wigs are the despair of costume committees who must economize. Sets of such costumes, so often used in high school plays, are better rented than made. By research work in the period in which the play is set, the designer will find what materials were most used, and she will then be able to determine what cheaper material may be substituted with best result.

The old idea that any children's play could be costumed with cambric and cheesecloth has lost much ground. Directors have discovered that better materials are not only vastly more effective, but far more serviceable; and schools that care to build a permanent wardrobe are buying materials which will last for several plays.

Many costumes there are for which cambric is good enough. Groups of children costumed as flowers or toy soldiers or frogs may very effectively be garbed in cambric. Individuals do not stand out, in such cases; general effect is all that is necessary. And the costumes may never be needed again. Indeed, cambric may be used (wrong side out) for full peasant skirts, tunics, and for many other garments which need not hang in soft folds.

Cheesecloth, however, is well-nigh useless for costumes. It has no body, it does not hang well, and it looks like nothing but cheesecloth. There may be occasional uses for it; but after one wearing, a costume made from it is likely to look so sad and hopeless that it is scarcely worth keeping.

One of the most useful materials for costumes which are to be dyed or decorated is unbleached muslin. True, it is stiff; but after being washed or dyed, it loses enough of the dressing to make it suitable for many types of garments; and when stenciled with an attractive design, it often looks surprisingly rich and beautiful.

Cotton flannel may be dyed to look like woolen material of good quality. For a certain fourteenth century play, an entire set of costumes was made from a discarded sky cyclorama of pale blue cotton flannel. The material was cut into pieces, dyed in many harmonious shades, and then made into costumes. The cost was nothing, and the effect was really lovely. Dyed Turkish toweling, too, has been used successfully to represent soft woolen material. Agnes Brooks Young's *Stage Costuming* and Grimball and Wells' *Costuming a Play* have each an instructive chapter on dyeing.

For costumes which are not to be dyed, Canton flannel is more satisfactory than cotton flannel, for it is heavier and smoother. It may be had in ten or twelve useful colors, and it has the effect of broadcloth when it is new. Men's coats and tunics, long capes, king's robes, and every other garment supposed to be of woolen cloth may be made from Canton flannel if the desired shade can be obtained.

For velvet, the cheapest substitute is corduroy. From the distance of the stage, it looks very much like velvet, and it can be made into handsome regal robes, richly trimmed mantles, Colonial and Louis XIV coats. Velveteen, too, is good, but it is considerably more expensive, and scarcely worth the difference in price.

A satisfactory substitute for brocade is hard to find,

QUEEN OR PRINCESS

for it must be heavy and rich-looking. Some of the less expensive tapestries are often satisfactory, though they are never really cheap. Curtain materials of various kinds are useful for costumes, and therefore the curtain department should never be overlooked in the search for suitable fabrics.

As a substitute for silk, sateen, or lingette is most useful. It has not, of course, as much sheen as silk, but it is lustrous enough to be attractive, and soft enough to hang in graceful folds. Few materials can be used in so many ways, and few cheap materials can be obtained in so many lovely shades. Satin rayon, too, is very beautiful on the stage, having the effect of satin.

For silken veils to hang from fine headdresses nothing can take the place of the thinnest—and cheapest—Japanese or China silk. This material is rather expensive for costumes, but the veils made from it are so beautiful, so easily dyed, and so useful that they are well worth buying for the costume boxes.

Cotton crêpe is good for costumes which should hang in soft folds. It is one of the best materials for Greek tunics, as well as for other cotton costumes which should have a soft effect and it may be obtained in a variety of colors.

Peasants may be dressed in burlap tunics or skirts, for this material gives the effect of being homespun. Cambric, too, is much used for their tunics and skirts. The skirts are made, also, of calico and of flowered cretonne. Tights may be made from underwear, dyed, though cotton tights bought from a costumer, are more satisfactory.

By haunting the basements of department stores, the costume committee will find many bargains in cheap materials. They will discover substitutes they had never thought of using. They will learn to look at the cloth on the counters, and see it as it will appear on a stage, under colored lighting. And they will remember that what counts in the costuming of a play is not realism but illusion.

CHAPTER XI

THE SCHOOL STAGE AND ITS EQUIPMENT

THE physical theater has always been a powerful influence in determining a people's drama. The great open-air theater of the Greeks demanded plays which were vast in conception, and actors who were mighty in voice and stature. The medieval pageant-wagons, with the audiences standing about, required simultaneous scenes, realistic properties, and an absolute lack of illusion in the acting. The Elizabethan playhouses, modeled after the inn yards, called for alternation between localized and non-localized scenes, with descriptive passages taking the place of lighting and properties. And so on, down through the picture-frame stage of the Restoration to the most modern of little theaters, one finds the plays and the acting following the type of playhouse in which the drama is enacted. True, theaters are gradually changed by the revolutionary souls who ever form the vanguard of new drama. But, in general, plays and acting must fit themselves to the stage on which they will appear.

All this has a bearing on the school stage. For the plays must be chosen to suit the size and type of the auditorium and stage. A huge, barn-like stage and theater will mean that the plays must be pageant-like. The spectacular will be the form of drama most successful in an auditorium where there is no possibility of intimacy. And children's voices are too thin for such a place.

Some stages are built with the proscenium arch, and, therefore, the curtain, halfway to the back wall, the idea being to leave a space for speakers in front of the curtain. Such a plan is obviously ill-advised, especially when children's plays are to be given here, for the large apron throws the action of the play so far back that contact with the audience is very difficult. Here, again, the plays chosen should be those that depend for their effectiveness on spectacle rather than speech. Regardless of whether the voices carry well enough, a stage apron is always a mistake, except, perhaps, in a very small auditorium, where a narrow apron may offer no disadvantage.

A tiny stage, again, limits the choice of school plays. Intimate plays with small casts will be the type best suited to such a stage. Plays which require little in the way of settings are necessary, in order to leave free and uncluttered space for acting. One-act plays will be better than those of several scenes with but a single play on a program, for changes are difficult on a little stage, and off-stage space, as a rule, is proportionately small.

The middle ground between these two extremes is, without question, the best. A stage which has a proscenium arch 35 feet wide and 18 to 20 feet high, and a stage depth of not less than 25 feet, is ideal. Practically anything except a large pageant can be given there; and to build a stage large enough for a huge production at the sacrifice of the far more valuable plays, indicates a lamentable want of foresight.

OFF-STAGE SPACE

For a dramatic director to persuade school authorities and architects to build a beautifully proportioned stage does not require a great deal of strategy. But it is another matter to convince them of the necessary amount of off-stage space. Every stage should have as much space divided between the wings as is included in the playing area. In order to accommodate plays which have changes of scene, a stage must have space to keep the settings and properties which will be needed. When such things are crowded together in corners, the confusion of changing scenes is distressing to stage crews and tiresome to audiences, for the waits are necessarily twice as long as they should be. If there is adequate space for the production crew to work efficiently, the scenes can be changed with the minimum of time and effort. When a new stage is being built, therefore, the dramatic director will do the school a lasting service if she can bring the powers that be to see the necessity of sufficient off-stage space.

A PLASTERED BACK WALL

One of the great joys of the producer who is fortunate enough to possess it, is a back-stage wall of smooth white plaster. For sky effects nothing can equal it, the opportunities for varied and beautiful lighting it affords being well-nigh limitless. For exterior scenes, backing for windows and doors, background for the projection of silhouetted trees, clouds, magical scenes, what not, it is infinitely superior to the muslin cyclorama, which is inevitably wavy or unsteady. Scarcely a play will be given on the stage in which it is not used, scarcely one which is not made more effective by it.

A plaster dome, which is merely an extension of the back wall, curving overhead and at the sides, is, of course, still better than the plain wall, since the edges are so easily masked. But it is so much more expensive that few schools can afford to have it. And since the wall is so satisfactory, the dome need not be regretted.

The one disadvantage of using the plaster wall is that it precludes crossing back stage during a scene. This is not often necessary, but there are occasions when either a player or a member of the stage staff must get to the opposite side. Some auditoriums are so arranged as to afford another way around. Ideally, there should be a passage behind the wall. A small hallway behind the stage would be the best solution to the difficulty, and in some schools this hall, besides being convenient for plays, would be found very useful to get quickly from one side of the building to the other.

If a school has been built with no chance of having such a wall, a dyed muslin cyclorama must be made to answer the purpose. It should be starch-dyed by a scene painter, if possible, the best color being pale blue, splashed with pink and yellow ochre paint of exactly the same value.

HEIGHT OF THE STAGE

Height in a stage is very desirable, though not absolutely necessary. Naturally, it must be high enough so that ropes and battens are above the sight line. The proper height is two and a half times the height of the proscenium opening. And elaborate productions can be managed much more easily if complete drops can be drawn up into the flies. Scenes from *The Blue Bird* or *A Midsummer Night's Dream*, for instance, requiring gauze drops, can be changed quickly and effectively if they can be kept in the flies.

CURTAINS

The front curtains are made, preferably of velours, of a color to harmonize with the auditorium. Soft gray-green, tan, blue, wine, whatever color best suits the theater is naturally chosen, though it is well to keep in mind the fact that they are also to frame the stage picture, and should be soft and harmonious.

The curtain track should be placed close to the proscenium arch, so that there will be no space between the curtains and the arch. This track should be a silent one —the best procurable; for noisy or uncertain curtain control can make the best play seem amateurish. The curtains should be hung so as to cross two feet past each other in closing, that there may be no danger of their being brushed apart during the changing of scenes.

THE CLOSE-IN CURTAINS

A well-equipped stage of medium size has three or four sets of close-in curtains, each set long enough to extend entirely across the stage. These curtains are so hung that they not only mask the back-stage space when open, but make the stage of various depths when closed. Mere

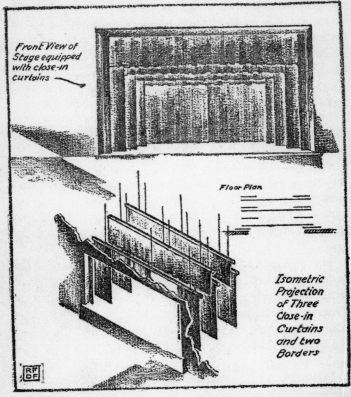

Front View of Stage equipped with close-in curtains

Floor Plan

Isometric Projection of Three Close-in Curtains and two Borders

TWO VIEWS OF STAGE EQUIPPED WITH CLOSE-IN CURTAINS

"legs," or narrow curtains masking the wings, are unsatisfactory, for they do but one thing. In any school innumerable occasions arise for a stage of different depths. Sometimes a shallow stage is desired for a speaker; again, about half the depth is needed for a playlet given as a curtain raiser, or to advertise a coming play. Then, for regular plays, the full depth may be required, with a door at the back through which will be seen the sky cyclorama.

On the very first occasion on which one fine stage was used, a program was to be given for the public by the glee club, a speaker, and a group from the dramatic department. "Legs" instead of close-in curtains had been provided, so that if the stage was used for the first part of the program, the set for the play could not be put in place until afterwards. Because this would necessitate a wait, the idea was rejected; and the outcome was that the stage was set for the play, and the curtains kept closed until after the first half of the program. Only the narrow space made by the depth of the proscenium arch was available, and this was used for the speaker and the glee club.

The advantage of being able to set one scene behind another, in school plays or other programs, is so great as to be worth more than it costs in the way of curtains. Programs move more smoothly and more rapidly; there is less excitement during the performance; and the scenes are better set for having been done before the last minute rush.

The material for such curtains varies according to the price a school is able to pay for them. Velours is sometimes used, but the cost is almost prohibitive when several sets are used. Rep is perhaps the most satisfactory of materials. It is firm, durable, and of good appearance; and it hangs in soft folds which take the light well.

Saxon plush, a material which is similar to Canton flannel, is considerably cheaper than rep, and very good for curtains except that it is a little light if unlined. The texture is soft and excellent for lighting.

Denim and sateen are two other possible materials for close-in curtains, but neither is so good as the other materials mentioned. Denim is durable but rather stiff and unlovely, and sateen appears hard and wears and soils badly.

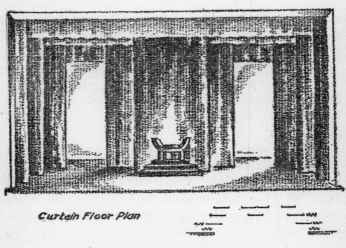

Curtain Floor Plan

CURTAIN ARRANGEMENT

In color, such curtains are usually neutral. Soft oyster-gray, gray-green, or sand are all good, for the curtains are to form the background for many colors in costumes, and, therefore, should harmonize with any possible combination.

No more borders should be used with these curtains than are absolutely necessary to mask the rigging in the flies. Ideally, the curtains should be long enough so that they can be hung above the sight line, making borders unnecessary. They are much more beautiful so hung, their long sweep giving height to the stage and simplicity to the general picture. If this is not possible, a border should be available for each close-in curtain, but the number actually used should be cut to the minimum, for they are heavy-looking and difficult to keep straight.

Close-in curtains may be hung permanently on tracks; or drapery hooks may be sewed at intervals along the tops, hooking into three-fourth inch rings strung on wires which are bolted into the side walls. In whatever way they are hung, they, too, should close well past each other. Each side should be on a separate pull, but all lines should be controlled from one side of the stage, preferably the switchboard side.

SETS

A standard set of flats for a stage with a 30-foot proscenium opening is the following:

5 plain flats ....5 feet 2 inches wide
2 doorway flats .....5 feet 2 inches wide (doors 2'9" ×
                                             6'8")
2 window flats ......5 feet 2 inches wide (window 2'9" ×
                                             6, 1'8" from floor)
5 jogs ....3 feet 2 inches wide
2 jogs ....2 feet wide
4 jogs ....1 foot wide
1 folding flat ....7 feet 6 inches wide (doors and
                                             windows each 2'10" × 7'8")
    (for double doors
    or French windows)
2 frames ....3 feet 2 inches wide

THE USE OF DIVIDED CLOSE-IN CURTAINS IN AN EXTERIOR SCENE

These flats should be at least two feet higher than the lower edge of the front valance.

The two frames are made to take doors in the set, as well as to make recesses for special windows, fireplaces, wall panels, and period windows and doors (Gothic, Tudor, Colonial, Moorish arches, etc.), or, with taping, to make leaded windows or French doors.

If more can be afforded, add casings (making the openings in the flats correspondingly larger), and add special pieces such as arches, fireplaces, parallels, platforms, and steps.

SUGGESTIONS FOR THE USE OF FLATS

Flats which are to be used together in a set should be hinged and stripped before being painted in order to avoid light cracks.

Recessed casings, which give depth to doorways and windows, should be used with curtains instead of ordinary flats.

Variety in setting a stage may be secured in many ways even though but one set of flats is available. Painted a neutral tone, matching or closely harmonizing with the close-in curtains of the stage, it can be used for almost any purpose without repainting. By changing the size, shape, and general plan of the room which is set up; by varying the placing of windows and doors; by using different levels; by altering the type of room by the use of period arches and windows; and by skillfully lighting the stage, the same flats can be used over and over again without the least monotony of effect. On a school stage, too, many of the plays and most of the other programs will require only the regular close-in curtains. Thus, one set can easily be made to answer all purposes.

For outdoor settings, several different devices may be used. Sections of the close-in curtains arranged irregularly, in small, bunched sections, give the effect of tree trunks better than painted scenery. A partial drop-curtain of net, on which painted foliage has been glued and then cut out, may give an excellent illusion of leafy boughs. Cut-outs of trees or shrubs may be used with good effect; and lighting can give a better illusion than anything else.

SCREENS

More imaginative in quality than conventional sets, and full of possibilities for interesting treatment, are settings made of screens, used against a dark back-drop or a cyclorama. The unusual theater in this country and abroad has obtained striking effects with them, and they could well be used more widely. Settings made of screens have no claim to realism. They do not imitate rooms and streets and courts. They merely suggest them. They stimulate the imagination of the audience, and, therefore, are especially successful with children. Practically, they are very useful, particularly when, because of lack of height or interference of borders, a ceiling cannot be used with a box set.

Such screens may be built from six to eight feet in height. Some of them will be in two panels, some in three, always so hinged that they can be turned either way. The top of the screens is preferably decorative in shape, but unless they can be skillfully done, they may

SCREENS

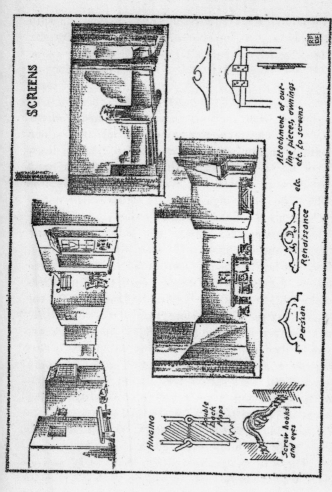

Persian   Renaissance   etc.

HINGING

Double back flaps

Screw hooks and eyes

Attachment of out-line pieces, awnings etc. to screens

SCREEN SETTINGS

Upper left: Street scene, showing use of properties, attached windows and a shop window set piece.
Upper right: Garden and terrace. The trees on the cyclorama are cardboard cutouts in front of floods.
Center: Dining room with set piece for fireplace. Height may be secured by projecting a sun spot over top of flat as if from high window.

better be left straight. In color, they should be a soft neutral tone, and if reversible, the other side might either be silvered or painted differently for each play.

The conventional lighting equipment, installed in schools by electrical companies whose business is not stage lighting, offers one of the most discouraging problems a producer of plays has to face. Rows of hard white borders and footlights, without so much as one adjustable light or a single dimmer, comprise the entire lighting equipment of thousands of schools. Even stage electrical companies may make bad mistakes in their recommendations for lights. If, when building a stage, the school authorities would consult an expert on stage lighting, as, for instance, Eugene Frost, the Hub Electric stage lighting adviser; Arvid Crandall of the Goodman Theatre, Chicago, or Dean Farnsworth, production manager for Clare Tree Major in New York, they would then start right in buying equipment. And if funds were limited, they could add to it gradually until their lights were satisfactory for all purposes.

Careful experiments have proved the following lighting equipment to be satisfactory for a school theater:

1. *A Sectional Border.*—Each light in this border is separate, having its individual reflector and color-frame holder. These lights, each of which may be as powerful as 500 watts, can be built in groups as desired. Sections of three are recommended as being the most satisfactory arrangement. These strips may be used in any position, for almost any purpose. If four sections of

three lights each are purchased, one or two sections can be used as footlights and the others for a concert border, or for lighting backings, or as any flood is used.

2. *A Strip of Footlights.*—Thirty-two lamps, on three or four circuits, is a sufficient number of footlights, for they should not extend across more than two-thirds of the proscenium opening. If there are four circuits, the colors should be red, blue, green, and pale amber or white. The bulbs used should be 60-watt naturals, a type which has the dye blown in the glass. They may be inside frosted, if desired.

When sectional borders are used with the regular footlights, they should be so placed as to flood the stage areas where the action will be especially important. For instance, a throne on the right could be made prominent by placing a section of the three powerful lights where it will illuminate that part of the stage. Or, it might be desired to light the face of a particular character with a weird, bluish light. The section of lights (with blue slides) could be so placed among the footlights as to do this effectively. They do not, naturally, focus on any limited area as intensely as does a spot, but they are very useful for localizing areas, whether used as borders or footlights. And being adjustable they can be placed so as to heighten materially the dramatic effect of each particular play.

3. *Baby Spots.*—These lights, which should be of a type taking any power lamp up to a thousand watts, are especially useful for definitely picking out playing areas. If possible, it is advantageous to have two fastened on the concert border—one at each side of the sectional border—and others, on standards, for special effects,

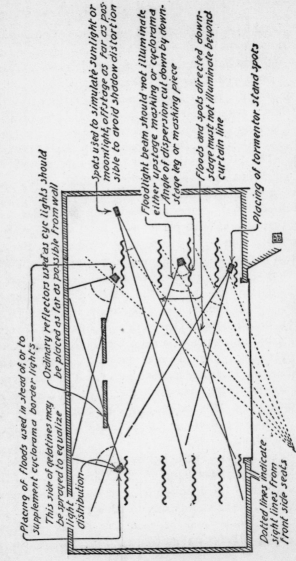

Placing of floods used in stead of or to supplement cyclorama border lights

This side of gelatines may be sprayed to equalize light distribution

Ordinary reflectors used as cyc lights should be placed as far as possible from wall

Spots used to simulate sunlight or moonlight, offstage as far as possible to avoid shadow distortion

Floodlight beam should not illuminate either upstage masking or cyclorama cut down by downstage leg or masking piece

Angle of dispersion

Floods and spots directed downstage must not illuminate beyond curtain line

Placing of tormentor stand spots

Dotted lines indicate sight lines from front side seats

FLOOR PLAN SHOWING PLACING OF LIGHT UNITS

such as sunsets and sunrises, window illumination, fire-light, etc.

4. *A Flood Light on a Stand.*—This is to be used especially to light backings of doors and windows. It may represent sunlight, moonlight, or simply the illumination in the next room. It, too, may carry as high as a thousand watts. In ordering this light, the type of flood with wings should be specified, in order to prevent light spill.

5. *Dimmers.*—Practically all stage lighting depends for its effectiveness on the use of dimmers. Without the power to vary the intensity of the lights, an electrician is so handicapped that he may as well not attempt light effects. Even the simplest of school lighting equipment should include dimmers if plays are to be given.

The use of dimmers makes possible the creation of mood in the staging of a play. A dim, mysterious light on the dark blue sky background, with a dazzling ray streaming down as if from the star over Bethlehem, will give more atmosphere for the shepherd scene in a Nativity play than the most skillful acting could do. The gradual illumination of the table spread with the feast, of the brazier of coals, of the fateful rosebush, gives a vivid impression of magic which thrills a child audience in *Beauty and the Beast.* There is no limit to the possibilities of lighting when a stage is equipped with dimmers, and a director whose stage lacks them will find no better use for the money earned by her plays than the purchase of several of them.

A large and complete school switchboard has from twelve to eighteen dimmers. This is very expensive, however—prohibitive to all but large, finely equipped schools. The alternative is a board of dimmers, wall-mounted, into which any circuits can be plugged. Five of these dimmers, three of them 440-watts, two of them 1100-watts, would cost about sixty dollars, not including wiring.

This completes a minimum standard equipment. The following lights should be added if more elaborate lighting is desired:

1. One flood.
2. Two high-powered spots of 2,000 watts capacity.
3. Up to ten baby spots, adaptable to both standards and teasers.
4. A Pevear revolving border to supplement the sections.
5. Two olivets—Pevears. This is a type of flood light which gives a perfectly diffused edge to the beam. Such lights are much more expensive than ordinary floods, but managed skillfully, they give more delicate and beautiful effects than any other kind.

6. *Cyclorama Lights.*—These lights should be especially designed by the manufacturer, from stage specifications, to suit individual cases. Pevear cyclorama lights are excellent, as are also those designed by A. Crandall of the Goodman Theatre, Chicago. For a small cyclorama backcloth, two 1000-watt floods may be used, one from each side.

THE UNTRAINED ELECTRICIAN

Stage lighting is a difficult art, but a fascinating one. Schools with no teacher who understands lighting must be content with the simplest effects. But every director who must be responsible for the lighting of her own plays

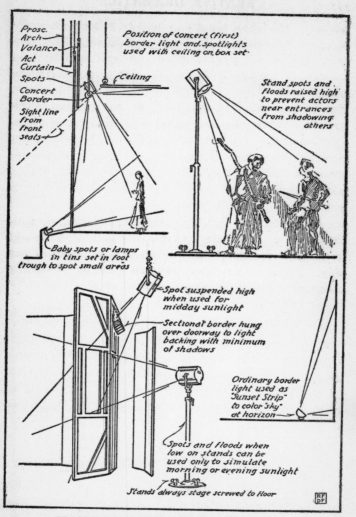

Prosc. Arch
Valance
Act Curtain
Spots
Concert Border
Sight line from front seats

Position of concert (first) border light and spotlights used with ceiling on box set.

Ceiling

Stand spots and floods raised high to prevent actors near entrances from shadowing others

Baby spots or lamps in tins set in foot trough to spot small areas

Spot suspended high when used for midday sunlight

Sectional border hung over doorway to light backing with minimum of shadows

Ordinary border light used as "Sunset Strip" to color "sky" at horizon

Spots and floods when low on stands can be used only to simulate morning or evening sunlight

Stands always stage screwed to floor

PLACING OF LIGHTS FOR SPECIAL USES

can learn enough of the art to manage a fairly elaborate lighting equipment with the help of a stage staff, appointed from the most capable and interested boys in school. If she has a chance to study with experts, she will go much further, naturally, than she can go alone. But in case this is impossible, she can gain much information from the electricians who install the equipment; and then, by constant experimenting, she and her staff will learn how to do more than merely illuminate the stage. At first they will get only the simpler effects, such as sunlight and moonlight. Then they will learn how to make certain characters and situations stand out by emphasis in lighting. And, finally, they will gain the power so to use color and intensity in lights as to add in no small degree to the beauty and significance of the play. There are no rules. It is all a matter of outside observation and inside experiment.

CHAPTER XII

CHILDREN'S THEATERS

PETER PAN, playing riotously on his fairy pipes, cries out to Wendy in elfish glee, "I just want always to be a little boy and have fun!" And the cry of Barrie's little hero finds its way to the hearts of countless boys and girls who, though they may no longer own a little house in the Never Never Land, yet steal back as often as they dare to taste the happiness that comes to all who never really grow up!

The fun of "make-believe" is such a glorious thing in the lives of children that nothing can quite compare with it. Whether they deck themselves out in cowboy regalia and play "Wild West," or go to a show to see it played for them, they live for the time being a life entirely apart from their own. They are transported to new environments, and thrilled by delightful new experiences.

The fascination which a play holds for children is almost universal. Yet few children ever have the opportunity to see a real play. No professional companies present children's plays; few amateur groups attempt them; with the result that the only opportunity for satisfying their hunger for the theater lies in the movies. Every mother and teacher knows how unsuitable for children are the average motion pictures with their adult emotions and passions. Yet children flock to them in such numbers as to cause real alarm to all who are concerned with their welfare.

EDUCATION FOR LEISURE

A children's theater would be a worthy project if established for the sole purpose of affording a substitution for the present type of motion pictures. Its possibilities, however, are much broader than this. To provide wholesome recreation is, indeed, its main object. But at the same time that it is giving joy to its youthful audiences, it is developing their artistic taste and thus educating them for leisure.

For the problem of the use of leisure time is a more significant thing than most of our schools have recognized. As long as children are allowed to grow up with no training in discrimination as to their pastimes, the standard of recreation in the country will be low. People go to amusement parks, cheap shows, and public dance halls because they know of no better way to entertain themselves. It is a pathetic spectacle to watch the crowds at such places trying to have a good time. They seem completely to lack the art of creating for themselves wholesome enjoyment. They make little discrimination in their pleasures, merely following the line of least resistance. If their appreciation for the beautiful in music, art, and drama had been trained in their youth, they would reject the tawdry and commonplace, and demand a type of recreation which would bring them genuine joy. Children's theaters give one of the best possible opportunities for this training; it is, therefore, a matter for gratification that they are being organized in so many cities.

WHAT IS A CHILDREN'S THEATER?

The general understanding of the term, *children's theater*, seems to be a theater in which children act. This is not its real meaning, if most of the existing children's theaters can be considered typical. Rather, the term means a theater in which plays are given for child audiences, whether the players are children or adults. In some children's theaters the players are all adult; in others they are all children; while a few theaters cast their plays with both children and adults.

From the point of view of the audience, there is a distinct advantage in having older and more skillful players predominate. When grown people play the adult parts, the illusion is far better, the characters are more convincing, and the audience, instead of thinking patronizingly of how "cute" the children are in the grown-up parts, identifies the player with the character, and gives itself over to the enjoyment of the play.

Many adult parts, even in a children's play, cannot be played by children with any degree of satisfaction. A youthful audience can appreciate far more than it can actually play. Such a character as Long John Silver in *Treasure Island* is thoroughly enjoyed by children, yet it is too subtle to be played adequately by a little boy. The foolish young mother in *The Poor Little Rich Girl*, the hypocritical governess, the kindly doctor, are impossible as children's parts, yet children can understand them sufficiently to get much joy from the play.

PLAYERS OR AUDIENCE

The question to be decided at the start is this, "Just what is to be the purpose of our children's theater?" And on the answer will depend the policy which should be followed. If the theater is organized to give the children a chance to act, the emphasis will be on the development of the players. If, instead, the main object is to provide the finest type of recreation possible for child audiences, the emphasis will be on the finished product rather than on the players. The director will use in her casts the most talented people she can find, whether they be children or adults; she will so direct the play as to gain the highest possible degree of effectiveness; and she will stage it as beautifully as her means will permit. She will think first of what she is giving her audience, and second of what she is doing for her players.

Now, in communities where there is no other dramatic activity for children, the sponsors are likely to decide that the benefit of a children's theater would be greater if the children played all the parts. The theater could thus provide not only a means of entertainment for child audiences, but an opportunity for hundreds of children to act. Such a policy was adopted, not only by the Children's Educational Theatre, founded in New York by Minnie Herts Heniger some years ago, but it has been followed by a few of the children's theaters at the present time.

There is much to be said both for and against this type of children's theater. The child players derive much joy from the experience of acting in the plays; they gain in poise, in skill, in personality. At the same time, there is danger that the applause and praise of admiring friends, which is sure to follow public performances, will turn their heads, and give them an exaggerated idea of their own importance. To a considerable degree this danger can be counteracted by developing a sensible attitude toward the work. And there are many children who, with a wise director, will never be spoiled by taking part in public plays. But some children cannot stand the kind of success which is likely to come with public performances. Especially with repeated performances, they become less spontaneous and childlike, and take on, if not an insufferable conceit, at least an unfortunate sophistication.

The value to a child of acting in a children's theater play is far less than the value derived from working in a creative dramatic class for the same length of time, granted that the directors are equally capable. The experience of taking part in a play which is worked out to a fine degree of finish is not to be discounted; but the development which comes from the original work of creating a play out of a story means still greater growth. A play director who is working for a finished production must impose her own ideas on her cast; she must be more or less arbitrary in order to get the best results in the least time. But a teacher of creative dramatics, not having to worry about an audience, can take time so to stimulate the thought and imagination of the children that their experience will be a richer one, and their growth accordingly greater than could be gained from any formal play.

The ideal situation is a combination of creative dramatic classes with a children's theater. In these classes all children are given the opportunity of participating in the active side of the work. The children's theater is the passive side—a source of inspiration for the original work. At the same time, if the cast of each play includes a few children, the pupils who have been doing the most excellent class work may be chosen for the parts. The knowledge that such chances may come to those who do superior work in dramatization, voice, and diction, proves an incentive to highest effort. One small boy, whose chum was chosen for a children's theater play, amazed his teacher by a sudden and inexplicable improvement in his class work. Not only did he outdo himself but he outstripped the whole class in planning scenes, analyzing character, and acting the various parts. And, having risen from mediocrity, he never slumped but remained at the top of the class for the rest of the year, ready for the chance which would come to those who achieved!

THE SPONSORS OF THE THEATER

Who is to sponsor the children's theater? An individual? A school? A civic organization? A record of the children's theaters in this country shows the following sponsors:

1. *Professional Schools.*—Probably the largest number of children's theaters in the United States are sponsored by schools of the drama. The Emerson College of Oratory in Boston, the Goodman School of the Theatre in Chicago, and the School of Speech of Northwestern University are three of the professional schools which have established children's theaters. Their object in

sponsoring such a project is, as a rule, twofold: first, to give their students training in producing children's drama, and second, to render a service to the community. Their students take an active part in the directing, producing, and acting of the plays, and gain valuable experience in managing a community enterprise.

The Children's Theatre of Evanston is sponsored not only by the School of Speech of the University, but by the public schools and the parent-teacher associations. The director is a faculty member of the School of Speech and also the supervisor of dramatics in the grade schools. The staging of the plays is done by the play production classes in the university, and the acting by speech students and by pupils in the dramatic classes of the public schools.

2. *High Schools.*—A few high schools have undertaken the production of children's plays, and substituted them for the adult plays they had formerly given. It is reasonable to believe that within the next few years many children's theaters will be founded in high schools, both because of the dearth of suitable adult plays, and because of the great opportunity offered by a children's theater of filling a community need.

3. *Civic Theaters.*—Here and there is a civic theater which is making a start toward a children's theater by producing one play a year for children. As civic theaters increase in strength, they will doubtless enlarge their activities to include more plays for young people.

4. *Drama Leagues.*—The Drama League of Chicago has for several years made a valuable contribution to the community by sponsoring the Chicago Civic Children's Theatre which provides creative dramatic work

for children on the Municipal Pier throughout the summer.

5. *Other Clubs and Organizations.*—One of the important activities of Junior Leagues over the country is the sponsoring of children's plays. The young women who make up the membership manage the productions and take all the parts in the plays.

Settlement clubs in New York and Chicago have done rather extensive work in producing plays for children, notably Christadora House in New York and Hull House in Chicago. Most of these plays have been acted by the children themselves.

6. *Individuals.*—In a few cases children's theaters have been sponsored by individuals who formed acting groups, and financed the project either by door receipts or by patrons.

THE ORGANIZATION

Whoever sponsors a children's theater should consider well the size of the undertaking before taking steps to organize it. For, to be a success, a children's theater involves a number of difficulties not met in an adult venture. The expense of children's plays is greater, as a rule, because of the large number of difficult settings and the many costumes required, while the income is less because children cannot be charged so large an admission. The children are too immature to be of much help on the stage staff, which must be larger than for adult plays because of the unusual number of scenes. The time for rehearsals is limited because no night rehearsals can be held. Such problems as these should be considered carefully before the project is undertaken.

And they all can be solved if a group of people have a real wish to establish such a theater. One or two trained people, with a number of untrained but willing adult workers, can overcome every difficulty. The productions can be simple at the start, with settings of curtains or screens, and few lighting effects. As the workers gain in experience and interest other workers in the fascinating project, the plays will grow in beauty and artistry until they attain real distinction. An organization with a stage of its own can soon make a children's theater self-supporting by interesting many children and giving several performances of each play.

If the regular staff of a theater or school undertakes the project of a children's theater, with unpaid helpers, the chief items of expense will be the following. Out of a $300 budget for four performances of a play, the royalty would be about $60, the printing $25, the costuming $50, the staging $150, the properties $5, the trucking $5, and the photographs $5. The expense is, of course, much larger when the staff is paid.

THE DIRECTOR

The responsibility of any amateur theater rests upon its director. And, as a rule, the director of a children's theater has a bit of everything to do. One minute she makes an important decision concerning general policy; the next, she telephones to find out which door will be open at night for the stage crew, or to inquire about the health of the small girl who had to miss rehearsal on account of a bad cold. She must sign requisitions, help the costume manager to plan costumes and buy materials,

THE ORGANIZATION OF THE CHILDREN'S THEATRE OF EVANSTON

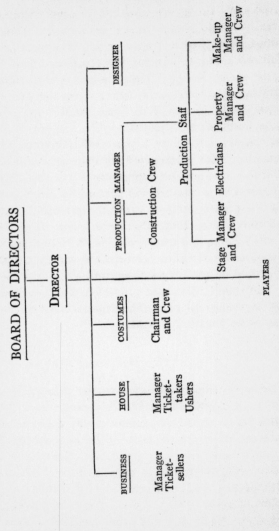

see that the publicity campaign is progressing satisfactorily, keep her eye on the progress of the settings, talk with the make-up chairman about additional materials, give the orchestra leader information about suitable music, see to complimentary tickets, photographs, difficult properties, dances—in short, keep her eye on every detail of the production. Incidentally, too, she must choose and direct the plays!

In order to be a really successful director, she must have not only a thorough knowledge of her profession, but a love and understanding of children and their needs and tastes. She must have high artistic ideals, but at the same time she must be thoroughly practical. She should have the point of view not only of a director of plays, but also of parents and teachers. This will be a guide in her management of the theater, and it will help her to get on with people; and this she must be able to do if she is to succeed. She should have imagination, good taste, and, oh, more to be desired than rubies—a delightful sense of humor!

THE PRODUCTION MANAGER

Second in importance only to the director is the production manager. No children's theater should be organized without a capable person in this position, for upon him rests the responsibility for the staging of the play. A woman may fill such a position, but a man is more often fitted to do the particular work it requires.

No small part of the success of a children's play depends upon the settings. A children's theater can succeed with very simple ones, but they should be effective and beautiful if they are to contribute to the artistic development of the young audiences. Most children's plays offer unusual opportunity for attractive and colorful settings. The dazzling underground cavern in *Aladdin;* the land of the unborn children in *The Blue Bird;* Davy Jones's locker at the bottom of the sea in *The Princess Who Would Not Say Die;* these represent the kind of setting that only an artist can do adequately—an artist, moreover, who appreciates the child's point of view.

Unless a children's theater has on its staff a designer, the production manager designs as well as makes the sets for the plays. If he is both artist and practical construction man, he studies the play, discusses the settings with the director, receives from her the floor plans with doors and windows correctly placed, designs the scenes, and then proceeds to supervise their construction. He is responsible for the entire production, and should relieve the director of all care concerning the setting, lighting, make-up, properties, and stage staff. In elaborate productions he may so organize the work that he himself merely supervises. In a small children's theater, he does much of the actual work himself, as a rule, gradually training his helpers so that they form a competent stage staff.

THE COSTUME MANAGER

This third member of the staff is highly important in a children's theater, for practically every play requires special costuming. Sometimes period costumes are needed, oftener fanciful ones, so that the costume manager may well be a student of historical costumes and an artist, as well as a seamstress. Unless the theater has a special designer, the planning as well as the executing falls to her lot. The director discusses with her the kind of costumes which will best express the characters, and the production manager has something to say about their harmony in line and color with the settings. Much of her value to the director, however, lies in the amount of responsibility she is able to take. If she has a feeling for the kind of costumes which are suitable, good taste in color, as well as skill in cutting, she can design and buy the costumes as well as supervise their making.

In schools of the drama, the sewing is ordinarily done by members of the play production or costuming classes. The domestic art classes often make the costumes in high schools, while special committees or hired seamstresses do them for clubs or other organizations.

THE BUSINESS MANAGER

A children's theater starts out, as a rule, on a small scale, requiring, or at least, having, very simple organization and only one or two trained workers. As it grows, it necessarily becomes more complex, requiring a larger staff, and more and more efficiency in its management.

The Children's Theatre of Evanston is perhaps a typical example of a project which is continually requiring more complex and more efficient organization and management as it takes on larger proportions. Therefore, to cite its experience in handling its business may, perhaps, be helpful to children's theaters which are only in their infancy.

The work of a business manager is, obviously, to take

charge of all receipts and expenditures; specifically, to sell tickets and pay bills. This sounded simple enough to warrant the appointment of untrained students for the position during the first three seasons. But as the theater grew, the financial problems became more and more perplexing. Bills appeared from everywhere, sometimes months after the play had been given. Responsibility for many purchases could not be fixed. No one could tell the expense of each particular play, nor the real financial status of the theater in general.

At the beginning of the fourth year a trained business manager was hired. A new and efficient system of bookkeeping was adopted; and for every purchase a requisition blank had to be filled out by either the director or the production manager. This gave an effective check on expenses, so that at any time the business manager could give a report on the financial condition and tell the exact cost of each play. The money saved to the theater by the ability to check back on all expenditures has not been inconsiderable; and that fact alone offers a strong argument for a trained business manager and a requisition system.

THE PUBLICITY MANAGER

Another valuable member of the staff is the manager of publicity. The work of this staff member might be a part of the job of the business manager if he could afford enough time to do both.

Upon the publicity manager depends the audiences, without which the theater cannot survive. No ordinary publicity will do for a children's theater. Advertise in all the papers, put posters all over town, and unless you have built up a following, you will have only a scattering few children whose mothers are particularly zealous about their children's interests. No, the publicity manager must not stop here. He must see that there are personal announcements in the schools and at parent-teacher clubs, and that these announcements are made in such a way that children and parents will remember them.

Perhaps he will send an announcer in a fantastic costume, only to find that the children are so fascinated by the costume that they do not heed the announcement. He may plan tiny scenes to be given at assemblies, get popular pupils to give clever little dialogues, send out striking handbills. He must think of original, attractive ways of announcing, and he must time them carefully. An announcement given shortly before the pupils are dismissed has a better chance of being remembered, but when it must be made in many schools, it cannot in every case be given at the best psychological moment. It must, too, be tactful and brief, else the schools and clubs will soon object.

A SEASON ANNOUNCEMENT

A children's theater may not be able to sell season tickets until its worth is proved by the plays of one or two seasons. But by the second or third year, it should be well enough known so that a season-ticket campaign may be launched with great success.

The following description is that of the publicity preceding the sale of the fourth year tickets in Evanston. Two thousand season tickets were sold by the parent-teacher associations in the week between the publicity stunt and the first play, and little publicity was necessary for the remainder of the season, the theater selling hundreds of single tickets for each play in addition to the season sale.

During the fall the director of the theater talked at many parent-teacher meetings, explaining the aims, policies, and plans of the children's theater, thus preparing the way for the campaign which was to follow.

Arrangements were made with the school superintendent to tour the grade schools with a five-minute scene from *The Wizard of Oz*, the first play of the season. Mimeographed letters had been sent out to all the principals and teachers, explaining the plan and giving information about the sale of tickets.

On two successive afternoons, then, the five principal characters in *The Wizard of Oz* were taken in an automobile from school to school to present their little scene. An exact schedule had been made out, allowing barely time to go from one school to the next. The announcer went ahead in another car, and on her arrival the principal of each school assembled the pupils. By the time she had told them the necessary facts about *The Wizard of Oz*, the season of four plays, and the coming ticket sale, the other cars arrived with the Tin Woodman, the Scarecrow, the Lion, the Dog, and little Dorothy—all in costume—and they went on the stage to do their scene. The fantastic characters, exactly like the pictures in the "Oz" books, the broad and obvious comedy in the lines, and the lively action, made an instantaneous hit with the pupils. Gales of laughter greeted the playing of the scene in each school, and one small boy said to his mother afterward, "Why, I laughed so hard at that one

THE WIZARD OF OZ.

little scene that I don't know what I'll do when I see the whole show!"

The advertising accomplished by the scene did not stop with the schools. Every one on the streets paused, surprised and amused, when the car passed with its queer passengers, for the Tin Woodman (a six-foot university student in a gorgeous tin suit) was forced to ride on the running board, not being able to sit down in his costume! Because the costumes were so fantastic, this play, though not of the caliber of most of the Children's Theatre plays, was an especially good one to advertise.

The success of such publicity as this is more sure than any other possible advertising. But it requires unusual coöperation on the part of the school authorities. It is no small favor to ask that every school program be disrupted for the sake of such an announcement. Two circumstances, in this case, made it easier. In the first place, the theater is a school project, not an outside institution; and in the second place, one big public stunt at the first of the season was less upsetting than a series of small announcements during the year. For after this first campaign, the only advertising in the schools was done by posters and by notices read in assemblies.

Newspaper publicity must, of course, be carried on throughout the season. Beginning three or four weeks before a play occasional articles are run, with two or three the last week. The general article about the play itself comes first, followed by one or two feature stories, an article about the cast, then a shorter article about the leading characters, with one or two pictures. The final story is likely to be general, reviewing some of the information of the other articles. Publicity needs to be carefully managed when children are in the cast so that they may not be conscious of their acting. It would be better for them if they were not featured at all, but play publicity demands a certain amount of it for the leading characters. Having been careful to choose children who were least likely to be spoiled, a director can prevent an overimportant feeling by a sensible talk about the reason for the publicity. Furthermore, she can, in this publicity, feature the characters of the play more than she features the players.

These things and more are in the province of the publicity manager, who needs must have a fertile brain and indefatigable energy to take advantage of all the channels of publicity.

THE ELECTRICIAN

A skillful, or at least, an ingenious electrician is a tremendous asset to any children's theater, for there is no limit to the possibilities of lighting in an imaginative children's play. The simplest of settings and costumes take on a soft richness with effective lighting. The mood of a scene, whether it be the strange mystery of Jim's meeting with Ben Gunn, in *Treasure Island,* or the delicate unreality of the Land of Memory in *The Blue Bird,* is heightened enormously if the lighting is well done.

A careful study of the play is necessary for the electrician if he is to light it intelligently. The cues, the changing moods, the climaxes, will be noted in the reading, and the important areas of the stage will be discovered when he sees it in rehearsal. For it is not enough to give the players acting light. The areas where the most significant action takes place require special lighting if they are to be dramatically effective. The table in the attic room in *The Little Princess*, where Sara gives her sumptuous party must not be dim like the rest of the room, and a good electrician will see to it that the soft light thrown on it from overhead merely emphasizes the candle in the middle of the table.

Makeshifts in lighting must be devised on most amateur stages, for equipment is seldom adequate. Ingenuity, therefore, is a necessary qualification of a good electrician. Floods made by using old pans, dimmers devised by homemade rheostats, color wheels for fantastic effects fastened to electric fans—these and numberless other devices will be a part of the contribution of an ingenious electrician. And if he stays with the children's theater throughout a season or more, he will be increasingly valuable to the director.

Several thorough light rehearsals are necessary for each play, if the first performance is to go well. First, the electrician and his assistants will see to it that the lights are all in order, for no part of a theater's equipment is so delicate and so constantly in need of repair as the lighting. Then they will experiment with the arrangement, trying their effects as well as can be done without the players. Next comes the preliminary dress rehearsal, when the lighting is tried out with the players —and usually found to be wrong! Some adjusting is done during the rehearsal, but the players should not be kept waiting for lengthy experiments. Instead, the director and electrician check up on all changes necessary, and before the final dress rehearsal these changes are made.

Much experience is necessary for really successful lighting, and it is advisable to attempt only the simplest effects at first. If the electrician is interested enough to stay with the theater, and if he has something of the artist in him as well as the mechanic, he will soon be able to play his part in making the production a lovely, harmonious whole.

THE CONSTRUCTION CREW

While rehearsals of the play are in progress, before the electrician and his assistants have begun the preliminary work on the lights, the construction crew, under the direction of the production manager, is engaged in building the sets. These sets have been designed and drawn to scale by the designer or production manager. If the crew is made up of untrained students, the work must be very simple, though a skillful production manager often gets remarkably effective results with an ordinary inexperienced crew. The most difficult of the pieces are often built by a professional scenic artist, a carpenter, or a manual training department, but the covering and painting of flats, the building of fireplaces and other stage furnishings, and the devising of quaint and unusual properties is usually done by the construction crew.

THE PROPERTY MANAGER

The property manager and assistants work first with the director, who gives them the list of necessary properties, carefully explaining the kind of properties required. In order that they may work intelligently, they, too, should read the play and watch a rehearsal or two. A conference is then held with the production manager, in order to determine just what things are to be made by the construction crew and which must be supplied by the property committee. The production manager and director must pass upon the properties in every case, that they may be entirely suitable to play and settings. They should be on hand for several rehearsals, in order that they may be placed correctly by the property committee and easily used by the players. To rehearse a play continually without properties is a risk, for a player, not having formed the habit of using them, is more than likely in the performance to go on pretending to light a candle or bring in a pail of water instead of actually using the properties supplied.

THE STAGE MANAGER AND CREW

When the day of the play arrives, the most important person on the production staff is the stage manager. By this time, the production should be in such shape that it could run with perfect smoothness without either the director or the production manager. The stage manager is commander-in-chief, and players and production staff alike must obey his orders. The production manager may, himself, act in this capacity, though in an elaborate production, it is well for him to be left free for general supervision.

The person who fills this important position should be an individual who can make his authority respected. He must know his business, give orders with firmness, and see that they are obeyed with dispatch.

An understanding of the exact way in which the scenes are to be set up and the furnishings placed is a first requirement of the stage manager. Knowing this, he next proceeds to organize his stage and staff so that the changes of scene can be made in the most efficient manner, and the play thus enabled to move swiftly and smoothly. Every member of the production crew is given his particular duties, and as soon as the curtains close on a scene he is expected to start work without the loss of a moment of time.

It is the stage manager who instructs the electrician when to signal the orchestra, and when to dim the house lights and bring on the foots for the opening of the acts. It is the stage manager who gives the order for the opening of the curtains, though he often undertakes this duty himself. And when the play is over, it is the stage manager who takes the responsibility of directing the crew in clearing the stage and disposing of the settings as the production manager has ordered.

THE MAKE-UP COMMITTEE

Many a young director finds herself without the help of a single person to make up her casts. Up to the last minute she must be making up the characters for her play, when her decisions are needed on fifteen other matters. Without delay, therefore, she should start giving lessons in make-up to several people who are willing to help her, for she can be much more useful as a director if she has no set duties just before the play is to begin. With several trained helpers acting as a make-up committee, she can act merely in an advisory capacity, and thus be left free for consultation on the many questions which only the director can decide.

As with the other members of the production staff, the make-up committee should know the play. By watching the preliminary dress rehearsal, they decide on the make-up for the various characters, and at the final dress rehearsal they try them out. If some of the make-ups are unsatisfactory, they are changed between acts, and by the end of the rehearsal, the staff knows exactly how to proceed on the day of the play.

Plenty of time should be allowed for making up at the regular performances. Two or three of the most difficult make-ups can be started an hour and a half before the performance if there are many to do, the others occupying the last hour. Hurry and confusion in making up a cast results in a general worried, unsettled feeling in opening the play, while a calm, leisurely procedure is reassuring.

THE ASSISTANT TO THE DIRECTOR

Throughout the rehearsals the director should have an assistant to relieve her of a small part of the responsibility, as well as of petty details such as the arranging for rehearsal space, the setting of the stage, and the notifying of players for special rehearsals. She has acted as prompter throughout the rehearsals, and does so at all the performances. When there are double casts, or scenes which do not duplicate characters, she sometimes conducts a second rehearsal at the same time the director is rehearsing. Occasionally she conducts a regular rehearsal if the director is unable to be present. After she has watched a scene rehearse for a time, she can be of much value by rehearsing it until the business is fixed in the minds of the cast. A capable assistant who shows herself willing to share responsibility is of great value to the director. And at the same time that she is giving assistance, she is developing, through observation and experience, the ability to direct plays of her own.

THE HOUSE MANAGER

Not all the staff of the children's theater is behind the scenes. The management of the audience, particularly in a children's theater, is as important an item as is the care of the stage. A house manager is, therefore, appointed to supervise the ushers, see to the darkening of the house, the giving out of programs, the taking of tickets, the conduct of the children, and any other matters which concern the welfare of the audience. He, or she, may take the tickets at the door, or act only as supervisor, free to go to any part of the house which requires attention.

The person in such a position needs decision, tact, and judgment, for the crowd is sometimes trying, and the questions which arise are perplexing. To keep a friendly, happy spirit in the audience, without allowing the children to become unruly, requires a combination of sympathy and firmness possible only in the person who sees the point of view of both children and adults.

THE USHERS

Ushers may be children or adults, or both. They should act throughout the season if they are to be of any great value to the house manager, so that they will know exactly how to find seats if they are reserved, and how to select seats for people if they are not. A neat uniform is highly desirable, better, probably, than any fantastic dress which may be devised. For, if the ushers' costumes suit the particular play which is being presented, they detract from the effect produced by those on the stage. If they are Mother Goose or fairy-tale costumes, they need to be varied from play to play, for the novelty wears off. And this involves more trouble and expense than is ordinarily advisable or possible. The style and dignity of a well-made uniform is more suitable, everything considered, than any manner of fantastic costume. And if uniforms are not possible, some form of neat insignia, in the shape of a badge or cap, will answer until such time as uniforms can be provided.

The Plays

THE NUMBER OF PRODUCTIONS

How many productions are desirable in a children's theater season? How many are possible? The answers to these two questions are likely to be quite different, depending on the community and on the producing group.

A small community, if it supported a children's theater at all, would doubtless patronize five or six plays a season. A large community would support as many as eight or ten after an audience had been built up by the production of a few plays. A performance every Saturday afternoon would soon draw part of the movie audiences if the children's theater plays were known to be cheap and good. Mothers would send their children off to the children's theater with far more assurance that they would see a suitable play than if they sent them to the average movie.

The amateur group, however, is seldom able to produce on such a scale as this, especially if its productions are at all ambitious. Four or five plays a year are enough for any group which does not give its entire time to the work, for every production requires many workers and much time.

The Children's Theatre of Evanston presents four plays during the regular season, with four performances of each play, and an additional play, produced in July by the Children's Theater class in the School of Speech summer session. This is as many productions as can be managed at present, though audiences could easily be gotten for several more plays.

THE CHOICE OF PLAYS

In the course of a season or two the director will learn many things about the choosing of plays. She will find that good plays are scarce; that the plays which draw the crowds are dramatizations of much-loved stories, like *Snow White, Robin Hood, Treasure Island;* that it is difficult to get audiences for new plays unless the children have season tickets. She will discover, too, that the simple, straightforward plays with big, compelling motives and true human interest in the working out of their plots will win young audiences far more than fantastic and subtle things, however beautifully done.

Knowing the popular taste, she will, if she is wise, follow its dictates. Until the theater has a following, she will choose dramatizations of popular stories. Then, when she is sure of her audiences, she will slip in, from time to time, something new in the shape of a charming little fantasy, a comedy with rather subtle humor, or an absurdly farcical little curtain-raiser. New plays of merit should, by all means, be produced; for one of the opportunities of a children's theater is to lead the children to a wider appreciation and enjoyment in the field of drama.

VARIETY IN PLAYS

The age variation in a children's theater is likely to be about four to fourteen, with the largest proportion between seven and twelve. Boys and girls seem equally interested. All classes of society will attend if the price is placed low enough so that the children of the poorer families can attend. How can plays be chosen for all?

A director who has such a problem to decide will inevitably come to this conclusion: that a variety of plays is the only solution. If she prefers to attract the little children, she may present a large proportion of such dramatizations as *The Three Bears, The Brownies, Rumpelstiltskin, The Wizard of Oz.* If she believes that the children's theater is of more value to the older children, she may give the preference to such plays as *The Prince and the Pauper, Treasure Island,* and *The Make-Believe Gentleman (Le Bourgeois Gentilhomme).* The Children's Theatre of Evanston prefers to attract the children of the upper grades, believing that their need of suitable recreation is far greater than that of little children.

Any children's theater, however, must give plays with a wide appeal if it is to be successful. And, fortunately, older children delight in seeing dramatizations of stories which they have loved years ago. Seventh and eighth grade children are keenly interested in seeing *Ali Baba, Beauty and the Beast, The Little Princess,* even though they read them years ago. This fact simplifies the problem of the director, who would find it impossible to get enough good new plays even if she cared to do so. She should, however, present one or two plays such as *A Midsummer Night's Dream* and *The Prince and the Pauper,* quite definitely for the older children.

The season may be divided between the fanciful and the realistic. *The Wizard of Oz* and *Alice in Wonderland* should alternate with such plays as *The Little Princess* and *Robin Hood.* The imaginative play has special charm for children from six to ten, appealing also to tiny children because it is colorful and picturesque. From ten to fourteen the appeal of the realistic is stronger, the boys particularly liking the adventurous and heroic play. From twelve on, the glamour of romance attracts both boys and girls, especially when it is combined with adventure. *Treasure Island* is a favorite at this time; so is *Robin Hood.* If there were a really good *King Arthur* play to be had, it would be assured of popularity. Few children over fourteen attend children's theaters, so that the problem of the director ends before the love element appears. And the many adults who come with the children find their enjoyment partly by experiencing again their childhood pleasure in the stories, and partly by watching the delightfully spontaneous reactions of the child audiences.

Programs of short plays offer more opportunity for variety than does one long play. Serious and comedy elements, realism and fantasy may all be combined in one production. One children's theater program opened with Stuart Walker's attractive little play, *Nevertheless*, which had a strong appeal for the younger children. Second on the bill was a half-hour version of *Rip Van Winkle*, done with puppets. This was a novelty to many of the children, and an interesting variation from the plays with real characters. The thriller for the boys came next. It was *The Crowsnest*, a 47 Workshop play by William F. Manley—not a children's play at all, strictly speaking. Expurgated a trifle, however, it proved an excellent choice, for the older children reveled in the mystery and excitement of it. Last came *The Slippers of Cinderella*, described by the author, Graham Robertson, as "an impossibility in one act." Clever and absurdly funny, it was a pleasing contrast to the weird play of the sea, and it sent the children home bubbling with laughter.

Such a program is, in itself, a good variation from the long play, and may be used, if desired, as often as once in a season. If the majority of players in a children's theater are children, most of the programs should be made up of short plays, since it is so difficult for them to sustain a long play. But if the players are chiefly adult, long plays are preferable, for, after all, they are the favorites of the child audiences.

THE BASIS OF CHOICE

Every play chosen for the children's theater should have literary and dramatic merit. It should be popular enough in type to make its success reasonably sure, but the standard should be unquestionably high. Starting with plays which children cannot fail to appreciate—plays such as *The Little Princess, Snow White, The Three Spinners,* all based on familiar tales, a children's theater should be able, gradually, to educate its youthful audiences to appreciate plays a bit more subtle and difficult. Children who have for several seasons enjoyed such plays as these, will grow to appreciate plays on the order of *Peter Pan, The Piper,* and *A Midsummer Night's Dream.*

Sophistication should be avoided in children's plays. It comes far too soon to the modern child, and the children's theater should be free from it. Love-making is entirely uninteresting to little children, though some little romance is tolerated, especially if it is a part of the poetic justice at the end. Snow White may marry her suitor and live happily ever after; the Beast may be transformed to a handsome prince and make Beauty his princess; Robin Hood may outwit the scheming Guy of Gisbourne and win the fair Marian. But as for the actual love-making, it is entirely out of their realm of interest.

Action is an absolute necessity in a children's play—plenty of it. The small boy who, at the close of a lively scene, jumped up and down, exclaiming ecstatically, "I liked that! I like a play where things happen!" only voiced what every child feels. The maximum of action with the minimum of dialogue is a rule for a play meant for little children, and every director finds it necessary to cut down long speeches if her play is to hold a young audience.

Symbolic plays are not childlike. Only the most obvious symbolism can be understood by children, and even what they can understand has no real interest for them. Every children's play must depend for its effectiveness upon plot and character rather than upon symbolism or beauty of idea or cleverness of dialogue, or any other thing. *The Blue Bird* is effective with children chiefly because of their interest in Tyltyl and Mytyl, rather than because of the symbolism in the search for happiness. It is a play thoroughly worth using in a children's theater because, in spite of all the underlying significance which children miss, it has enough of surface interest and beauty to make it charming to them.

Modern writers of children's plays have a strong tendency to introduce satire into their work. For many adults this adds a spice more delightful than the naïveté of the truly childlike production. But one has only to study the reaction of an audience of youngsters to a satirical play to realize how useless it is for them. Except for a few older children, the satire fails to make any impression whatever, and it should by all means be saved for adult plays. Louise Saunders' charming little play, *The Knave of Hearts,* is liked, not for the satire, but for its delightful characters. Alice C. D. Riley's *Ten Minutes by the Clock* is popular, not because of the fun it pokes at silly conventions, but because of funny little Dux and Dox.

The child's point of view must be kept by author, director, producer, and players if the play is to be truly successful. The outlook on life must be simple and democratic, the standards and ideals clean cut, the sympathy rightly placed at all times, and the end characterized by poetic justice. This does not mean that the play should be goody-goody. Not at all! *Snow White, Robin Hood, The Prince and the Pauper* are not goody-goody, yet they conform in every respect to this formula. In them the children see the wheels of life go around, and they sit in justice on the good and evil deeds which are done. No adult in a children's theater audience can fail to recognize the thrills of sympathy for the gentle and forgiving Snow White, the chivalrous Robin Hood, or the sturdy little prince, nor the scorn with which they regard the jealous queen, the cowardly Sheriff of Nottingham, or the cruel John Canty. Ideals, here built into something they love, have an influence more powerful than sermons.

PRACTICAL CONSIDERATIONS

Finally, in choosing plays, there is the practical side to be considered. Is the royalty prohibitive? For the payment of royalty is necessary and right, and no director should try to escape it. Is the stage large enough and well-enough equipped for an adequate production? Will the settings be too expensive? Are the changes of scene few enough so that the audience will not become restless? Are the right players available for the particular parts? Can the play be adapted to run an hour and three quarters including the *entr'actes?*—an ideal length for a children's theater play. These and similar questions should be carefully considered before a final choice is made. When they cannot be answered satisfactorily, a play, even though it has worth and charm, should be postponed until it has a really good chance to succeed.

PLAYS WHICH HAVE BEEN PRODUCED IN THE
CHILDREN'S THEATRE OF EVANSTON

Snow White and the Seven Dwarfs....................
JESSIE BRAHAM WHITE (French)
Crossings ....WALTER DE LA MARE (Knopf)
The Little Princess...............................
FRANCES HODGSON BURNETT (French)
Ali Baba and the Forty Thieves....................
LOUISE ARMSTRONG (Longmans, Green)
Robin Hood..................OWEN DAVIS (French)
The Prince and the Pauper........................
ABBY SAGE RICHARDSON (French)
Ten Minutes by the Clock...ALICE C. D. RILEY (Doran)
The Bubble Peddler........ALICE C. D. RILEY (Doran)
Treasure Island........Dramatization of Stevenson's tale
Beauty and the Beast..Dramatization of the old fairy tale
The Make-Believe Gentleman
(Le Bourgeois Gentilhomme)..................MOLIÈRE
Dick Whittington...........M. JAGENDORF (Brentano)
The Three Spinners....FLORENCE KIPER FRANK (Vinal)
The Poor Little Rich Girl......ELEANOR GATES (French)
Aladdin................THEODORA DUBOIS (Manuscript)
Make-Believe..................A. A. MILNE (French)
The Wizard of Oz......ELIZABETH GOODSPEED (French)
The Blue Bird....MAURICE MAETERLINCK (Dodd, Mead)
Nevertheless.............STUART WALKER (Appleton)
The Crowsnest.......WILLIAM F. MANLEY (Brentano)
The Slippers of Cinderella........................
GRAHAM ROBERTSON (Little, Brown)
A Midsummer Night's Dream...WILLIAM SHAKESPEARE
The Scotch Twins.....ELEANOR PERKINS (Manuscript)

PLANNING FOR ENTR'ACTES

To choose a play and produce it well would seem to be enough to occupy the whole attention of any director. But not so in a children's theater! Careful plans must be made for the time between the acts if the performances are to be happy occasions for all. Children need to relax after each period of concentration; they need to talk, to stir about. But if nothing fills in the time between the scenes, there is a crude break, a sudden drop from the lovely, imaginative, make-believe world to the everyday commonplaces of facts and realities. Each of the usual five or six scenes must pull the audience back to the story, and the abruptness of the change destroys the right "feel," or atmosphere, for the beginnings of the scenes.

What can be done with the intervals? The Children's Theatre of Evanston tried several plans during its first year, including music by a three-piece adult orchestra, dramatic interludes, and clever announcements of plays to come. The orchestra was a mild success; the interludes (consisting of story dramatizations) were entertaining, but distracting to some of the younger children, who thought they belonged to the play; the announcements were successful, but too brief to be of much use in filling in the time between scenes.

By the second season a plan was hit upon which proved ideal. The orchestra of the intermediate school (seventh and eighth grades) offered to play for all of the productions—to become a regular part of the organization. It made a happy combination. The orchestra director felt that it was a fine experience for his orchestra to play regularly for an audience of children, and an incentive to practice. The Children's Theatre management felt that the gain was all on the side of the theater, for the audiences from the first took great delight in the young players. The children could still relax and chat between the scenes, for the orchestra made no claim to great skill, and felt the more at ease that they were not on exhibition. As far as possible, music suited to the play was used, and thus the break between the scenes was softened and the atmosphere preserved.

Probably every children's theater sponsored by a school can have such an orchestra, for there are few public schools without them, and they are glad both for the chance to play for the productions and to earn a little money. Even when a theater is under other auspices, it should be able to obtain a student orchestra at a very moderate price.

THE AUDIENCE DURING THE ENTR'ACTES

As long as the children in an audience feel a bit strange and awed in a theater, they are on their best behavior. But little by little, as they begin to feel at home, they are likely to take on more freedom than is good for them or their neighbors, and, unless they are restrained by the presence of many adults, they will in time become really lawless.

The management of a child audience is a problem not easy of solution. To police the house with stern-faced adults may keep it quiet, but will induce a bad attitude among the children, who continue to be noisy as soon as they know they are not watched. To give them complete freedom is worse, for mob psychology will lead them eventually into real lawlessness.

The best solution appears to lie in a group of adults who are understanding and sympathetic, yet possessed of an authority which will be respected. A few teachers who are truly interested in the children's theater and its audience, stationed about the house to see that no lawlessness so much as starts, can, by speaking kindly but firmly to children who are not conducting themselves in an orderly manner, not only avoid any trouble, but actually build up a loyal, coöperative spirit in an audience.

Other factors which help in audience management are short waits between scenes; good ventilation, and little talks from the stage upon various aspects of the children's theater. Such talks may give the children in the audience a voice in the selection of plays by allowing them to vote on the plays they would most like to see, and those they hope to have revived; they may awaken special interest in plays which are to come; or they may indirectly build certain attitudes and appreciations which will lead to a sense of responsibility in audience courtesy and a finer discrimination in their enjoyment of plays.

ATTRACTIVE EXTRAS FOR THE THEATER

There are endless possibilities for adding to the charm of a children's theater. Attractive wooden signs pointing the way to the theater, if it is at any distance from the street; an artistic sign at the door; large, colorful posters or "tapestries" about the auditorium, painted to represent favorite fairy tales; ushers in attractive uniform; a distinctive symbol for the program—these and many other devices may help to make the theater a magic place where anything delightful may happen.

On the stage there are opportunities for novel and captivating extras, even apart from the plays. When a program of one-act plays is to be presented, a clever idea of linking them into a unit will add greatly to their charm. One such program, consisting of several plays chosen for their pleasing variety, was unified by an elfish child, who ran out from between the curtains to announce each play in a funny little rhyme adapted from Mother Goose. Another program, consisting of an English, an Irish, and a Chinese play, had a clever little prologue and several interludes made up of the conversations of an Englishman, an Irishman, and a Chinaman. The Stuart Walker idea of a Prologue and Device Bearer may be adapted; or the program can be presided over by two pages, who converse about the play, make quaint announcements, and appear to open the curtains for the scenes.

With imagination and ingenuity, any number of surprising and delightful additions to the regular program may be devised. Good taste will require that they be used with restraint, in order to avoid a multiplicity of impressions. So used, however, they can provide a piquancy and charm which will make the theater a place of distinction to the youthful audiences who frequent it.

FINALLY

The experience of the Children's Theatre of Evanston may not be typical. Findings from other theaters may contradict much that has been written here. But children are much the same wherever and whenever they live. That is why they have always loved *Snow White* and *Cinderella* and *Ali Baba*. That is why they can be counted on to love them when they see them on the stage. It is only the universal things, after all, which are important. Details, local conditions, popular taste can easily be learned. If a director will give the children what is truly beautiful in life and art, keeping always the child's point of view as she chooses and directs her plays, she will find, wherever she may be, that the children will come to her theater, eager to share the joys and sorrows of the folk that lived "once upon a time."

PLAY LIST

A short, carefully selected list of plays is always more valuable than a general catalogue; therefore, only such plays are suggested here as can be definitely recommended for the sixth, seventh, eighth and ninth grades, and for the children's theater. They are listed by authors, but only the plays which, in the present writer's estimation, are the most suitable and effective for the purposes mentioned have been chosen from each collection.

ARMSTRONG, Louise Van Voorhis:
> *Ali Baba and the Forty Thieves* (Longmans, Green). Hour pantomime with interesting possibilities. Music suggested. For school or children's theater.
>
> *The Old History Book, The Drama Magazine,* January, 1922. Pageant play based on life of Lincoln.
>
> *Dolls* (Longmans, Green). A Christmas nonsense play. Might be acted by ninth grade for children's theater.

BARRIE, James M.:
> *Peter Pan* (Scribners). The most delightful of all plays for a children's theater, and at the same time, the most difficult, both as to acting and setting. To be attempted only by the most experienced and skillful groups. Not available for amateurs at the time this list is made.

BURRILL, Edgar White:
> *Master Skylark* (Century). Eighth and ninth grades. Children's theater.

COOKE, Marjorie Benton:
> *The First Thanksgiving Dinner* (Dramatic Publishing Co.). Good one-act play for eighth or ninth grade.

CORNEAU, Perry:
> *Robin Hood and the Widow's Three Sons* (Drama League of Chicago). Good one-hour play for eighth grade.

DAVIS, Owen:
> *Robin Hood* (French). Delightful three-act play with strong climaxes and exceptional comedy situations. Needs

much cutting for a children's theater, but is highly effective when played for children by adults.

DuBois, Theodora:

Aladdin (manuscript). Author, Dongan Hills, Staten Island, New York. A dramatic and colorful play in seven scenes, based on the Arabian Nights' tale. An elaborate children's theater play.

Field, Rachel Lyman:

Six Plays (Scribners).
Three Pills in a Bottle. A charmingly fantastic one-act play which can be done by junior high school pupils.
Theories and Thumbs. An easy and appealing little play for junior high school girls. The setting is a museum.

Forty-Seven Workshop Plays (Brentano's).
The Crowsnest, by George Manley. A thrilling one-act play for boys not younger than ninth grade. Effective when done by one boy and three men for a children's audience. The setting is the crow's nest of a ship.

Frank, Florence Kiper:

Three Plays for a Children's Theatre (Vinal).
The Three Spinners. A delightful three-act play of an hour's length, based on the story of *Rumpelstiltskin.* Can be used for upper grades or for children's theater.

Fyleman, Rose:

Eight Little Plays for Children (Doran). Some of these charming little plays are suitable for young children, others for sixth or seventh grade. They make good curtain-raisers and interludes for a children's theater.
Darby and Joan. The two little figures who show what the weather is to be. An adorable little play for sixth grade and older.
The Weather Clerk. Excellent for sixth grade.
The Fairy Riddle
Naughts and Crosses } Tiny plays which may be
The Fairy and the Doll } used effectively as inter-
Cabbages and Kings } ludes in a children's theater.

Garnett, Louise Ayres:

Three to Make Ready (Doran).
Hilltop. An attractive little morality play, suitable for sixth or seventh grade.

Gates, Eleanor:

The Poor Little Rich Girl (French). A long and difficult play. It is very effective for a children's theater if cut and acted by adults. The staging is unusually difficult.

GOODSPEED, Elizabeth Fuller:
> *The Wizard of Oz* (French). For a children's theater. A Junior League play.
> *The Land of Oz* (French). Children's theater.

GREGORY, Lady Augusta:
> *The Dragon* (Putnam). For a children's theater.

JAGENDORF, M.:
> *Pantomimes for a Children's Theatre* (Brentano's).
>> *Dick Whittington.* A good pantomime of an hour's length, suitable for sixth or seventh grade. Music supplied.
> *Short Plays for Young Folks* (Brentano's).
>> *Five Ghosts.* A humorous Hallowe'en play for sixth or seventh grade.

McFADDEN, Elizabeth:
> *Why the Chimes Rang* (French). One of the loveliest of all Christmas plays. For junior and senior high schools.
> *The Knights of the Silver Shield* (French). A dramatization of Raymond McDonald Alden's fine little story. Junior and senior high schools.

MACKAY, Constance D'Arcy:
> *The House of the Heart and Other Plays* (Holt).
>> *The House of the Heart.* A morality for sixth grade.
>> *The Christmas Guest.* An unusually good short Christmas play for sixth or seventh grade.
> *The Forest Princess and Other Masques* (Holt).
>> *The Forest Princess.* Attractive play in three short acts, based on *The Sleeping Beauty.* Sixth grade.
>> *A Masque of Christmas.* Three short acts. Sixth grade.
> *The Silver Thread and Other Folk Plays* (Holt). These plays are suitable to sixth, seventh and eighth grades.
>> *The Silver Thread.* The best of the collection. Hour length.
>> *A Brewing of Brains.* Good short play of Colonial days.
>> *The Three Wishes.*
>> *Troll Magic.*
>> *The Forest Spring.*
>> *The Foam Maiden.*
>> *Siegfried.*
>> *The Snow Witch.*

MAETERLINCK, Maurice:
> *The Blue Bird* (Dodd, Mead). An elaborate and beautiful play for a children's theater. May be acted by ninth grade students.

MEIGS, Cornelia:

> *Helga and the White Peacock* (Macmillan).
> *The Stedfast Princess* (Macmillan).
>> Both are excellent three-act plays for sixth or seventh grade.

MINCHIN, Lydia:

> *The Jester's Purse* (Harcourt, Brace).
>> *Sir Richard Serves His Queen.* A very good Robin Hood play, about an hour in length. Seventh or eighth grade.
>> *On the Tower of the Shadows.* An Indian play, poorly written but with a very fine central idea. Eighth or ninth grade.

MOLIÈRE:

> *Le Bourgeois Gentilhomme* (Putnam). Under some such title as *The Make-Believe Gentleman* or *The Tradesman Turned Gentleman,* this play is admirably suited to a children's theater. It could be acted by ninth grade pupils who had had two or three years of dramatic training.

MORSE, Katherine:

> *Goldtree and Silvertree* (Macmillan). Some of the plays in this little book are best suited to fourth or fifth grade, but the following have been used successfully in the sixth:
> *Goldtree and Silvertree.*
> *The Pudding Pan.*
> *The Proud Princess.*

MOSES, Montrose J.

> *A Treasury of Plays for Children* (Little, Brown). This and Moses' other collection are the most useful of all books to the director of the children's theater. Most of the plays are best suited to children's theaters in which grown-ups play the adult parts, though some of them may be done entirely by children.
> *The Little Princess,* by Frances Hodgson Burnett. One of the greatest favorites in the children's theater. Not difficult as to setting. Could be done by ninth grade.
> *The Silver Thread,* by Constance Mackay.
> *The Testing of Sir Gawayne,* by Marguerite Merington. A King Arthur play in one act for eighth or ninth grade.
> *Six Who Pass While the Lentils Boil,* by Stuart Walker.
> *Alice in Wonderland,* by Alice Gerstenberg. The best available dramatization of Lewis Carroll's story.
> *The Toymaker of Nuremberg,* by Austin Strong.
> *Another Treasury of Plays for Children* (Little, Brown).

Treasure Island, by Jules Eckert Goodman. An elaborate dramatic version of this fascinating story.

The Slippers of Cinderella, by Graham Robertson. An exceptionally clever and humorous one-act play which can be done by eighth or ninth grade. Described as "an impossibility in one act."

Don Quixote, by Anne Stoddard and Tony Sarg. Written for marionettes. Ninth grade.

The Racketty-Packetty House, by Frances Hodgson Burnett. Good children's theater play for little children.

Abraham Lincoln, by John Drinkwater. Ninth grade.

The Birthday of the Infanta, by Stuart Walker. Unusual play for eighth or ninth grade. One act.

Snow White and the Seven Dwarfs, by Jessie Braham White. The finest version of this loved story. Can be done by eighth or ninth grade. Six scenes.

Make-Believe, by A. A. Milne. A most charming play which can be acted by eighth and ninth grades.

NICHOLS, Dorothy:

Lost Children (manuscript). Author, Palo Alto, California. A charming Christmas play in one act. For eighth or ninth grade.

Sounding Brass. An excellent Christmas play for ninth grade and above.

PEABODY, Josephine Preston:

The Piper (Houghton Mifflin). This version, though beautiful, is too mature for young children. Older children would appreciate it.

PERKINS, Eleanor Ellis:

The Scotch Twins (manuscript). Author, Evanston, Illinois. An exceptionally good dramatization of the book by Lucy Fitch Perkins. In four acts. Especially suited to a cast of adults and children, though it might be done by ninth grade. A splendid children's theater play.

PRICE, Olive:

Plays from American History and Literature, Vol. I (French). These plays would be far more useful if written in fewer scenes.

Lantern Light. A play about witchcraft.

Little Lady Dresden. About Washington.

Around the Blue Wigwam. About Pocahontas.

Plays from American History and Literature, Vol. II (French). Most of these plays are not worth the staging they require. The best is:

West o' the Alleghenies. A short Christmas play which has Daniel Boone as one of its characters.

RICE, Adams T.:

Pinocchio (manuscript). Author, Bonstelle Playhouse, Detroit, Michigan. A rather elaborate play based on the popular story. For children's theater.

RILEY, Alice C. D.:

Ten Minutes by the Clock (Doran). A clever one-act play for ninth grade or children's theater.

The Blue Prince (Drama League of Chicago). Sixth or seventh grade.

The Bubble Peddler (manuscript). Author, Evanston, Illinois. Sequel to the Red Riding Hood story. An attractive little play in three scenes for sixth grade or children's theater.

SAUNDERS, Louise:

The Knave of Hearts (Longmans, Green). An unusually clever, one-act play, suitable for eighth grade or children's theater.

SCHAUFFLER and SANFORD:

Plays of Our American Holidays (Dodd, Mead). Interesting and usable little plays.

Twelfth Night Festivities, by Knox.

The Snow Queen, by Grimball.

Two Plum Puddings, by Colin Clements.

An April Fool, by Virginia Olcott.

The King of Sherwood, by Ivy Bolton.

The Three Thanksgivings, by Faith Van Valkenburgh Vilas.

Sojourners, by Harnwell and Meaker. An excellent short play of the Pilgrims in Holland. Eighth or ninth grade.

At the Turn of the Tide, by Georgia Stenger.

Faith of Our Fathers, by Anne Marble.

SYRETT, Netta:

Six Fairy Plays for Children (Dodd, Mead). Especially for girl casts.

The Dream Lady.

White Magic.

The Wonderful Rose.

THACKERAY, William M.:

The Rose and the Ring (Baker). An extravaganza in four acts suitable for a children's theater.

THOMAS, Charles Swain:

The Atlantic Book of Junior Plays (Atlantic Monthly

Press). One of the very best collections of plays for junior high schools.

What Men Live By, by Virginia Church. From Tolstoy's story. An exceptional one-act play which can be done by ninth grade.

Kinfolk of Robin Hood, by Percy MacKaye. Play in four short acts for eighth and ninth grades.

The Dyspeptic Ogre, by Percival Wilde. A very clever and humorous one-act play for seventh grade.

The Fifteenth Candle, by Rachel Lyman Field. One of the finest of serious one-act plays for eighth or ninth grade.

The Bellman of Mons, by Dorothy Rose Googins. Play in three short acts for ninth grade.

A Marriage Proposal, by Anton Tchekoff. A good Russian farce, though difficult for ninth grade.

Jephthah's Daughter, by Elma Levinger. A highly dramatic one-act play based on the Bible story.

The Play of Saint George, by J. M. C. Crum. A rollicking farce based on the story of *Saint George and the Dragon.*

The Birthday of the Infanta, by Stuart Walker. See page 287.

The Christmas Guest, by Constance Mackay. See page 285.

WALKER, Stuart:

Portmanteau Plays (Appleton).
Six Who Pass While the Lentils Boil. See page 286.
Nevertheless. Funny and whimsical little play which can be done by seventh or eighth grade children.
Portmanteau Adaptations (Appleton).
The Birthday of the Infanta.

WEBBER and WEBSTER:

Short Plays for Young People (Houghton Mifflin).
The Stolen Prince, by Dan Totheroh. Richly comic one-act play done in the Chinese manner. Junior high school.
The Shutting o' the Door. From an old ballad.
One-Act Plays (Houghton Mifflin). Suitable for ninth grade and older.
The Boy Comes Home, by A. A. Milne.
The Romancers, Act I, by Rostand.
My Lady's Lace, by Knoblock. The Dutch scene of *My Lady's Dress.*

Nevertheless, by Stuart Walker.

WILDE, Percival:

Alias Santa Claus (Appleton). One-act play with street urchins as the principal characters. Seventh or eighth grade.

The Enchanted Christmas Tree (Appleton).

Kings in Nomania (Appleton). Excellent Christmas play for sixth and seventh grades. By adaptation it can be used at other than holiday time.

SOME LITERATURE FOR DRAMATIZATION
IN THE SIXTH, SEVENTH, AND EIGHTH GRADES

Alice in Wonderland, Lewis Carroll (Appleton).

American Folk and Fairy Tales, Rachel Field (Scribners).

Arabian Nights. Versions by many publishers.

The Bee Man of Orn, Frank Stockton (Scribners).

The Birds of Killingworth. Longfellow (Houghton Mifflin).

The Birthday of the Infanta, Oscar Wilde (Modern Library).

A Book of Ballad Stories, Macleod (Stokes).

A Book of Legends, Scudder (Houghton Mifflin).

The Boy's King Arthur, Sidney Lanier (from Malory), (Rand, McNally).

The Boy Who Cried Wolf, Æsop (Harpers).

The Children's Blue Bird, Maeterlinck (Silver, Burdett).

The Children's Book, Scudder (Houghton Mifflin).

The Children's Hour (10 vol.), Tappan (Houghton Mifflin).

Children's Literature, Curry-Clippinger (Rand, McNally).

The Christmas Carol, Charles Dickens (Lippincott).

East o' the Sun and West o' the Moon, Gudrun Thorne-Thomsen (Row Peterson).

Stories: *The Cock and the Fox, The Lad Who Went to the North Wind, The Parson and the Clerk, The Squire's Bride, Why the Sea Is Salt.*

Hans Brinker, Mary Mapes Dodge (McKay).

In the Days of Giants, Abby Farwell Brown (Houghton Mifflin).

King Arthur books, Howard Pyle (Scribners).

The King of the Golden River, Ruskin (Lippincott).

The Knights of the Silver Shield (in *Why the Chimes Rang*), Alden (Bobbs-Merrill).

The Legend of Sleepy Hollow, Washington Irving (McKay).

Legends of the Middle Ages, Guerber (American Book Co.).

Little Cosette, Victor Hugo (*Les Misérables*), adapted in *For the Children's Hour*, Carolyn Bailey (Milton Bradley).

Midas (in *The Golden Age of Myth and Legend*), Bulfinch (Stokes).

Nature Myths and Stories, Flora J. Cooke (A. Flanagan).

The Nuremberg Stove (Ouida), adapted in *The Story Hour*, Wiggin and Smith (Houghton Mifflin).

The Odyssey, Palmer's translation (Houghton Mifflin).

Old Pipes and the Dryad (in *Fanciful Tales*), Frank Stockton (Scribners).

The Old Woman and the Tramp (in *Tales of Laughter*), Wiggin and Smith (Macmillan).

The Paradise of Children, Nathaniel Hawthorne (Houghton Mifflin).

The Prince and the Pauper, Mark Twain (Harpers).

The Princess and the Vagabond, Ruth Sawyer (*Outlook*, Nov. 1911).

Rip Van Winkle, Washington Irving.

Robert of Sicily, Longfellow (Houghton Mifflin).

Robin Hood, Howard Pyle (Scribners).

Sara Crewe, Frances Hodgson Burnett (Scribners).

The Selfish Giant (in *Fairy Tales*), Oscar Wilde (Modern Library).

The Shakespeare Story Book, Macleod (Gardner Darton).

Siegfried (in *Sigurd the Volsung*), William Morris (Longmans, Green).

Some Great Stories and How to Tell Them, Richard Wyche (Newson).

The Story of the Rhinegold, Chapin (Harpers).

Story Telling, Edna Lyman (McClurg).

Story Telling Ballads, Frances J. Olcott (Houghton Mifflin).

This Way to Christmas, Ruth Sawyer (Harpers).

Especially good stories: *The Voyage of the Wee Red Cap* and *The German Clockmaker*.

To Your Good Health (in *The Art of the Story Teller*), Marie Shedlock (Appleton).

Treasure Island, Robert Louis Stevenson (Scribners).

REFERENCES

For the Teacher of Creative Dramatics

Voice and Diction

AIKIN, W. A., *The Voice* (Longmans, Green). An excellent handbook for the teacher.

AVERY, DORSEY and SICKELS, *First Principles in Speech Training* (Appleton). For small children.

FOGERTY, Elsie, *First Notes on Voice Training* (Dutton).

Word Practice. A little handbook of drills which may be obtained from Miss S. Wellesley-Reade, 44 Fairholme Road, West Kensington, London, W. 14.

Costume

CALTHROP, Dion, *English Costume* (Black).

DABNEY and WISE, *A Book of Dramatic Costume* (Crofts).

GRIMBALL and WELLS, *Costuming a Play* (Century). Probably the best of the smaller books on period costumes.

HAIRE, Frances, *The Folk Costume Book* (Barnes). Good for peasant costumes of all nations.

MACKAY, Constance: *Costumes and Scenery for Amateurs* (Holt).

YOUNG, Agnes Brooks: *Stage Costuming* (Macmillan). Practical directions for dyeing and making costumes.

Miscellaneous

BROWN, Corinne, *Creative Drama in the Lower School* (Appleton). An excellent book for the teacher of dramatics in the kindergarten, first, second and third grades.

CATHER, Katherine, *Educating by Story Telling* (World Book Co.). The chapters on the story interests of childhood are particularly good.

CHUBB, Percival, *Festivals and Plays* (Harpers). A book which is both inspirational and practical.

CURTIS, Elnora, *The Dramatic Instinct in Education* (Houghton Mifflin).

DEAN, Alexander, *Little Theatre Organization and Management* (Appleton). An excellent book for those who expect to organize a theater.

DEWEY, John, *Human Nature and Conduct* (Holt).

HERTS, Alice M., *The Children's Educational Theatre* (Harper).

HILLIARD, McCORMICK, OGLEBAY, *Amateur and Educational Dramatics* (Macmillan).

KILPATRICK, William H., *Foundations of Method* (Macmillan). An exceptionally helpful book for the teacher of creative dramatics.

KREADY, Laura, *A Study of Fairy Tales* (Houghton Mifflin).

LEE, *Play in Education* (Macmillan).

MACKAY, Constance D'Arcy, *Children's Theatres and Plays* (Appleton). An account of children's theaters in the United States and Europe, with many suggested plays. *How to Produce Children's Plays* (Holt).

MACCLINTOCK, Porter Lander, *Literature in the Elementary Schools* (University of Chicago Press). One of the best of books for the preparation of the teacher.

MEARNS, Hughes, *Creative Youth* (Doubleday, Doran). An inspirational book, telling how the creative impulse of high school students was released in the writing of verse. *Creative Power* (Doubleday, Doran). A later book dealing with the process of freeing the creative impulse.

MERRILL, John, *The Value, Place and Use of the Dramatic Instinct in Education,* also, *Creative Effort* (Year Books of Francis Parker School).

MILLER, Elizabeth, *Dramatization of Bible Stories* (University of Chicago Press). A helpful little book for a dramatic director of a Sunday school.

NEILSON and KITTREDGE, *Facts about Shakespeare* (Macmillan). Very good material to use in the Shakespeare course.

NORSWORTHY and WHITLEY, *Psychology of Childhood* (Macmillan). One of the best child psychologies.

OVERTON, Grace Sloan, *Drama in Education* (Century). Much of this book has to do with drama in the church.

QUENNELL, *History of Everyday Things in England* (Scribners). Very useful for background material in the years between 1066 and 1799. Manners, customs, modes of living.

ROLFE, William James, *Shakespeare the Boy* (Harper). Excellent material for the Shakespeare course.

RUGG and SHUMAKER, *The Child-Centered School* (World Book Co.). An interesting account of the changes in curriculum and method which are going on in the progressive schools of to-day. Every teacher of creative dramatics should be familiar with the book.

SIMONS and ORR, *Dramatization* (Scott Foresman). High school classics dramatized.

SMITH, Milton, *A Book of Play Production* (Appleton). One of the best in the field.

TAYLOR, Emerson, *Practical Stage Directing for Amateurs* (Macmillan). Contains useful definitions of stage terms.

Some Addresses Which May be Useful to Play Directors

SCENERY AND LIGHTING

NEW YORK

P. D. Ackerman, 140 West 39th St. Scenic studio

Beaumont Scenic Studios, Inc., 443 West 47th St.

Robert W. Bergman, Inc., 142 West 39th St. Scenic studio

Display Stage Lighting Co., 410 West 47th St.

J. R. Clancy, Inc., Syracuse, N. Y.
    Stage rigging and hardware

Dean Farnsworth, 53 Washington St., Pleasantville, N. Y. Stage and lighting adviser

BOSTON
Pevear Color Specialty Co., 71 Brimmer St.
Stage consulting engineers. Lighting apparatus
PHILADELPHIA
Amelia Grain, 819 Spring Garden St. Scenic studio
COLUMBUS
Schell Scenic Studios
CHICAGO
Robert P. Carsen Scenic Studio, 1507 N. Clark St.
Chicago Stage Lighting Co., 55 Wacker Drive
Electrical equipment and parts. Gelatines
Arvid Crandall, Goodman Theater. Lighting expert
Eugene Frost, Hub Electric Co. Stage lighting adviser
Furolin Service, Inc., 1330 N. Halsted St.
Textile fireproofing for muslin curtains
Hub Electric Co., 2225 W. Grand Ave. Switchboard
Manufacturers
LOS ANGELES
Calkins Scenery, 935 S. Broadway
Los Angeles Scenic Studio, 1215 Bates St.
Martin's Scenic Studio, 4140 Sunset Blvd., Hollywood
SAN FRANCISCO
C. J. Holtzmueller, 1108 Howard St.
Theatrical appliances. Stage lighting

COSTUMES

NEW YORK
Brooks Costume Rental Co., 1437 Broadway
Eaves, 151 West 46th St.
Tams, 318 West 46th St.
PHILADELPHIA
Van Horn & Son
Miller, Costumier, 236 South 11th St.
CINCINNATI
Wm. Beck & Sons, 2102 Highland Ave.
CHICAGO
Kettler Wig Co., 162 N. State St.
New York Costume Co., 75 W. Lake St.
Fritz Schoultz, 58 W. Lake St.

Minna Schmidt, 920 N. Clark St.

MINNEAPOLIS

Minneapolis Costume Co., 9th and La Salle Sts.

ST. PAUL

Martin Gieson, 76 West 4th St.

ST. LOUIS

Andrew Frieger, 3236 Olive St.

Robert Schmidt, 206 South 4th St.

KANSAS CITY

Harrillson Costume Co., 1327 Main St.

OMAHA

Theo. Lieben & Son, 1514 Howard St.

DENVER

Colorado Costume Co., 1751 Champa St.

SALT LAKE CITY

Salt Lake Costume Co.

SEATTLE

Brockland Costume Co., 1624 Eighth Ave.

LOS ANGELES

Western Costume Co., 955 S. Broadway, and 5533 Sunset Blvd., Hollywood

Publications

Drama Magazine, Church and Drama League, 289 Fourth Ave., New York, N. Y.

Theatre Arts Magazine, 7 East 42nd St., New York, N. Y.

Index

(1)